ROUTLEDGE LIBRARY EDITIONS:
EDUCATION 1800–1926

Volume 8

ELEMENTARY SCHOOLING AND THE WORKING CLASSES 1860–1918

ELEMENTARY SCHOOLING AND THE WORKING CLASSES 1860–1918

J. S. HURT

Routledge
Taylor & Francis Group

LONDON AND NEW YORK

First published in 1979 by Routledge & Kegan Paul Ltd

This edition first published in 2017
by Routledge
2 Park Square, Milton Park, Abingdon, Oxon OX14 4RN

and by Routledge
711 Third Avenue, New York, NY 10017

Routledge is an imprint of the Taylor & Francis Group, an informa business

© 1979 J. S. Hurt

British Library Cataloguing in Publication Data
A catalogue record for this book is available from the British Library

ISBN: 978-1-138-22412-4 (Set)
ISBN: 978-1-315-40302-1 (Set) (ebk)
ISBN: 978-1-138-21641-9 (Volume 8) (hbk)
ISBN: 978-1-138-21643-3 (Volume 8) (pbk)
ISBN: 978-1-315-44228-0 (Volume 8) (ebk)

Publisher's Note
The publisher has gone to great lengths to ensure the quality of this reprint but points out that some imperfections in the original copies may be apparent.

Disclaimer
The publisher has made every effort to trace copyright holders and would welcome correspondence from those they have been unable to trace.

ELEMENTARY SCHOOLING AND THE WORKING CLASSES 1860–1918

J. S. Hurt

LONDON: Routledge & Kegan Paul

*First published in 1979 in Great Britain
by Routledge & Kegan Paul Ltd
and in Canada and the United
States of America by
University of Toronto Press
Toronto and Buffalo
Set in 10/12pt Press Roman by
Hope Services, Abingdon, Oxon.
and printed in Great Britain by
Lowe & Brydone Ltd
Thetford, Norfolk*

British Library Cataloguing in Publication Data

*Hurt, John
Elementary schooling and the working classes,
1860–1918. – (Studies in social history).
1. Education, Elementary – English – History
2. Labour and Labouring classes – Education –
England – History
I. Title   II. Series
371.9'67   LA633   79-40050*

*RKP ISBN 0 7100 0275 0
UTP ISBN 0 8020 2353 3*

To Grenda

Contents

Preface

In common with many readers of this book my family's educational background is rooted in the period that it describes. My grandfather and grandmother attended Church schools in the St Marylebone area of London when the Reverend C. D. Du Port (p.9) was supervising them. They had eleven children, the eldest two of whom attended a private school next door to their home, a school now destroyed without trace thanks to a preliminary onslaught of the *Luftwaffe* and a follow-up attack by property speculators. The middle range of children attended a Church school until my grandparents, convinced of its insanitary condition and ignoring the entreaties of its clerical manager, gave their support to the secular arm. Thus the youngest children, including my father, attended the Princess Road Board School, Marylebone; fortunately, this was after the consequences of E. R. Robson's negligent supervision had been made good and the drains repaired (p.170). Coming from a family that respected learning and enjoyed modest prosperity, the younger children earned books and medals for their diligence, punctuality, regularity of attendance and, in one case, for a faithful reproduction of a lecture on temperance. At least two of the children went to higher-grade schools, one to train as an elementary-school teacher just in time to receive one of the first compulsory courses in health and hygiene (p.171). Thus their experiences at a school in a 'non-necessitous' area were not those of many of the children described in these pages.

However, there was one classmate of my father's who was frequently caned for arriving late at school until the schoolmaster learned the reason: this boy had had to wait at home until his mother had earned some money by charring and could buy him his breakfast (p.108). When my father's master found this out, he gave the boy a halfpenny or penny to buy some food in the mornings. Readers will see that I have been aware of these family stories and my own affinity with the past while writing this book and I expect some of my readers will have their childhood memories of parental anecdotes similarly revived.

I have finally the pleasant task of thanking all those who have made this work possible. My thanks are due to Professor Harold Perkin and Dr Eric Evans of Lancaster University for their encouragement, advice, and meticulous editing of the text. I also wish to place on record my gratitude to Ms Pamela Mumford for the calculations that appear in the appendix to Chapter V. I have also to thank the University of Birmingham for financial assistance and study leave that have facilitated the necessary research and writing. I acknowledge permission from the Reverend C. Buckmaster, principal of St Peter's College, Birmingham, to quote from his college's archives; from the Greater London Council to quote from their archives; and from the British Library to reproduce material from the *Englishwoman's Domestic Magazine*. My thanks are also due to Joan Maddocks for typing much of the final draft. Last, my greatest debt is to my wife, Grenda, whose encouragement, support, and scholarly advice have proved invaluable.

Part One

The Working Classes and the
1870 Act

I

Our Future Masters

The Elementary Education Act of 1870 created school boards for those parts of England and Wales in which there were insufficient school places for those children whose station in life was held to destine them for the elementary school. These boards possessed power to enforce the attendance of their pupils. Ten years later this power became a duty that devolved also on the school attendance committee, a body created under an act of 1876 in the non-school-board areas. As certain groups of children had been forced to attend school before 1870, the idea of compulsory education was not new. The number previously affected by a miscellany of legislation that included the Factory Acts, the Reformatory and Industrial Schools Acts and the Poor Law Acts, had been comparatively small. What was new about the legislation of the 1870s was the extent of its operation. For the first time in history the nation's children had to attend school on a full-time basis for a minimum of five years, a period that extended to nine for many by 1914.

The new laws had an important effect on the working-class way of life. No longer could parents take for granted the services of their children in the home and their contributions to the family budget. Traditional working-class patterns of behaviour, when continued, did so in defiance of the law. The state had interfered with the pattern of family life by coming between parent and child, reducing family income, and imposing new patterns of behaviour on both parent and child.

Any analysis of the impact of compulsory education between 1870 and 1914 on working-class culture has to recognize the great diversity of practice and belief that this term conceals. In reality there were several working classes and many cultural differences in the period

3

under examination. Mid-Victorians were well aware of the complexity of this cultural mosaic as their frequent preference for the term 'working classes', in contrast to 'working class', demonstrates. As well as giving recognition to gradations within the working classes based on differences of income, occupation, and the degree of reliability of earnings, they were also aware of regional diversity.

The *modus operandi* of the commissioners appointed under the chairmanship of the Duke of Newcastle in 1858 to inquire into the state of popular education in England—a brief that was extended without protest in those pre-devolutionary days to includes Wales—illustrates this point. In tackling the problem of producing a balanced account of the existing state of affairs without the advantage of today's knowledge of statistically reliable sampling techniques, they chose two contrasting agricultural regions, two manufacturing, two mining, two maritime, and two areas in London for detailed examination. Yet, as will be argued, their omission of many of the largest cities and some of the poorest parts of London obscured the major failing of the elementary schools of the day. The children of the poorest classes—the 'residuum', the 'street arabs', the 'dangerous and perishing classes', to quote a few contemporary terms—were virtually untouched by the existing state-aided voluntary schools managed by the religious societies. The most important of these were the Anglican National Society and the nonconformist British and Foreign School Society which between them provided over 90 per cent of the voluntary-school places.

If, broadly speaking, the children of the poorest received no education apart from that offered in those unflatteringly designated institutions, the Ragged Schools that flourished mainly in Bristol and London, it follows that the new laws bore the most heavily on the least articulate. Hence any evaluation of the impact of compulsory education in the period under examination is heavily dependent on the writings of their social superiors, be they middle-class observers or the leaders of the trade-union and labour movement. To stipulate a further caveat, the term compulsory education is used as a synonym for compulsory schooling. Although this is not entirely accurate it accords with contemporary and popular usage. It must not be forgotten, though, that for the greater part of historical time children have received their education outside the classroom. Schooling has been the experience of the minority of mankind before the present century. Such phrases as 'got his book-learning' or 'got his schooling' vividly demonstrate the way in which the distinction between formal and informal education lives on in the minds of the elderly.

Our discussion must start with an examination of the position in the 1860s just before the new laws reached the statute book. There are two interrelated problems. The first is that of defining the social groups for whom the elementary schools were intended. As the parental consumer had a free choice of sending his child to an elementary school, a private school, or to no school at all, the second problem is that of establishing whether the social composition of the classroom reflected the will of the bureaucrat.

As an answer to the first question the Education Department used a simple social and demographic equation. One-seventh of the population belonged to the upper and middle classes who were expected to make their own arrangements for the education of their children. As a corollary it was argued that these parents would not have wanted their children to attend a school in the company of those of the remaining six-sevenths. The latter, the labouring classes, came within the orbit of the state system. Although the methods by which these proportions were determined do not stand up to a close scrutiny, they provided a working basis for the implementation of the 1870 Act. When it became law, officials used this rule-of-thumb formula to determine whether a particular district possessed sufficient school accommodation. Since this was the first great nineteenth-century exercise in social planning the Departmental guide-lines merit closer scrutiny.

The ratios of one- and six-sevenths were derived from calculations made by Dr W. Farr, of the Registrar-General's Office, and others for the Taunton Commissioners' investigation of the middle-class endowed schools in the 1860s. Farr used the returns of the Department of Inland Revenue. These showed that 519,991 of the 3,739,505 houses in England and Wales were assessed for inhabited house duty at an annual value of £20 or more in the financial year, 1861−2. He calculated that the corresponding figures for 1864 were .575,779 and 3,893,233 respectively. He also found that the number of marriages by licence, at a fee of £3 4s, in 1864 was 26,579. On the other hand 153,808 couples had chosen the more economical and leisurely method of marriage by banns at a cost of about 12s. The proportions in the two cases, 14,789 and 14,730 to 100,000 were close enough to convince him that there was a causal connection and that they provided a satisfactory means for determining the number of children in the middle and upper classes. 'Taking the country generally', he pronounced, 'it is considered right and becoming for the higher and middle classes to marry by licence, and for the rest of the population to marry after the publication of banns.' He concluded that despite the difficulties involved in drawing the line between[1]

what are called the working classes and the middle classes, requiring such an education as the Commission is inquiring into . . . . We have broad lines drawn by the people themselves, and recognized for practical purposes by the Chancellor of the Exchequer. From the one class he collects the house tax, and he does not now venture to go lower.

Other investigators, who followed different routes, reached similar conclusions. Although D. C. Richardson, Assistant Commissioner and Registrar to the Commission, quite legitimately attacked Farr's assumption, he broadly agreed with his result. Richardson showed that the relationship Farr had attempted to establish between social class, the occupation of houses assessed at £20 a year or more, and marriage by licence, did not stand up to close scrutiny. For instance, 44·2 per cent of the houses in London and 6·2 per cent in Westmorland were assessed at £20 a year or more. Yet the percentages of marriages by special licence in the two areas were 14 and 39 respectively. Richardson accordingly carried out a survey based on information derived from the *Court Directories*. He chose for investigation the towns of Woodbridge and Bury St Edmunds, in Suffolk, and the large villages of Kimbolton, Huntingdonshire, and Stradbroke, Suffolk, a sample biased heavily in favour of a rural and pre-industrial England of a century earlier. From an analysis of this material he decided that 155 in every 1,000 belonged to the upper and middle classes. A third person to tackle the problem was J. G. Fitch, another assistant commissioner to the Taunton Commission. After examining the parental background of children in the schools of York, Sheffield, Halifax, and Selby, he calculated that 17·8 per cent of the boys and 19·7 per cent of the girls belonged to the class that paid for the education of its children. His slightly higher proportions, he argued, were consistent with Farr's figures because they were inflated by the longer stay at school made by children in 'the middle and upper ranks'.[2]

A contemporary study, R. D. Baxter's *National Income* (1868), provides little further guidance on the matter. Baxter calculated that 4,870,000 of the estimated population of England and Wales belonged to the upper and middle classes. The balance, 16,130,000, were members of the manual labouring classes. However, Baxter's classification

6

was based on an amalgamate of social esteem imputed to a particular occupation and status ascribed by income. He had used the Occupational Returns of the 1861 census to make his allocation of individuals to his broad social categories. Similarly, his general conclusion that there were 2,053,000 people with independent incomes in the upper and middle classes and 7,785,000 in the manual labouring class gives little further guidance in answering the question what proportion of the population could afford to pay school fees of over ninepence a week, the upper limit of the charge made in public elementary schools. Since Baxter was concerned with establishing the total number of independent incomes, his aggregate figures include estimates of the earnings of both married and single women, and children. Moreover, his estimates of upper- and middle-class income are made from the dubious evidence of income tax returns. Somewhat naively he assumed that only the working classes would have been so unscrupulous as to practise tax evasion.[3] Thus Baxter's enquiry does no more than broadly confirm the accuracy of the one-seventh and six-sevenths formula of the Education Department, it by no means proves its reliability. His estimates, in common with those already cited, are open to other objections. Any calculation of the number of children whose education had to be subsidized needed to take into account, not so much individual income, as total family income. It also had to allow for such quantifiable variables as the size and age structure of the family as well as the non-quantifiable one of parental interest in education.

In any discussion of social class and school attendance it must be remembered that mid-Victorian observers had some, but only a limited, justification for equating willingness with ability to pay school fees. In today's society parental value-judgements on the worth of higher education for children vary not only between various income levels but within them as well. In the nineteenth century this was equally true of elementary education. Apart from other factors, readiness to pay school fees was determined both by income and occupation. One perceptive inspector, the Rev. D. J. Stewart, whose district included the university city of Cambridge, showed his awareness of this in his *Report* for 1856.[4]

In thirty-one schools . . . I saw 3,505 children. Of this number, only 1,629 were children of the labouring class; the others were the children of farmers; small shopkeepers, farm bailiffs, household servants, college servants, petty tailors, shoemakers, and etc., many of whom are, no doubt worse off than labourers in full work.

Although Stewart's main concern was to demonstrate that children other than those of the labouring class used the schools receiving a government grant, his comments show that there was no simple correlation between income levels and attitudes towards education.

Granted that some of the farmers and small businessmen may have been worse off than the labourer in full employment, others were not. Hence the social structure of England and Wales by the 1860s was too complex to make a cut-off point of one-seventh valid. The Taunton Commissioners gave considerable attention to this social borderline where the lower middle classes and the more prosperous members of the working classes overlapped. They found that 'the education of what is sometimes called the lower section of the middle class is at present often conducted in the National and British schools', the very schools that had been surveyed by the Newcastle Commissioners during their enquiry into the education of the independent poor. Not surprisingly they commented, 'our inquiry into this most important part of our subject has been attended with unusual difficulties.'[5]

In their *Report* they had envisaged that the sons of 'the lower section of the middle class'—the sons of 'the smaller tenant farmers, the small tradesmen, the superior Artisans'—would attend a 'third-grade school' where they would receive a thorough grounding in the basic skills of reading, writing, and arithmetic. This level of attainment broadly corresponded with that expected of the top class of a voluntary school. Under Standard VI of the Revised Code, introduced by Robert Lowe in the early 1860s to monitor the scholastic performance of the schools and to determine the amount of their annual grants, a child was expected to 'read a short ordinary paragraph in a newspaper', write a similar passage of prose from dictation, and calculate 'a sum in practice or bills of parcels'. The mastery of such accomplishments would have qualified a boy for a clerkship in a mercantile office or some comparable career, the level of parental ambition of many from the top end of the working classes or the lower end of the middle. The duplication of the syllabuses paralleled that of the institutions. 'The lower divisions of the third-grade schools do not differ from good national schools except in as far as a higher fee may secure schoolmasters either of a higher social rank or of a greater professional skill.'[6]

The demands made by this socially amorphous group gave school managers an easy and acceptable market to satisfy. The children were seen as easier to handle and more highly motivated than those of the poorer sections of the working classes. Their regular attendance together with the opportunity of charging higher fees made the voluntary schools financially secure. When a school manager decided to go up-market he frequently did so at the expense of the very children for whom the school had been founded in the first place. Poor children were either excluded because the fees were too high or, if admitted to the bottom classes at a low fee, were accorded the lowest priority in the allocation of teaching resources. In 1895 H.M.I. Du Port described his experiences as a young curate at Holy Trinity Church, Marylebone, in the early 1860s.[7]

I was behind the scenes as a curate-manager of large and highly esteemed schools in London, teaching in them daily; and very pleasant hours did I spend with those 40 first-class boys over their Euclid, their history, and their arithmetic. My occasional visits to the second class, too, were, though, in a less degree, interesting and encouraging; but . . . the lower two-thirds fraction of the school was little better than an unorganized mass of children of all ages; of teaching properly so called they had none; . . . educational training began at the *second* class.

In this school the children of the skilled artisan travelled first class, those of the poor were in the steerage, the captain seldom came below deck.

School managers who provided a more advanced form of teaching had little reason to fear for the future prosperity of their schools. In making their schools the precursors of the higher elementary schools run by the school boards in the last decades of the century, they were remedying one of the major deficiencies of the English educational system. 'The schools that are wanting everywhere', the Taunton Commissioners declared, 'are good schools of the third grade.' This was demonstrably true of London where almost all schools 'are badly placed, inadequate in buildings and accommodation, and worst of all unsatisfactorily taught and conducted.' More than half of London's population were without any local endowment for education at all. Outside London the situation was little, if any, better. Apart from Birmingham and Liverpool, none of the remaining twelve towns with a population around the 100,000 mark, had an 'endowed school specially provided for boys in the third grade'. In fifty-four towns with populations between 20,000 and 100,000 there were only three or four at the most with any 'systematic provision of third-grade schools adapted to the wants of the lower middle classes'. Of the 52,000 boys reputed to be in endowed and proprietary schools offering secondary education in England and Wales, only 11,077 day scholars and 1,764 boarders were reported to be attending third-grade endowed schools. Yet some 255,000 boys alone were thought to require secondary education. This missing 80 per cent 'educated in private schools, or at home or not at all' provided ambitious voluntary school managers with a potentially rewarding market to tap.[8]

Businessmen patronized such schools in the belief that they offered their sons a sound education that would equip them for the commercial world. James Bryce, at this time an assistant commissioner to the Taunton Commission, found this view especially prevalent in South-East Lancashire, an area bounded by Burnley, Warrington, Wigan, and Stalybridge. This rapidly expanding manufacturing 'frontier' district he likened to parts of America and Australia. Here he detected little social pretension among the *nouveaux riches*. He depicted a 'society . . . in an unsettled and fluctuating state'. In this region he continued, 'Men almost, sometimes wholly, illiterate, have risen to prodigious wealth . . . . A millionaire has cousins or even brothers among the operatives, and is socially on a level with his own workpeople, to whose class he belonged a year or two before.' Hence the Privy Council schools were used to a very large extent 'by those of what would be accounted [elsewhere] a socially superior class, the shopkeepers, the publicans, the foremen, and overlookers in the mills, nay even by the manufacturers themselves'. In some of the local towns and villages, where the National and British schools were the only ones available, the managers ran special classes. For a fee of 6d or 1s a week a pupil could receive instruction in history, geography and even Latin. Bryce found what he described as a misuse of government funds in both Manchester and Liverpool. Parents who could afford to pay the total cost of their children's education were using the voluntary schools thereby accepting state assistance intended for the independent poor. Bryce noted that the pupils included the children of shopkeepers, clerks, well-to-do artisans, and warehousemen earning up to £200 a year, men whom he considered well able to afford a fee of 15s or £1 a quarter for a private school. Such parents doubtless agreed with the archetypal businessman to whom Bryce attributed the opinion, 'I want my boy to write a good clear hand, and to add up figures quickly . . . . Too much schooling oftener mars a man of business than it makes him'.[9]

Other assistant commissioners to the Taunton Commission provided similar evidence. J. L. Hammond, who investigated the counties of Northumberland and Norfolk, thought that the introduction of the Revised Code had made the voluntary schools more attractive than the 'private schools of the lowest class'. This was because 'the first and indispensable requirement not only of the working but also of the trading classes, is a sound instruction in reading, writing, and arithmetic, no school will meet with much favour if it sacrifices the essentials to any other branch of study . . . .' Concentration on the basic skills allowed a boy to finish his 'education' as soon as possible, thereby not only enabling his parents to save on school fees but allowing them to profit from his contribution to the total family budget. As in parts of Lancashire so in Northumberland, Hammond found, 'there is no social feeling to prevent a farmer or tradesman from sending his child to a Government school, the improvements caused by the grant in the form, if not the substance, of instruction are seriously affecting private educational enterprise.'[10]

J. G. Fitch observed the same phenomena in the West Riding of Yorkshire. 'In many of the good schools under inspection and in receipt of aid . . . , I find an increasing number of children belonging to a class above that for which the schools were intended. The small shopkeepers, clerks, and superior workmen', he added, 'find the education given in a good National school is better suited to their needs than that which is to be purchased in small private academies.' Some of these schools had developed senior classes in which the fees were above the ninepence limit stipulated in the Revised Code. Such a step, debarring the pupils from qualifying for the government grant, enabled the managers to employ better qualified masters. Thus the syllabus of the Leeds parish school included geometry, algebra, and Latin. Similar classes were held at British and National schools in York, Doncaster, and Hull.[11]

The Independents and Baptists, after their secession from the British and Foreign School Society to form with others the Voluntary School Society, found that their bid for spiritual freedom had brought them the secular advantage of liberation from the social and monetary restrictions of the Revised Code. Instead of offering an elementary education for the children of the labouring poor at a cost that did not exceed ninepence a week, they had set up secondary schools that charged as much as 1s 3d a week. These schools, known as 'training schools', prepared their pupils for the middle-class examinations recently started by the universities of Oxford and Cambridge. Some National-school managers had followed the example set by these prosperous nonconformists. They had given up all pretence of fulfilling their pastoral duty to the poor. They had farmed out their school to the master. This enabled him to run it as a business concern unaided either by government grants or private subscriptions. He kept the balance of the fees he charged after meeting the running expenses out of his pocket. Fitch found that 'Cases of this kind are daily multiplying.' These changes had been made at the expense of the poor for the schools had become 'essentially middle class, self sustaining and semi-private schools . . . not accessible to the children of the poor.'[12]

A few years earlier the Newcastle Commissioners had also given some thought to the social composition of the classroom to see whether the government grants were reaching the class for whom they were intended. While the inquiry was still in progress the Education Department categorically stated in its codification of the existing regulations 'The object of the grant is to promote the education of the children belonging to the classes who support themselves by manual labour.'[13] During the course of his evidence R. R. W. Lingen, Secretary to the Education Department, stated that in the British and Wesleyan schools charging threepence or fourpence a week 'the parents . . . consist, to a very great extent of that class which is either at the top of the working class or at the bottom of the shop-keeping class.' Later on when asked 'Do you see a clear line between the classes now receiving aid and the classes immediately above them?', he hedged 'I think it is an exceedingly difficult line for the State to lay down, but it is found in practice that the feeling of independence acts very strongly, and that as soon as people can pay for their education, as a matter of fact they do so.'[14]

On this point the Commissioners' faith in the canons of established contemporary social theory came to their assistance. 'The feelings which tend to make the offer of gratuitous instruction unpopular, tend also to incline the parents to pay as large a share as they can reasonably afford of the expense of the education of their children.' In addition the Newcastle Commissioners alleged that the large majority of parents 'mistrust the value of a purely gratuitous education'. This was not entirely the product of that healthy spirit of independence that middle-class commentators so readily fathered on their social inferiors. Parents, who were able to afford a fee of three or fourpence a week, did not want their children sitting next to the verminous and unkempt sons and daughters of the near-pauper classes. For them there were the ragged schools that catered for 'that class which cannot associate with the children of respectable labouring men'.[15] Hence J. D. Morell, an inspector of British schools in Lancashire, could argue that the most successful schools were those very ones that charged a fee of twopence to sixpence a week, a range that virtually excluded the children of the manual labourer from all but the bottom classes. He believed that the effect of reducing fees to a penny a week would be to empty the schools. 'A few children of the lowest classes would go in', he predicted, 'and then the mechanics, who considered themselves to be a little above those classes, would not let their children go in and learn with them.'[16]

When attempts were made to reduce the level of public expenditure after the Crimean War, one obvious economy the Education Department could make was to ensure the strict observance of the expressed intention of the grant they administered. Confinement of the benefit of the grant to the children of the labouring poor would dissuade better-off parents from relying on state aid, a practice that if it became habitual was believed to lead its adherents to lose all self-reliance. This was the primrose path that ended at the gate of the workhouse. Hence Lingen, notwithstanding his earlier hesitation, attempted to lay down the 'exceedingly difficult line' between those parents eligible for state assistance and 'the classes immediately above them.' In January 1864 he issued a series of instructions to assist the inspectorate in deciding whether a particular child belonged to the classes supporting themselves by manual labour. In drafting these regulations, Lingen showed he realized that a man's occupation could not necessarily be related precisely to his social class. For instance the term 'clerk' which, prima facie, has a connotation of occupational homogeneity, by the 1860s covered a wide socio-economic spectrum. The Department, adopting a somewhat Marxist stance, argued that men in skilled trades such as those of the mason, carpenter, tailor, blacksmith, mariner, or fisherman, who employed labour were *ipso facto* ineligible for financial assistance from the state towards their children's education. As employers, they profited from the labour of others. They did not support themselves by their 'own labour alone'. Humbler folk such as simple policemen, coast-guards, and dock and railway porters, presented no problem. They could 'commonly be regarded as working men'. Their immediate superiors, 'petty officers in those services, excisemen, pilots and clerks of various kinds', taxed the skill of the amateur social classifier to the utmost. In making their decision, inspectors were urged to ask about the father, 'Does he rank and associate with the working men or with the tradesmen of the place?' Such a question took the decision out of the hands of the inspectors for it recognized the social classification made by the working classes of one of their fellows as the effective one. Another consideration enjoined on the inspectorate also posed problems. They could ask themselves whether it was unreasonable to expect a particular parent to pay ninepence a week for the schooling of each of his children.[17] Yet the parent who could have afforded nine-pence a week for one child, let alone more, was well outside the ranks of the labouring poor. The choice of the ninepenny limit had been determined by administrative not social criteria. It represented the average *per capita* weekly cost of the maintenance of a child in a government assisted elementary school. Even a rigorous application of Lingen's instructions would have left plenty of room in the classroom for the children of a skilled worker and householder, the man who received the franchise in 1867 and for whom standard histories of education tell us the Elementary Education Act, 1870, was intended. The members of the inspectorate, schoolmasters, and school managers alike, had good reason to frustrate the intent of these regulations. Schoolmaster and school manager, with a vested interest in the size of the annual grant, had every temptation to devalue the social origins of those pupils who came from a financially superior background. Such children made Standards V and VI, the top classes where the highest fees were charged, their stronghold. 'Standard VI', HMI the Rev. G.R. Moncreiff wrote, 'is composed of the flower of the school, not so much the cleverest, as the steadiest in attendance oftener of a slighly higher social grade, or the children of parents of a slightly higher social tone'.[18]

The inspectorate knew full well that the Revised Code was already unpopular enough with the school managers. To have conducted a minute examination of the children's social background by referring to regulations that possibly created more problems than they solved would only have fanned the flames of resentment still further. The greater part of the inspectorate, preferring discretion to valour, made little effort to comply with their instructions. For instance, in the year ending 31 August 1867 only 15,343 passes, that is approximately the equival-ent of 6,000 children tested in reading, writing and arithmetic, out of a total of 592,005 children examined in England and Wales, were deemed ineligible for the annual grant.[19] One inspector justified his inactivity on the somewhat tendentious grounds that the new rules did not actually debar such children as those of tradesmen and farmers from the purview of the grant. On the other hand he advocated a policy of charging such fees as the parent could bear. He instanced the case of a school at Woodside, near Dudley, 'a populous mining and manufactur-ing district', where the weekly fees rose from threepence to sixpence a week on a sliding scale related to parental incomes that varied from £1 to £2 a week. He had perforce to admit that even such a cut-and-dried scheme as the one he described was 'most difficult . . . in large towns where the different classes of society so run into one another.'[20] In this particular case it does not seem that the managers even considered the possibility that the children of the unskilled labourer might be pupils of the school. The lower limit of a wage of £1 a week was more than the average earnings of the unskilled manual worker at this time.

Of all the inspectors J. G. Fitch, who dealt with British schools in South Lancashire, probably made the most consistent effort to carry out his instructions. In 1867 alone, he excluded some 450 children from the benefit of the grant. However even he considered that he had done no more than to touch the tip of the iceberg. The task of filling up the necessary forms, he complained, was 'very frequently evaded'. He was convinced that the 'exceptions ought in equity to have been much more numerous'.[21]

Other inspectors who were concerned over the enforcement of Lingen's instructions included Matthew Arnold, his brother the Rev. Edward Arnold, and the Rev. D. R. Fearon. The Arnold brothers took the hard line that the ninepenny limit was too high. Edward pointed out that the average cost, per pupil, in his district of Cornwall and Devon was £1 5s 8¾d and not £1 10s a year. The latter figure included such non-local costs as the expense of central government administration and other disbursements that did not affect the schools directly. School managers, E. P. Arnold complained, forgot these facts when assessing parental willingness, that is ability, to pay. His brother Matthew, conscious of the social anomalies of the ninepenny limit, wanted to reduce it to sixpence. In this way 'plenty of well-to-do parents in the middle classes' would be excluded from the benefit of a state-aided education for their children. Last, Fearon was another inspector who wanted to confine the education grant to its stated purpose. 'The number of well-to-do persons who were not ashamed, under the Old Code', he wrote in 1865, 'to provide their children with elementary education at the public expense is much diminished by the new system.' He sympathized with the dilemma confronting the middle-class parent who frequently had no suitable school to which he could send his children. He accordingly advocated the reform of the endowed grammar schools. Once this was achieved,[22]

Members of the middle class will, when able to obtain suitable education, no longer endeavour, as so many of them do, to educate their children in the annual grant schools intended for the poor, and an unjust burden will thus be taken off from the whole nation, while more money is left for the use of the poor.'

Clearly it is difficult without considerable research in a carefully chosen sample of localities, using such documents as admission registers of individual schools, rate books, census enumerators' reports, and other local material, to give a quantitative precision to the hypothesis so far advanced from a study of literary evidence. However, a consideration of the course of domestic politics in the late 1860s makes the picture of a voluntary-school system serving mainly the more prosperous working-class parent, and by inference neglecting the poorer—an issue to be examined separately—a more convincing one.

When Gladstone and Disraeli introduced their measures for the extension of the franchise, they argued that the skilled working man was not only ready for the vote but had earned his right to it. The years since 1848, when other European capitals had been shaken by revolution while London remained virtually unscathed, had been a period of growing social stability and increasing prosperity. Far from trying to deny the artisan access to the polling booth on the grounds of his illiteracy, the two statesmen maintained that his self-improvement since 1832, when an estimated 87,000 working men had been enfranchised, had earned him the right to come within the pale of the constitution. Their proposals for reform, they consequently argued, would not rupture the fabric of society as their opponents feared. On the contrary their suggested legislation would strengthen it.

Hence when the Rt Hon. W. E. Gladstone, Chancellor of the Exchequer and leader of the Liberal Party in the House of Commons, moved the first reading of the unsuccessful Reform Bill of 1866, he reminded Members of the great advances his intended beneficiaries had made:[23]

Whether we take education in schools; whether we take social conduct; whether we take obedience to the law; whether we take self-command and power of endurance, shown under difficulty and privation; whether we take avidity for knowledge and self-improvement . . . there can be no doubt at all that if the working man in some degree was fit to share in political privileges in 1832 he has, at any rate, attained some considerable degree of additional fitness now.

A year later the Rt Hon. Benjamin Disraeli, Gladstone's successor as Chancellor of the Exchequer in the new Conservative administration

16

headed by Lord Derby, echoed his political rival's sentiments when he introduced the bill that eventually became the Representation of the People Act, 1867.[24]

I would say that looking to what has occurred since the Reform Act of 1832 was passed—to the increase of population, the progress of industry, the spread of knowledge, and our ingenuity in the arts—we are of opinion that numbers, thoughts, and feelings have since that time been created which it is desirable should be admitted within the circle of the constitution.

Despite their well-known antipathy both political leaders were in agreement on a further point. A carefully controlled measure of electoral reform would help to cement and stabilize the existing social order. Gladstone urged the House:[25]

Give to these persons new interests in the Constitution—new interests which, by the beneficient processes of the law of nature and of Providence, shall beget in them new attachment; for the attachment of the people to the Throne, the institutions, and the laws under which they live is . . . at once the strength, the glory, and the safety of the land.

Disraeli gave the House a similar assurance only twelve months later. His bill, he claimed, conferred a popular privilege that was 'consistent with a state of society in which there was great inequality of condition'. He carefully pointed out that it did not confer democratic rights which 'demanded that there should be equality of condition as to the fundamental basis of the society which they regulate.'[26]

During the subsequent committee proceedings, Disraeli exploited his party's confidence in the willingness and ability of the proposed newly enfranchised classes to act rationally, the hallmark of the receipt of sound popular education, by accepting the leadership of their social superiors. In the words of Lord Elcho, a former cohabitant of Robert Lowe in the cave of Adullam, 'Working men are as open to reason as any other class; and if the upper classes will in their sphere do their duty, and exercise their moral influence over the people, they will find them much more reasonable than some suppose them to be.'[27]

Thus the Conservative Party, sustained by a belief in its innate capacity for successful leadership in a deferential society that had been educated on sound principles, accepted the crucial amendments to the bill—the lodger franchise, the enfranchisement of the householder who had compounded his rates, the lowering of the residential qualification

17

for the boroughs from two years to one, and the inclusion of the £12 householder, the £5 long-leaseholder and the copyholder in the counties.

Recent studies have suggested that these concessions were not as far-reaching as their bare recital suggests. In the boroughs the difficulties facing the lodger deterred all but the most resolute from claiming their newly acquired constitutional rights. Likewise the residential qualification required of the householder kept the more nomadic and impoverished working man off the electoral roll. For instance, only 47 per cent of the adult male occupiers were on the 1868 register. Furthermore the safeguard in the Reform Act for the householder, whereby the widespread practice of rating the owner of dwellings instead of the occupier was discontinued, was resumed just two years later. Payment by the owner came to be deemed payment by the occupier for the purpose of the franchise. Even if these difficulties were surmounted there remained another obstacle for the working man who wished to exercise his right to the franchise. The hours of polling were less than those of the working day both for parliamentary elections and, as we shall see, for school-board ones as well before the mid-1880s. The manner of the redistribution of parliamentary seats provided yet another 'bulwark against democracy'. The twenty-three smallest boroughs with about 28,000 electors in 1868 returned forty-five members. The nineteen largest ones with a combined population of about 5,000,000 possessed forty-six members. In a number of non-parliamentary boroughs the artisan, who did not qualify under the more restricted county franchise, had no vote at all.[28] If one takes into account the probable social composition of the classroom as well, the combined effect of these features of the Reform Act of 1867 is to make it seem unlikely that the onward march of democracy had outstripped the progress of popular education.

The time required to compile a register of the new electorate gave the government a breathing space. They could have introduced legislation elementary education if there had existed a consensus of opinion between the main political parties that such a step was a prime necessity for the preservation of the *status quo*. However, when parliament met for the first time after the passing of the Reform Act the government showed, through its lack of any such sense of urgency, confidence in the future. Although Disraeli claimed that the reference to public education in the speech from the Throne was 'not a rhetorical flourish', he undermined his credibility by adding that the government did not feel justified in referring more specifically to their efforts and intentions in that direction. The Earl of Derby, another temporiser, alleged that the subject 'requires much more information than we possess and I cannot but feel', he added, 'that the time is hardly ripe for coming to a definite conclusion in regard to it.'[29] Yet any minister anxious and ready for action could have found information enough. To cite only some recently published official sources, he would have had at his disposal the six volumes of the *Newcastle Report* published in 1861, the two volumes of evidence collected by the Select Committee on Education in 1865 and 1866, as well as the annual *Reports* of the Education Department and its inspectorate. Even such a committed advocate of the extension of popular education as W. E. Forster shared the official view. He pointed out that 'If the Reform Bill was likely to do harm, the harm would be done before their measure took effect.'[30] In other words if the recent Reform Act had enfranchised the uneducated classes, a comprehensive measure for the extension of education would be doing no more than closing the stable door after the electoral horse had bolted at the hustings.

Despite earlier ministerial equivocation the Duke of Marlborough introduced an Education Bill in March 1868. Its most radical proposal was an administrative one, not an educational one. The Bill contemplated the creation of a sixth Secretary of State at the head of a unified education department. As an educational measure, it did little more than to try to give the existing voluntary system a new lease of life and ward off the creation of any system of popularly elected boards vested with rating powers, thereby assuaging the fears of the Duke's fellow landowners. Possibly to conciliate his noble audience the sponsor took pains to disavow any suggestion that the bill was 'a complete measure'. Sweeping changes were unnecessary and fraught with hazard. 'If we should take a false step', he warned, 'or arrive at a hasty conclusion, we might commit an irretrievable error.' Precipitate action was inappropriate since the wants that had to be supplied were not 'so great as to demand any violent or extraordinary remedy'. Indeed the government's main positive proposal for the extension of the voluntary system was to raise the level of the grant for building new schools from 2s 6d a square foot to 4s 0d.[31] Understandably the bill, with its avoidance of the rating system and its commitment to the maintenance of the voluntary schools, was 'well received' by the National Society. The Conservative Party was serving the Established Church well. The Bill had received its first reading on 24 March, its second on 27 April, only to be withdrawn on 18 May. The exigencies of political life had halted its passage through parliament. In the early hours of 1 May Gladstone had carried a resolution for the disestablishment of the Irish Church. Three days later, Disraeli announced his intention of seeking a dissolution and fighting a general election on the basis of the new register when it was ready in the autumn.

The question of the status of the Irish Church dominated the subsequent electoral campaign. When education received mention, it was included along with other issues for which reform was advocated. For instance William Rathbone of Liverpool declared himself in favour of 'a full measure of national education, the disestablishment of the Irish Church, an amendment in the laws of land tenure in Ireland, a greater economy in all departments of the State, and a reform of our municipal and parochial taxation'. In the course of two speeches at Bradford, W. E. Forster mentioned education but in neither case did he make it a major theme. Gladstone made lengthy speeches at Liverpool, Warrington, Newton, and Leigh, Lancashire. Although some of these occupied six or more columns in *The Times*, he does not seem to have touched on the need to reform elementary education at all. Even Robert Lowe's main concern in his address to the graduates of London University was that of the manner in which expenditure on public education should be financed. If the reports of election speeches provide a reliable guide, there was no obvious alarm over the way in which the franchise had been extended before a system of nationwide and comprehensive education—in the nineteenth-century sense—had been developed.[32]

Accordingly it is not surprising that when members of parliament met early in 1869 to hear the Speech from the Throne they heard no reference to the problem of elementary education. Gladstone, the Anglican who had earlier been involved in the National Society's counter offensive of the late 1830s, defended this omission. 'There is no greater temptation to a government . . . than that of promising . . . a great number of measures of vast and widely extended interest, without any careful reckoning or calculation of the time at their disposal for carrying them into law.' The government had enough on its plate. It had just stated its intention of introducing two measures on rating, as well as bills on bankruptcy, education in Scotland, and the Endowed Schools. In addition there was the most contentious issue of them all, the bill for the disestablishment of the Church in Ireland. Thus it was not until the following session that W. E. Forster was able to put forward another equally controversial bill, that in its original form was in some respects almost as displeasing to the radical non-conformist conscience of his own party as it was to the Anglican Toryism of the Opposition, containing proposals for the extension of elementary education.[33]

Despite the recent extension of the franchise, the poorer working-class child had been put firmly at the end of the legislative queue. The task of safeguarding the funds available for the education of the children of the aristocracy and middle classes had received priority. The Public Schools Act, 1868, and the Endowed Schools Act of the following year, frustrated the intent of those who wanted the misappropriated endowments of those bodies used for the good of the community at large. The propertied classes had safeguarded their stake in a hierarchially structured educational system by timely and judicious reform before turning their attention to the needs of the poorer working classes.

The delay in introducing the 1870 Act, coupled with one historian's failure to detect any sense of urgency in the private papers of the leading politicians of the period, raises legitimate doubts about the interconnexion that is so widely thought to have existed between the extension of the franchise in 1867 and the passage of this later act. The often quoted—and frequently misquoted—warning of Robert Lowe has received undue attention. His remark 'I believe it will be absolutely necessary that you should prevail on our future masters to learn their letters' was made by a member of the House of Commons whose virulent opposition to the extension of the franchise made him atypical of the House as a whole. Lowe, who had returned from Australia a confirmed anti-democrat, saw the Bill as a 'new dangerous . . . desperate expedient'. 'It is the order of Providence that men should be unequal,' he explained, 'and it is in my opinion the wisdom of a State to make its institutions conform to that order.'[34]

Lowe did not share the view held by some that a generous settlement of the franchise question would provide political stability for a considerable time. 'The Bill so far as it has any principle at all,' he pointed out, 'is founded on the principle of equality.' The new Act far from ushering in a period of stability would inaugurate an era of rapid change. With a political prescience and realism that few others possessed, Lowe warned that the county electors would not remain content with a £12 limit nor the lodgers with a £10 one. 'When you have once taught the people to entertain the notion of the individual rights of every citizen to share in the government, you impose on your-selves the task of remodelling the whole of your institutions, in reference to the principles you have set up.' There would be, he pre-dicted, an elected prime minister, elected judges, and elected army officers. In particular he feared the power that would now accrue to the trade unions, 'the most dangerous political agencies that could be conceived', a judgement made against the background of the Sheffield outrages.

Lowe was so alarmed about the future that he announced he had completely changed his views on the educational question. He with-drew all his earlier opposition to increasing centralization and the prospect of an educational rate. With a complete disregard for the finer nuances of the class structure of a rapidly expanding economy he denounced the new Act as entrusting the 'masses', the great bulk of whom he alleged were uneducated, 'with the whole power of the country'. This evil could only be remedied by 'the most universal measure of education that can be devised. I believe,' he continued, 'it will be absolutely necessary that you should prevail upon our future masters to learn their letters . . . .'.[35]

This question is now no longer a religious question, it has become a political one . . . . For the moment that you intrust the masses with absolute power their education becomes an absolute necessity, and our system of education . . . must give way to a national system . . . . You have placed the government in the hands of the masses . . . . You must now take education up [as] the very first question, and you must press it on without delay for the peace of the country.

Lowe's speech shows his failure to comprehend the social gradations that existed within the working classes. He was also unaware of the extent to which the more skilled man already possessed some education either as a result of his own efforts or through attendance at school in the past. Such men who helped to provide the readership of the new popular Sunday newspapers, the family journals, the earlier *Penny Magazine*, and the more popular literature investigated by Louis James in his *Fiction for the Working Man, 1830–50* (1963) had already learnt their letters. In similar vein R. K. Webb has argued that two-thirds to three-quarters, or even more, of the working classes of early Victorian England could read. Although one may legitimately wonder just what they could read and with what fluency, one can accept his assertion, together with its converse, that the greatest proportion of the totally illiterate were amongst the lowest sections of society.[36] Finally,

Lowe's concern to see that the sons of those who were about to be enfranchised were educated involved a remarkable volte-face. As putative author of the Revised Code and Vice-President of the Committee of the Privy Council on Education, he had tried to keep some of those very children out of the schools.

Practitioners of a quasi-Whig school of educational history assisted by reinforcements from the battalions of social-conflict theorists of history have given Lowe's dictum the sanctity of the Tablets. However, parliamentary reform can be seen as much the response to change that has already taken place as the catalyst of further reform. The removal of a series of legislative shackles and the humanizing of the criminal code were only two of the important improvements made to British institutions in the decade before 1832. Even the manner of the passing of the Reform Act itself, the coercion of the House of Lords by the Monarch's promise to create sufficient peers to secure the passage of the bill, shows the extent to which the balance of power in the constitution had already shifted in favour of the Lower House. In this light the initiation of the building grant for schools in 1833 'so often made the starting point for optimistic histories of educational progress, can be more helpfully and accurately read as the belated triumph of pre-Reform, pre-modern legislation.'[37] Such initiatives as the Younger Pitt's Bill of 1796 to set up schools of industry, the Factory Acts of 1802 and 1819, Whitbread's bill of 1807, Lord Brougham's Select Committee of 1816 and his bill of 1820, provide eloquent testimony of the interest a section of the unreformed parliament showed in the education of the children of the poor.

The reform of parliament together with the repeal of the Corn Laws in 1846 removed the more demonstrably indefensible bastions of privilege. From this two important consequences flowed. First, the new propertied classes were able to use their political power to block reform that conflicted with their propertied interests. Public health and education were issues of great social concern between 1832 and 1870 where thoroughgoing reform posed the double threat of rates on landed property on all types and elected boards. After 1832 a series of acts shored up, but did not radically modify, the voluntary-school system. The industrial Schools Acts of 1857, 1861 and 1866; the Reformatory Schools Acts of 1854, 1857 and 1866; and the Education of Pauper Children Act of 1862, all helped local authorities to tackle the problem of the education of the 'residuum', the class the voluntary schools had neglected.[38] When these efforts of pre-1867 parliaments had failed and the voluntary system had lost credence as the means of educating the children of the nation, then and only then, did the 1870 Act belatedly and reluctantly 'fill the gaps'.

A second effect of the Acts of 1832, 1846 and 1867, was that they deprived the agitating classes of their potential leaders who were absorbed into the ranks of those with a vested interest in the preservation of the status quo. A consideration such as this seems to have been in Forster's mind in 1867 when he acknowledged that the Reform Bill of that year made the question of education a less, not a more, politically urgent matter. As one of the sponsors of the Education of the Poor Bill of that year – the last such measure to bear this socially discriminatory title – he remarked, 'A great deal has been said in the course of the session about a 'residuum'; but he had no fear of that portion of the community, since the suffrage had been extended by the Bill which had occupied so much of their attention of late; still it was the duty of the House to prevent the children of the class which formed the 'residuum' growing up to be no better than their parents.'[39] In other words the extension of the provision of elementary education after 1867 had become a matter of social policy, it was no longer a matter of political necessity.

II

♦♦♦

The Parental Consumer

♦♦♦

Much of the history of education has been written from the top, from the perspective of those who ran and provided the schools, be they civil servants or members of the religious societies that promoted the cause of popular education. Little has been written from the viewpoint of those who were the recipients of this semi-charitable endeavour, the parents who paid the weekly school pence and the children who sat in the schoolrooms of nineteenth-century England. Hence historians have tended to neglect one important way in which the 1870s mark a great divide for the parental consumer. Up to 1870 the voluntary system was a voluntary one for both principal parties. Not only was the establishment of schools a matter of individual choice for local persons, the sense in which the system is usually seen as a voluntary one, it was also a voluntary one for parent and child alike. Before this date the majority of parents could decide how much, if any, formal schooling their children should receive. After the decade of the 1870s they lost this freedom of choice. The state decreed a minimum that all had to receive. Parental choice was, and still is, limited to deciding the maximum.

An examination of the twenty years before 1870 can reveal much about working-class attitudes towards the education of their children before the state imposed its will. Parents, as a whole, were slightly more concerned about the education of their sons than of their daughters. In his report on education in the 1851 Census Horace Mann analysed the household returns relating to more than a quarter of a million children, 253,425, aged between 3 and 15. These returns included all social classes and covered 'a selection of localities in the various counties'. He found that 45 per cent of the boys and 43 per cent of the girls were described as scholars and that 15 per cent and 9 per cent respectively

25

TABLE 1   *Children at school, work, or at home, 1851*

	Boys							Girls						
	Scholars		Employed		Undescribed		Total	Scholars		Employed		Undescribed		Total
Age	*No*	*%*	*No*	*%*	*No*	*%*	*Total*	*No*	*%*	*No*	*%*	*No*	*%*	*Total*
3	1,881	16·8	—	—	9,341	83·2	11,222	1,885	17·0	—	—	9,199	83·0	11,084
4	3,526	30·9	—	—	7,889	69·1	11,415	3,227	28·6	—	—	8,040	71·4	11,267
5	5,890	50·2	19	0·1	5,831	49·7	11,740	5,285	46·4	27	0·2	6,077	53·3	11,389
6	6,515	58·3	46	0·4	4,612	41·3	11,173	5,967	54·1	42	0·4	5,016	45·5	11,025
7	7,122	63·6	95	0·8	3,995	35·6	11,212	6,328	58·4	89	0·8	4,413	40·8	10,830
8	6,668	62·4	314	2·9	3,704	34·7	10,686	6,049	58·6	187	1·8	4,079	39·6	10,315
9	6,465	61·9	638	6·1	3,342	32·0	10,445	5,975	58·3	335	3·3	3,944	38·4	10,254
10	6,049	55·3	1,389	12·7	3,500	32·0	10,938	5,794	55·3	760	7·3	3,916	37·4	10,470
11	4,939	48·9	2,180	21·5	2,990	29·6	10,109	4,880	50·2	1,085	11·1	3,761	38·7	9,726
12	3,935	38·6	3,498	34·2	2,781	27·2	10,214	4,248	42·6	1,829	18·3	3,897	39·1	9,974
13	2,588	27·8	4,468	48·1	2,242	24·1	9,298	2,790	30·0	2,676	29·7	3,548	39·4	9,014
14	1,628	15·9	6,485	63·4	2,122	20·7	10,235	1,825	19·4	3,848	41·0	3,717	39·6	9,390
3 to 15	57,206	44·4	19,132	14·9	52,349	40·7	128,687	54,253	43·5	10,878	8·7	59,607	47·8	124,738

Source: 1851 Census: Great Britain: Reports and Tables on Education: England and Wales, Parliamentary Papers, 1852–3, XC, p.xxvii.

Note: This table is based on the household census which, together with the census of public worship and attendance at Sunday schools was taken on Sunday, 30 March 1851. The census of attendance at evening schools for adults was taken the previous day, that of attendance at day schools on Monday, 31 March.

were in employment. The balance, 40 per cent of the boys and 48 per cent of the girls, were unclassified in the census returns. It is reasonable to assume that the majority of the girls from working-class homes who were in the unclassified category gave unpaid help at home. Girls not only assisted their mothers in the daily routine but also stood *in loco parentis.* Mann pointed out that in agricultural areas, for instance, the eldest girl frequently stayed at home to look after the rest of the children while the mother worked in the field.[1] The difference between a girl's wage and that of a full-grown woman made this a profitable arrangement for the family.

Similarly the 40 per cent of the boys shown as unclassified were not necessarily idling their time away at home. In the countryside Mann alleged that they might have been helping on the family patch or following their fathers around the fields hoping to catch the farmer's eye by acquiring 'a character for aptitude such as may induce the master to employ them'. In towns also boys frequently watched their fathers on the job, for the parents believed that they thereby obtained 'a species of industrial education much more valuable, as bearing on their future temporal lot, than would be the instruction to be gained at school . . . .' Table 1 shows the percentages of the children in the various categories used by Mann. It will be seen that the age range 6—10 provided the peak years for the schooling of the working classes. Above the age of 10 education became more and more a middle-class prerogative, under the age of 6 it was more of a custodial than an educational process. Since the date of the census was 30 March, a time of the year when there was not a high demand for children's labour, especially in the countryside, the bulk of those shown at work were probably in permanent employment. During the course of a year a child might successively be at work, at school, or at home. In addition the designation 'scholar' may have had an aura of respectability. Hence one cannot assume that all those shown as 'scholars' were in regular attendance throughout the year. Last, the practice of keeping children at home was not an exclusively working-class one. Mann pointed out that of 654 children aged between 3 and 15, 'of the upper section of the middle classes' resident in some of the more respectable squares and private streets of London, 343 were neither described as being at school nor engaged in business. However, it is unlikely that these children were following their father round and providing employers with what was, in effect, unpaid labour.[2]

The 1851 Census Report also suggests that the schooling of girls

TABLE 2 *Boys and girls and the curriculum, 1851*

Description of schools	All day schools		Public day schools		Private day schools	
	Males	Females	Males	Females	Males	Females
Number of scholars to whom the returns apply	988,615	829,409	699,167	540,926	289,448	288,483
Percentage of scholars instructed in						
Reading	88·0	89·0	89·5	89·9	84·4	87·4
Writing	62·5	56·0	67·7	61·3	50·1	46·0
Arithmetic	56·4	44·2	61·0	48·3	45·4	36·5
English grammar	27·3	22·3	25·6	18·2	31·4	30·0
Geography	30·6	25·6	31·0	24·8	29·4	27·0
Modern languages	4·0	3·4	2·3	1·0	8·3	7·8
Ancient languages	4·3	0·3	2·7	0·2	8·2	0·6
Mathematics	3·6	0·2	2·8	0·1	5·9	0·3
Drawing	5·5	1·8	5·1	1·0	6·6	3·4
Music	9·9	9·3	12·6	9·6	3·1	8·8
Industrial occupations	2·0	38·6	2·5	43·0	0·9	30·4

Source: 1851 Census: Great Britain: Reports and Tables on Education: England and Wales, Parliamentary Papers, 1852–3, XC, cxxxii.

was both qualitatively and quantitatively more restricted than that of boys. Table 2 shows the extent to which the two sexes studied various subjects. For a number of reasons the absolute figures need to be treated with caution. As the school managers and proprietors supplied the information on which the Table is based, it is likely that it gives an optimistic picture. Even the terms 'reading', 'writing' and 'arithmetic' have their pitfalls for the unwary cliometrician. For instance, a school that did no more than teach children their letters could legitimately claim 'reading' as part of its curriculum. In similar fashion 'writing' might have been limited to making a few pothooks. When the Newcastle Commissioners made their survey at the end of the decade, their assistant commissioners actually visited the schools. J. Winder found that in Bradford and Rochdale, 'Grammar varies from the mere teaching of the parts of speech to the parsing and analysis of complex sentences; geography, from a mere outline of British geography to a complete survey of the world . . . .' In private schools 'History, grammar, and geography, though always professed, are little more than nominal. By history, I found ordinarily meant reading Goldsmith, and by geography and grammar, the repetition of a portion of a text-book. Religious instruction is for the most part practically ignored. It rarely amounts to more than the use of the Bible as a reading-book.' In these circumstances one can do no more than assume that the compilers of the schedules exaggerated their claims without discriminating between boys and girls. In all the academic subjects, except reading, girls were the losers. A similar pattern emerged from the smaller survey made by the Newcastle Commissioners except that in private schools more girls than boys learnt geography, grammar, history and music from notes. To some extent what the girls lost academically they gained domestically. The main constituent of the industrial occupations that 38.6 per cent of all girls followed in 1851 was needlework. Similarly the *Newcastle Report* shows that three-quarters of all girls in private schools learnt needlework and less than six per cent studied some 'other industrial work', undoubtedly of a role anticipatory nature for womanhood in the nineteenth century.[3]

Cutting across the vertical division of society into male and female there were the horizontal ones of social class that also played a part in determining parental expectations and worldly assessments of the utility of formal schooling. A century before the advent of the 'meritocratic' state the idea that education could provide an avenue of social mobility had few disciples except amongst those close to the growth points of the mid-nineteenth-century economy. Even then it was widely held that a man could prosper without much education. The legacy of centuries of slow economic growth and social change was a low level of expectation. Parents from all grades of society, Mann argued, were content to give their children an education suitable to their own status. In general a parent in whatever his station of life might be, Mann wrote, 'takes himself and his own social *status* as the standard up to which he purposes to educate his offspring . . . .' Amongst the working classes this attitude was reinforced by the way in which they had 'for some generations past been tutored not to look *beyond their station*'. Hence the education of 'the sons of all engaged in manual industry,' that is the unskilled, was seen as completed 'as soon as they possess the manual strength and skill required for such pursuits.'[4] This failure to see education as a means of achieving upward social and economic mobility still persists in some circles today. In 1966 the Report of the Central Advisory Council for Education in England, *Children and their Primary Schools* (The Plowden Report), while dealing with the problems of social and educational deprivation in inner-city areas, observed 'In a neighbourhood where the jobs people do and the status they hold owe little to their education it is natural for children as they grow older to regard school as a brief prelude to work rather than an avenue to future opportunities.'[5]

A hundred years ago when the parental consumer of education was sovereign, he could act on his belief that the purely mental training which his children passed through could rarely be 'an influence upon their future temporal prosperity . . . .' He withdrew his children because he believed that 'a thorough education of this character' was not worth the time and money needed for its acquisition. In many instances the father knew full well that the work his children were going to do for a living was, in Mann's phrase, such that the 'rudiments of sciences and arts learnt with great labour *must* soon be forgotten from the want of any stimulus for their continued application.'[6]

Ten years later Cumin, in his report to the Newcastle Commissioners, found much the same restricted view on the amount of education for which parents were prepared to pay. 'If the opinions of the parents were taken upon the matter, I do not doubt that they would unanimously consider reading, writing, and arithmetic, as the essentials, and the others as accomplishments, to be acquired if time permitted.' For the majority of working-class parents and children time did not permit. Parents could not afford to take other than a restricted view of the formal education they deemed necessary for their children. In addition most were not culturally equipped to do so. 'The result which they wish to secure is that which they can themselves appreciate, namely a knowledge of reading, writing, and arithmetic, of the elements of religion and of the principles of good conduct.' Other assistant commissioners reported on similar lines. In the ports of Hull, Ipswich, and Yarmouth, the majority of parents were said to be 'perfectly content with moderate skill in writing, and arithmetic, vote superfluous grammar, geography, history, and all that kind of thing.' In the eastern agricultural counties parents, it was alleged, 'do not, indeed, commonly set any value upon anything beyond reading, writing, cyphering, and sewing. If there is a choice, they sometimes prefer a school in which no time is devoted to geography, grammar, or music.' In the south west parents were equally pragmatic. 'Their measure of the efficiency of a school is generally a very simple one - the rapidity with which children learn to write well.' In the agricultural districts of the north east and north west, the Newcastle Commissioners were informed, 'chiefly, but not exclusively, there is a strong feeling among parents that grammar, geography, history, etcetera are not of any value to children who will have to work with their hands for their bread.' In the colliery districts of the same regions there was an economic incentive to learn but to learn fast. 'There can be no promotion in the collieries from the position of a mere pitman to that of overman, deputy, or viewer, without some knowledge of writing and arithmetic as well as reading; and the general feeling is, that the more quickly these can be acquired the better.'

Although such parents were prepared to pay for formal instruction, they showed little regard for the socialisation function of the school, the 'regulation of the thoughts and habits of the children' to conform to contemporary middle-class norms. In the colliery areas of Durham and Northumberland, the assistant commissioner who surveyed the region complained,[7]

Time for school attendance is spared only with a view to its being preparation for work. Parents have no idea that there is any advantage in children spending so many years at school if the same amount of learning can be acquired in a shorter time. In short, they regard schooling, not as a course of discipline, but only as a means of acquiring reading, writing, arithmetic, sewing, and knitting, as a preparation for the main business of life - earning a living.

The literate youth not only possessed the *sine qua non* for promotion underground, he also had a good chance of avoiding the pit altogether in a supervisory job on the surface.

Such attitudes help to explain parental opposition to the Church schools. It was, for instance, a frequent complaint of the clergy that parents conveyed the impression that they were doing the incumbent a favour by sending their children to school at all. Spending time in school, mastering the minutiae of Biblical history, a pastime often confused with religious education, was a waste of that child's short school career and of the father's money. While their children were at school, parents wanted their money's worth in the shortest possible time. The puddlers and colliers of the Black Country were reputed to value the annual tests under the Revised Code. They 'wish schools to be a reality and not a sham; and that the inspection should be strict and searching; in fact, they look to the inspector to give a trade mark to the goods . . . .'[8]

Although the Black Country was a district of rapid economic growth, its inhabitants seem to have shown little enthusiasm for formal education when George Coode came on behalf of the Newcastle Commissioners. In the industrial villages between Birmingham and Wolverhampton a man could become a small-scale capitalist as a result of his innate shrewdness, determination to work and succeed, together with a little luck, without ever having to learn to read or write. The easily accessible seams of coal, ironstone, and limestone, were exploited without the need for much capital at this time. 'All this mineral wealth is to be had for the taking,' wrote Coode. The nail-making and chain-making industries provided similar opportunities for a humble man to attain a position of comparative wealth. Furthermore the typical work unit in this nineteenth-century boom region was the eighteenth-century one, the family in which the children worked as soon as they were able. In this materialist atmosphere public opinion held that education could ruin a man. 'It is a common thing to say "The father went to the pit and he made a fortune, his son went to school and lost it." ' Despite evidence that some employers were beginning to value a literate labour force, others could manage without one. 'Clerks and book-keepers, though very highly paid, are scarce and not efficient, and rude practices of accounting and reckoning survive here that are wholly extinct in places where the familiarity with the operations of the counting house is greater.'[9]

What was good enough for a Black Country merchant, still making do with the accounting methods of a non-literate society, did not satisfy those in the vanguard of the nineteenth-century industrial revolution. The directors of the Great Northern and the London and North Western Railways refused to employ boys who could not read and write. In the St Pancras area, which contained the London termini of these lines, this gave many a working-class parent an incentive to keep his boy at school long enough to qualify for a job highly rated for the security it offered. Here the dividend that investment in education yielded was clear enough. The secretary of the G.N.R. explained to the Newcastle Commissioners, 'We do not insist upon certificates for our lad porters from a schoolmaster, but they must all read and write. If they are decently educated they often rise and become clerks. All come in at one rate of pay, and rise to the better situations by ability and steadiness. We have many clerks who joined as porters, and some have charge of good stations, and receive from £70 to £100 a year, with house.'[10]

Near St Pancras there were the Working Men's Literary Institute, the Working Men's College, and the Jenkins' Secular Sunday School with a programme of French, history, geography, grammar, and natural philosophy. There were both the means of educating an artisan class and the appropriate occupational opportunities. Such men were themselves sufficiently educated to see the value of education in terms of job opportunities for their sons. Thus assistant commissioner J. Wilkinson's area of St Pancras, St George in the East, and Chelsea, stood highest among the ten investigated by the Newcastle Commission for the proportion of children learning arithmetic, and second for algebra, Euclid, elements of physics, and drawing (79·9 per cent, 1·3 per cent, 1·2 per cent, 8·7 per cent, and 18·7 per cent respectively).[11]

Similarly Patrick Cumin found that the skilled artisan class of Plymouth and Bristol, the masons, carpenters, and engineers, valued drawing. 'They find it extremely useful in explaining their ideas, and in understanding those of others.' As one carpenter explained in a comment that reveals the gradations that could exist within one trade,[12]

I am a carpenter, and my son will probably be a carpenter also. Now, a carpenter who can make staircases gets better wages than a carpenter who does not. To make staircases a man must be able to draw, and therefore, in order to give my son the best chance of getting on, I send him to learn drawing; and what is more, I give a penny a week extra for the purpose.

In seeking the determinants of what children studied at school and how long they remained there, one is virtually putting the same question in two forms. Those who were at school for only a couple of years or so and were intermittent attenders at the best seldom progressed beyond the three Rs. Those who stayed longest, the children from the more affluent working-class families, were there long enough to receive a wider education. After questioning children in over 300 schools in 1859 one school inspector concluded that just under 25 per cent, 24·58, reached the first class where[13]

The more advanced lessons given in our elementary schools – the lessons in geography, in grammar, in English history, and in the higher parts of arithmetic, in drawing, in cutting out and fixing for needlework are reserved, for the most part, to the first class, and are brought within the reach of only one-fourth part of our scholars.

As a generalization one can postulate that the closer families were physically and culturally to the new forces of nineteenth-century industrialized society the readier they were to spend money on their children's education if they could afford it. In contrast parents in rural areas showed less readiness and had less ability to pay for schooling. These statements require qualification. Statistics of school attendance, if reliable, show no more than the effective demand for formal schooling. There is no means by which one can quantify latent demand effectively and measure the gap beween parental intent and parental action. Similarly school attendance data do not reveal the extent to which parents, unable to send their children to school, valued education and learning.

The economic pressures on working-class parents in the group the mid-Victorians described as the independent poor not to send their children to school or, at best, just to allow them to acquire the three Rs were considerable. Parents faced a double cost. They had not only to find the money for the school fees but they also had to forgo the child's earnings. The opportunity cost of losing a child's wages was a far greater burden than the mere payment of the weekly fee. By the time of the Newcastle Commission's Report the break-even point at which a child's earning power – 2s 6d to 4s a week – could equal the cost of his maintenance in many a working-class home was around 8 to 10 years of age. James Fraser, later Bishop of Manchester and one of the more compassionate assistants to the Newcastle Commission, thought that wages of 1s 6d for a boy of 10 and 2s for one of 11 were enough to 'outbid the school'.[14] As boys got older the incentive to send them to work increased. From about the age of 10 the cost of feeding and clothing children begins to rise rapidly until by late adolescence it exceeds that of an adult. At the same time as children grow stronger they can earn more. Thus the economic interest of the family conflicted with the educational interest of the child. The age band during which it was possible to give a child a rapid training in the three Rs was the very one when the attractive force of the labour market began to outbid the school.

The outcome of the decision whether to send a child to school or to work depended on other factors such as the size of the family and the child's position within that family. 'It can hardly be a matter of surprise,' another assistant commissioner commented, 'that when three children in a family, above 8 years old, can double the weekly income of the house, parents should withdraw their children from school,' especially if there were younger ones to keep. It is probable that the younger children had a better chance of staying at school than their elder brothers and sisters who had had to leave early to supplement the family budget or, in the case of girls, assist at home. Luckiest of all was the youngest child kept at school by the earnings of his elder siblings.

For the independent poor the financial sacrifice involved in sending children to school was an immediate one that brought the family prolonged problems. The reward was remote in time and to many must have seemed uncertain. Those who were most culturally and economically circumscribed had the least likelihood of realising that the schools might offer their children a means of escape into a materially better life. Moreover although outside observers saw that the poor needed education, it was a want the poor could not afford to satisfy. It was their social superiors who wanted them to be educated and eventually provided the means. They failed, however, to tackle the social problems that the imposition of compulsory school attendance exacerbated. The family unit, deprived of juvenile earnings, found it harder to stay alive.

For the poorest even the restricted objective of compulsory instruction in the three Rs after 1870 must have seemed an imposition forced on them by their social superiors that was unrelated to their immediate physical needs and daily lives. In this context the experience of R. Thabault, a French educationalist who visited parts of Southern Morocco in the 1930s, is illuminating. Thabault found that, although the French had built the schools for the indigenous Muslim population, the Jewish parents and not the Muslims sent their children to them.

The Jews, he decided, saw the schools as a means of initiation into the three Rs, symbols needed for communication at a distance and for keeping records. They provided, in his view, part and parcel of an economy of change. The Muslim farmers, still living and working in a closed economy that relied on face-to-face encounters, felt no need for these symbols. The Jews, who were artisans and traders, did.[15] It is arguable that a similar division existed within the English working classes for much of the nineteenth century. Some led a narrow life in town or country circumscribed by poverty and near illiteracy. Others enjoyed a sufficiently high enough standard of living to lead a fuller life that was enriched by the possession of literacy. To many a board school child at the end of the nineteenth century the limited educational desiderata enunciated by James Fraser in the Newcastle Report back in 1861 must have seemed of little point. Fraser had wanted every child to be able to read a newspaper 'with sufficient ease to be a pleasure to himself and to convey information to listeners', to write a letter that was 'both legible and intelligible', and to make out a common shop bill.[16] Yet Seebohm Rowntree found that 27·84 per cent of the inhabitants of York lived below a poverty line drawn with such a stringency that it did not allow for the purchase of either a halfpenny newspaper or a penny stamp.[17] Children whose parents lived at this level had little opportunity or need to read or write outside the class-room. By and large they followed occupations in which their hard earned acquisition of literacy and numeracy gradually atrophied.

The independent poor had been caught by the nineteenth-century version of the poverty trap. They were not so poor that they had to look to the poor law guardians for succour. On the other hand they were poor enough to have to send their children to work to avoid the workhouse, a parental decision that the Newcastle Commissioners found commendable. For these children the call of duty was clear.

Independence is of more importance than education; and if the wages of the child's labour are necessary, either to keep the parents from the poor rates, or to relieve the pressure of severe and bitter poverty, it is far better that it should go to work at the earliest age at which it can bear the physical exertion rather than it should remain at school.

So wedded were the Newcastle Commissioners to a moralistic attitude towards the poor that they virtually denied poverty to be a cause of absenteeism from school. In their view, poverty was more often used as an excuse than a justification. Although they admitted that there were instances of parents being unable to clothe and shoe their children, they maintained that such cases were rare. The main determinant of absenteeism was a moral deficiency, not a financial one. 'The commonest cause, however, of an entire absence of schooling is to be found in the intemperance, apathy, and recklessness of the most degraded part of the population.' They were equally unsympathetic to those parents who could afford to send their children to school but failed to do so. Towards those children, since their school attendance did not make the family dependent on the poor rates at the expense of the propertied classes, the Newcastle Commissioners could afford to feel altruistic at the expense of the parents.[18]

The child has a moral right to as good an education as the parent can afford . . . . We think . . . that if a parent is in receipt of an income which, independently, of the child's earnings, will support his family, he has no moral right to send his child to work merely for the sake of increasing his income . . . .

Likewise, those parents caught in the poverty trap received short shift. Harry Chester, Assistant Secretary to the Education Department, had suggested that the poor law guardians should receive authority to pay the fees of those children whose parents, not in receipt of relief, could demonstrate their inability to pay the school pence themselves. The Newcastle Commissioners dismissed his suggestion for it 'obliterates *pro tanto* the distinction between the pauper and the independent labourer'. They sought refuge in the arguments that had been used to abolish the old poor law system in 1834.

The semi-pauper will be in the situation of the labourer relieved under the old allowance system or under the old labour rate-system. Though earning wages, he will have to ask for money on the grounds of his destitution. Few things can be more demoralizing.

So fearful and recent were the fears of the taint of hereditary pauperism that they alleged, 'Even the receipt, on the grounds of poverty, of gratuitous medical relief is found to be a step towards pauperism.' They then returned to their belief that the financial obstacle was largely an imaginary one:[19]

In the second place we believe that those who among the independent poor labourers who are intelligent enough to value education will almost always be able to afford what is the least part of its cost, the school pence; and thirdly, we are told by almost all our witnesses, that the education which costs nothing is valued at nothing.

Middle-class observers looking at working-class behaviour from the outside could only describe what they saw, what they thought were the beliefs of the working classes, and what they wanted to believe about them. The technique of the in-depth interview still awaited development. However, the Newcastle Commissioners made an attempt to overcome these problems. They instructed their assistants to enquire whether parents neglected education 'on the ground that it is not adapted to their wants, and, if so, are they right or wrong in that opinion, and what is the proof that they are right or wrong.' These questions, the instructions continued, could only be 'answered by detailed enquiry amongst persons of intelligence of either sex conversant with the locality.'[20] Thus the opinions of the working classes reached the commissioners through the filtration of 'intelligent', that is knowledgeable, local middle-class mouthpieces whose evidence received the embellishment of a further gloss from the assistant commissioners. To their credit Cumin and others on occasion actually sought the views of working-class men and women directly.

Moreover the part played by the school before the 1870s in spreading literacy and knowledge may not be as clear cut as has been usually assumed. Historians, for instance, are speculating about the extent of literacy in pre-industrial society and how this was achieved. Before the age of mass compulsory education parents may have been a more important educative influence with their offspring than historians of education, taking a rigidly institutional approach, have yet conceded. To parents who had obtained their learning at their home or workplace the rapidly spreading schools may have seemed no more than an institutionalized means of doing what previous generations had done informally. However much parents may have valued learning, cruel necessity made many value the earnings of their children more and discount the schoolmaster's worth.

The communities that made up mid-Victorian society showed marked regional and occupational variations. Even today only the most alienated and insensitive traveller would be unaware of these differences as he moved about the country. A century ago with less well developed means of transport and mass communication regional individualism was far more marked. Even a predominantly agricultural county could show a marked lack of uniformity. Dr W. B. Stephens has examined the proportions of brides and grooms signing the marriage registers in the census districts of Devonshire for the years 1865 to 1870. He found that the remote farming areas with declining populations had higher than average illiteracy rates for the county. In contrast those districts possessing good modern communications with the coming of the railway, a growing population, or were ones of urban prosperity, had lower illiteracy rates. There was also a tendency for illiteracy rates to be higher and school attendance poorer in those parts of the country where the agricultural holdings were small.[21] Parts of Lincolnshire, South Durham, and Somerset provide further instances of educational backwardness accompanied by a similar structure of landownership. The owner of a smallholding, unable to afford the wage of a full-time adult labourer, had to make do with the unpaid services of his children. In those districts where agricultural wages were low, agricultural labourers' families supplemented their earnings with the income derived from such cottage-based handicraft industries as glove making, lace making, and straw plaiting. The regions in which these crafts were practised were amongst the educationally most backward of all in rural England. So strong was local resistance to the school attendance acts that succour did not come to the children until the collapse of these industries following technological innovations that made labour intensive methods obsolete, and the loss of markets through changes in fashion or foreign competition.

In contrast, where wages were high because the farmer had to compete with the economic and social lure of the towns, labourers could afford a better schooling for their children. Regional geological differences played their part as well. On heavy clay soils farmers had little use for the services of boys under the age of 12 as they were not strong enough to guide the plough. Again, predominantly pastoral areas made fewer demands on childrens' services than did the arable and market gardening regions with their succession of harvests.

Amongst the best educated countryfolk of all were those of Northern Northumberland. Here labourers were hired by the year at a wage of 15s to 18s a week. Children remained at school until the age of 11 or 12, and then worked in the summer only until they were 14. A Presbyterian minister at Bellingham, near the border with Scotland, paid them this tribute.

A few shepherds on the hills keep a schoolmaster among them, and they lately commissioned me to procure for them Virgil, Horace, and Caesar. Such are the shepherds of the Cheviot Hills, a class always spoken of with great respect, as themselves highly educated for their station, making great sacrifices for the education of their children, and possessing great knowledge of the Bible.

From an entirely different cultural background were the tenants of the Great Dodford Estate, south west of Birmingham. As late as the 1880s there were still 17 of the original 39 participants in one of Feargus O'Connor's land schemes of 1849. The remaining 22 tenants were surviving relatives of the original mortgagors, many of whom had been north-country artisans. The Chartist legacy had made these smallholders engaged in market gardening exceptions to the rule. 'Generally the educational standard of the inhabitants, long before school boards were dreamed of was far beyond that of their surrounding neighbours.'[22]

As the example of the Great Dodford Estate suggests, even neighbouring parishes varied. In the close village, under the benevolent despotism of one resident landowner, more pressure could be put on parents and children alike to use the school than in an open parish owned by several landowners, some of whom were non-resident. Much also dependend on how readily the incumbent struggled against the open hostility and opposition of the farmers. Only further research will reveal how typical was the Norfolk cleric who wrote to *The Times* in 1899 telling of his fifty-year crusade to educate the children in his pastoral change sufficiently well to leave home. For if they stayed the prospect was dismal, 'Low wages, hard labour, and when old age begins to creep on and the labourer is bent nearly double then the union workhouse or half-a-crown a week and two loaves of bread.' His policy, he declared, was in accord with the teaching of the Church of England for the Holy Catechism enjoined a man 'to do his duty in that state of life unto which it shall please God to call him' and not as the farmers seemed to think 'unto which it has pleased God to call him'.[23]

As in the countryside, so in the towns, the demand for juvenile labour, the level of wages, and the structure of industry, all played a part in determining the effective demand for formal schooling. The county of Staffordshire provides an example of this diversity. In this county the educational plight of urban children in some instances was worse than that of their rural brothers and sisters. The pottery towns of Northern Staffordshire made heavy demands on juvenile labour before the working conditions of women and children were regulated under the Factory Acts Extension Act of 1864. Conditions seem to have been worst in Longton, a centre for high quality chinaware, a specialism where the work was lighter than elsewhere and the opportunities of using juvenile labour greater. Although the town had five parochial schools not under government inspection, it was reputed to be the only town of over 15,000 inhabitants without one under inspection and in receipt of an annual grant. The Rev. H. R. Sandford, the inspector of the area, found that whereas 13 per cent of 3,550 children in actual attendance in the schools of the Potteries were over the age of 10, 32 per cent of 895 in rural schools in North Staffordshire were over this age. The corresponding figures for those over 12 were 3·6 per cent and 17 per cent respectively. In the Potteries the high season for school attendance was between August and Christmas.[24] Parents having bought new clothes for their children for the Stoke wakes could send their children to school respectably clad for a while. Work in the pottery kilns was dirty. Hence, even if parents could spare their children from an occupation in which the family usually worked as a unit, it was difficult for them to move from the kiln to school unless they had a change of clothes. In this respect the children of the Potteries were said to be worse off than those in the cotton mills.

Because of the heavy demand for juvenile labour during the working week, the Primitive Methodist and the Methodist New Connexion Sunday School of the Potteries had given a secular bias to their instruction. The socially more respectable Anglicans and Wesleyan Methodists gave their secular instruction in evening schools. These schools, as was the frequent practice in other industrial areas, usually met on Mondays as the observance of St Monday made possible good attendances. If evening schools met later in the week, attendance fell because of the long hours of work. For a number of reasons the Sunday school was an inadequate substitute for the day school. Even in those schools that taught reading and writing, attendance at some form of church or chapel service cut down the amount of time available for the teaching of reading, writing and arithmetic. In addition both pupils and teachers were frequently tired. Lack of suitable clothing debarred many of the poorest. In Hanley George Foster, aged 10, told the Commissioners on the employment of children and young persons in trades and manufactures in 1842, 'I got Sunday clothes.' He was one of the lucky ones. Less fortunate were Ann Taylor, aged 11, 'I do not go to Sunday school because I have not another frock,' and John Orton of Fenton aged 8, 'I can't read, can't write; I went once to church-school but don't go now cause I've got no trousers.' By the 1860s the parents of the Potteries were readier to ignore the conventions, possibly because they were more concerned to see that their children had some schooling than they had been twenty years earlier. 'The majority of the children who appear in rags while at work, come in better clothes to school on Sunday. There are exceptions, and latterly I have observed,' stated one superintendent, 'the children are not so well dressed.'[25]

It would be wrong, however, to present a harrowing picture of swarms of toddlers streaming in and out of the kilns. There was little demand for the labour of very young children. The 1851 Census shows that only 688 of the 7,261 boys and girls, in the age range of 5 to 10, worked in the earthenware industry in the registration district of Stoke-on-Trent. The heavy demand for labour came later, at the very age when children could have profited most from two or three years at school. In the next age band, up to age of 15, the kilns employed 4,924 out of a total of 6,810. The Pottery towns were unique in the nineteenth-century economy for the extent to which they depended on a single manufacturing process. Since a child's future working life was so easily determined, a lifetime in an industry in which literacy was not a prerequisite for entry, there must have seemed little point in paying for his formal education before he started work.

In the industrial villages of the Black Country in the southern part of Staffordshire the educational record was slightly better. HMI the Rev. H. R. Sandford put South Staffordshire above the Potteries for school attendance but below other areas where he had inspected schools. These were Shropshire, Cheshire, Hampshire, the cotton manufacturing districts of Lancashire, and the North and East Ridings of Yorkshire. In South Staffordshire 5½ per cent of the children in school were over 12, while 16 per cent were over this age in the rural schools of Yorkshire. Again he described 23 per cent of those in South Staffordshire in school over the age of 12 as middle class and 16 per cent of those in the Yorkshire schools as being in this social classification. In other words working-class parents kept their children at school longer in Yorkshire than in the Black Country. He also found that the level of literacy apparently varied from one industry to another. The percentages of those boys attending a night school who could not read were 64 per cent for colliery boys, 41 per cent for those in ironworks and whose trade required them to work at night every other week, and 33 per cent in the foundries. Attendance at night school required resolution and stamina. In Wolverhampton and Bilston, such were the long hours of work, that there was no point in starting teaching before 8 p.m. Girls in the nailing trade of Cradley were said to persuade their parents to allow them to stop work early so that they could wash and go to night school.[26]

It is unlikely that many of the boys and girls in the unskilled trades attended Sunday School. An analysis of the occupations of 168 boys attending the New Meeting Sunday Schools in Birmingham in 1841 shows 2 iron founders, 2 metal rollers, and 24 brass founders. The majority excluding 22 at school and 5 at home, were in skilled and semi-skilled trades ancillary to the metallurgical industries. Twenty years later the superintendent of the Baptist Sunday School in Great King Street, Hockley, Birmingham, observed much the same phenomenon. 'The school is an average one; the scholars are the children of artisans almost exclusively . . . . There is a class below these, not paupers, who do not attend Sunday school for want of clothes.' What was true of Birmingham was true of the country as a whole by the 1850s and 1860s. The social pressures to conform sartorially were strong enough to prevent the poor, ashamed of their lack of clean clothes, from either attending church or chapel or from sending their children to Sunday school. 'Unless a mother can dress her child decently she will not send it to Sunday school,' Patrick Cumin told the Newcastle Commissioners. His experience was that Sunday schools[27]

Never contain so poor or so low a class as that which attends the week-day schools. The children in the dissenting schools are always from a higher class than those in the Church schools, but even in the Church schools the really poor are fewer on Sundays than on the other days of the week.

Although conditions undoubtedly varied from one industrial town to another, one point stands out. By the 1860s the exploitation of the labour of the very young was the exception rather than the rule. In this respect there had been an improvement since the 1840s. Instances of the employment of children under the age of six were now comparatively rare, except in the straw-plait schools, where children of 3 and 3½ were still working long hours. Apart from this and other rural handicraft industries, employers had little use for very young children. This seems to have been true even of agriculture if the following analysis of the members of certain public gangs in the eastern counties in the 1860s can be regarded as typical. Of a total membership of 3,699 children, young persons and women, only 27 were children under the age of 7. The largest group, 1,740, were in the 7-to-13 age range. Of the remainder, 1,195 were between 13 and 18 and 737, including 663 women, were over 18.[28]

The findings of the commissioners on the employment of women, young persons, and children in trades and manufactures reveal much the same pattern. They estimated that there were 19,500 boys and girls working in the hardware and other manufacturing trades of Birmingham in the early 1860s. Of these 1,500 were thought to be between 8 and 10 and a further 500 under the age of 8. The millinery and allied trades employed over half a million in all, 573,380, but only 16,560 were returned as being under 15. Seamstresses, shirt makers, and boot makers, constituted another large group. Of the 366,497 in these trades, 57,164 were under 20. The Lancashire metal trades employed 139 boys under the age of 10 and 160 girls under 18 out of a total of 51,748 men and 603 women in 1861. Last, in the lace trade, 8,000 to 10,000 of a possible 150,000 unprotected by any existing legislation were children and young persons under the age of 18.[29]

Despite the emphasis given to them in many histories of education, the children working in factories protected by the Factory Acts were not numerically a significant group. In the two decades from 1835 they had become both relatively and absolutely a smaller element in the labour force. In 1835 the cotton, wollen, worsted, and flax factories, employed 354,684 in all. By 1856 these factories, together with silk manufactories, had a labour force of 682,497. Yet over the same period the number of children under the age of 13 in them had shrunk from 47,373 to 44,385.[30] Under the 1844 Factory Act, employers could deduct schoolpence at a rate not exceeding twopence a week or a penny in the shilling of the child's earnings. In effect the school fee was a form of income tax. Parents, who failed to send their children to school, were liable to a fine ranging between 5s and £1. In comparison with the fines employers faced, these penalties were harsh. The wealthier employer risked the prospect of a fine varying between £1 and £3, or £5 if the act were contravened at night, through the illegal employment of children.

Moreover, the provisions of the act were not stringent enough to ensure that parents received their money's-worth for the fees they paid. Under the Act a factory inspector could annul a schoolmaster's certificate if he were dissatisfied with him, 'by reason of his incapacity to teach them to read and write, from his gross ignorance, or from his not having the books and materials necessary to teach them reading and writing'. The Act did not require the schoolmaster to teach any arithmetic. Indeed, strictly speaking the Act did not require him to teach at all. He had only to be capable of teaching.

The standard of the factory schools, as the high standard of the London Lead Company's school at Middleton, county Durham suggests, varied considerably. There is evidence to suggest that parents, once they overcame their initial hostility, did their best to see that the school fees were spent to advantage as better schools became available.

Striking a eulogistic note H. Seymour Tremenheere, school inspector involuntarily turned colliery inspector, informed the annual meeting of the National Association for the Promotion of Social Science in 1865,

> There has been I have been informed by both inspectors of factories ...,
> a very great improvement; and so much have the schools in general
> improved, and so ready are the manufacturers to send the half-time
> children to the best in the neighbourhood, that the factor inspectors
> are satisfied with the law as it is.

After this last exaggeration he continued, 'All the badly furnished and ill-taught schools are said by them to be fast disappearing, and they believe that in a short time half-timers will be found attending none but the best local schools.'[31] An investigation organized by Alexander Redgrave, a factory inspector, in 1870, gives some precision to Tremenheere's statement. He instructed his sub-inspectors to examine the schools in his area which were not subject to government inspection and were attended by factory children. He found that only 5,000 out of a total of 70,000 part-timers attended such schools. These schools were still in the old tradition for even in the best of them 'the average attainments of the children would not bear comparison with those of children at a medium school under inspection.' Unfortunately it is not clear whether Redgrave meant schools inspected annually for a grant under the Revised Code or those schools, usually of an inferior standard, that were inspected only occasionally. Nevertheless, his findings suggest that no more than a small proportion of factory children were now at schools reminiscent of the more lurid accounts of the 1840s. Moreover, he thought that even the uninspected schools in the factory districts were superior to those in other districts where the half-time system did not apply. For instance, he stated that the sub-inspector's report on Suffolk, where the Factory Act of 1867 was beginning to be implemented, 'calls to mind most forcibly the state of the manufacturing districts as they existed years past.' The improvements in the schools of the factory districts and the large proportion of children in inspected ones he attributed to the fact that parents and masters realized that 'if children must go to school they had better do something to make the school attendance useful.'[32] Whether or not one can accept Redgrave's contention that working-class parents acted as rational economic men in the choice of schools for their children is a matter for speculation. The improvement that he detected may have been part of a wider one resulting from growing parental awareness and ambition for their children. Whatever reservations one may have, it is difficult to reject the general tenor of his findings.

A study of the coal-miners' campaign for compulsory education reveals something of the conflicting pressures to which parents were subject. The coal-miners, the spear-head of the working-class movement, formed the industrial group that has probably the longest tradition of making this demand on behalf of their children. As early as 1842 the miners of Barnsley had resolved, 'The ignorance of the children of colliers is very great, and the reason is that their wages are not sufficient to enable the colliers to give their children education, and they earnestly desire to have better means of education.' Members of the Primitive Methodist congregation at Knott Lanes, Oldham, were of like mind. They believed that plenty of colliers 'would send their children if they could afford it, and it grieves their mind that they do not.' In 1854 the miners of Durham and Northumberland petitioned that children between the ages of 10 and 14 should attend school for part of the day and that colliery owners should be compelled to build schools. They stated their readiness to give twopence a week provided 'they had the appointment of the schoolmasters, the control over the funds thus subscribed, and to see them properly and well applied, so as to procure for their children a good and moral education.'[33]

Miners as a whole tended to have a high regard for learning. To some extent they wanted education for their children for its own sake. They also knew that knowledge was power. Without educated men from their own community they could not negotiate effectively with the owners, colliery inspectors, and members of parliament for better and safer working conditions. Education also enabled them to produce ministers for the nonconformist chapels from their own ranks.

Yet as the 1854 petition from the men of the north east suggests, there were other issues at stake. There were religious and political considerations concerning the nature and control of the education provided. The politically articulate man, who did not accept the social and religious teachings of the Established Church and the wealthier nonconformist sects, had much to resent if he had to send his children to a voluntary school. If his employer provided that school he had added grounds for his resentment. Men frequently suffered a deduction from their wages for the upkeep of the factory or colliery school whether or not they had children of school age.

In South Wales for example, where one school inspector estimated nine-tenths of the labour force to be dissenters, the majority of

46

employers did take the wishes of their employees into consideration. However, in some instances the employers used the stoppages from wages to establish Church schools 'and bring up in Church principles a set of children whose parents are generally dissenters in the proportion of at least nine to one.' Although the Education Department cited a county court case that cast doubt on the legality of this practice, it continued after 1870. As late as 1894 the Huddersfield School Board considered a complaint that a local firm had made it a condition of employment that their half-time employees should attend a particular Church school and that, if necessary, they should leave the local board school to do so. The facts of the case were not denied at a meeting of the school board. Unfortunately for the complainant, A. H. D. Acland, the Vice-President of the Council on Education, decided that the Education Department 'have no power to interfere with any conditions which private employers may choose to lay down in refusing employment to half-time children except on condition of their attending a certain school.'[34]

Added to the religious and political grievance was a sense of financial wrong. Men suspected the disinterestedness of their employer's paternalism. A recent study suggests that they had good reason. In South Wales it appears that the amount deducted from the paypacket more than covered the cost of running the works' schools there. For instance receipts at the copperworks schools at Hafod and Llanelli were £300 10s 2d in 1869 while expenditure was no more than £219 13s 11d, leaving a healthy surplus that many a clerical school manager would have envied.[35]

This practice extended beyond South Wales. From County Durham a correspondent to the *Miner* in 1863 complained about the weekly deductions of sixpence for physic and a penny for schooling made by the owners of the Consett Coal and Iron Works. The writer calculated that the doctor, who in addition to his weekly fee charged for any medicine he provided, made a clear profit of £1,650 a year. The teachers were thought to have an income of £150 a year. To add insult to injury the children had to bring a penny a fortnight for the teachers to buy coal, presumably from the Consett pits. Yet this was an area where two-thirds of the population were said to be Roman Catholic, but the school was affiliated to the nonconformist British and Foreign School Society. Before the creation of school boards there was little miners could do to remedy the situation. A year earlier the editor of the same journal had suggested to the miners of Usworth, near

Gateshead, who complained that they were paying fees 'much in excess of the running costs of the school', that they should band together to employ a teacher. Despite the *Miner*'s offer of free advertising space to obtain a teacher, nothing came of the suggestion.[36] The issue of financial control was part of a bigger whole. To the extent that miners saw the task of the schools as that of producing their future leaders and colliery owners saw it as producing a docile labour force, the aims of the two parties were incompatible.

Colliers were not only concerned to see that their children went to school but that they did so during the normal working day. From the 1840s onwards they had begun to campaign for an eight-hour day, a legislative goal they did not reach until 1908. They saw an extension of the Factory Acts as a means of restricting the length of the shift worked. Hence they opposed a plan put forward by H. S. Tremenheere in 1854 to extend the Printworks Act of 1845 to the coal-mining industry. This would have allowed boys between 10 and 14 years of age to receive 150 hours of schooling every half-year with a maximum of five hours in any one day. As there was no daily minimum, boys would have been able to attend whenever it suited the owners. Tremenheere wanted the boys to attend school when the men were not working. He suggested such times as 'idle' Monday – an institution he considered indicative of the 'low moral and intellectual state' of the mining districts – when trade was bad, or when machinery was being repaired. He saw the evening school as another means of meeting the miners' demand for education without inconveniencing the owners by shortening the working day. He did not think that boys who had worked underground for twelve hours would be too tired to attend. As he explained to the Select Committee on Accidents in Coalmines, 'The employment of boys underground is . . . to sit down all day and open and shut air-doors; there can be no fatigue arising from that.' He did not even consider a twelve-hour stint of loading and hauling the filled tubs of coal to be unduly tiring. Boys had frequent intervals of rest 'and the actual amount of their labour during the day was inconsiderable', he maintained.[37] As Tremenheere's proposals would not have taken the young lads out of the pit during normal working hours, the colliers' convert objective, they rejected them. They stuck to their demand for an extension of the Factory Acts to their industry, an objective they never attained.

Miners had a further non-educational reason for wanting to restrict child labour underground. Young children in the mines were a danger not only to themselves but to all who worked alongside them. In addition they were particularly accident prone. Herbert Mackworth, an inspector of mines in South Wales and elsewhere had found that in his area between 1851 and 1855 'on the average of the whole of the underground accidents, double the due proportion of boys under the age of 15 are killed, while men between 20 and 30 enjoy greater immunity from accidents than other colliers.' Their inexperience constituted a danger to others. 'Explosions are not infrequently caused by such boys neglecting to attend to the ventilating doors, or by their being allowed to enter dangerous places. A strong argument is afforded in favour of preventing boys entering the mines at so early an age as ten years . . . .' Thus in demanding compulsory education for their children miners saw it as a means of improving the safety conditions in the pits. As John Normansell, secretary to the South Yorkshire Miners' Association, admitted to the Select Committee on Mines in 1866, 'We do not really ask for education for the boys simply for the purpose of educating them particularly (that is one cause of course, and one great cause why we ask for these things); but we think that a child ought to have a proper knowledge of the dangerous position of the mines, because if a boy is placed behind a trap-door, we wish that boy to be so educated and so old as to understand the position he is placed in.'[38]

In common with other working-class groups miners faced a cruel dilemma. As parents many of them did not want their children to go underground at too early an age. As heads of households they found the immediate economic argument overwhelming. They needed their children's earnings. Unfortunately this was frequently more persuasive than any long-term abstract economic argument. The contention of the *Workman's Advocate* that 'The real fact is that the employment of child labour robs the home of the toiler of its comforts instead of adding to them. The child, too often, displaces the man. Capitalists alone thrive by the present system', was an argument that made little appeal if the larder was bare.[39]

In their evasion of the laws regulating the employment of boys underground parents and employers derived considerable assistance, albeit unwittingly, from the imprecise drafting of the statutes. The Mines Act of 1842, which had the intention of debarring boys below the age of ten from working underground, did not even have the rudimentary, but unreliable, safeguard of requiring a surgeon to certify a child's age. This Act was widely defied in South Wales, where the thin seams put a premium on the services of small boys, and in the coalfields of Yorkshire, Staffordshire, and north-east England, where as late as 1860 A. F. Foster found boys of the age of six and upwards working underground. He estimated that 10 per cent of the collier boys under the age of 15 in the Union of Auckland and 15 per cent of those in the Union of Durham were also under the age of 10. The Mines Act of 1860 did little to remedy the situation. Under this Act a boy under 12 years of age had to obtain a certificate from a competent schoolmaster stating that he could read and write. The Act, however, did not lay down any standard of competence either for the schoolmaster or for the pupil. Even if a humane employer wanted to enforce the law he could run into difficulties as the following experience of Foster shows. 'In a collier dwelling I was shown the fly leaf of the family Bible, in which the dates of the children's birth had been manifestly altered, so as to add two years to the age of each, in order to enable a widow to get her boys employed.' Before the registration of births became compulsory under penalty in 1874, parents could vary the declared age of their children according to circumstance. As one school inspector for the industrial regions of the North West wrote, 'I have been informed by a teacher in my district that in asking for the ages of children he has frequently received as the immediate reply, "What age do you want, school age or factory age?" '[40]

Miners' leaders, who advocated the introduction of compulsory education, knew full well the gulf that existed between themselves and their rank and file. Thomas Burt, the general secretary of the Northumberland Miners' Confident Association from 1865 to 1918 admitted this to the 1866 Select Committee on Mines. Although he did not want boys to start work underground before the age of fourteen, he expected that opposition to such a measure would come as much from the colliers as from the masters. William Pickard, the miners' agent for Wigan, thought that even the more modest proposal of banning boys under the age of twelve would divide the miners. When pressed later in his evidence he struck a more optimistic note. If an act were passed making education compulsory on condition that two-thirds of the miners of a district adopted it, that act could become law in Wigan. Another witness, Samuel Cartlidge, a working collier from North Derbyshire, pointed to the miners' ambivalence. Although there was a general feeling in his district that boys should stay at school longer, parents readily colluded with employers over the infringement of the 1860 Act. They needed the money. The Rev. H. R. Sandford, the Anglican school inspector for Staffordshire saw the failure of the

voluntary system in moralistic social terms. 'The voluntary system ...
just reaches those who want to improve themselves, this respectable
class of colliers – but if we are to reach the class who do not seek education of their own accord, and yet want more of it, perhaps, more
than anybody else, we must have more efficient compulsion than we
have at present.'[41] This was the task of the Elementary Education Act
of 1870. It coerced the parental non-consumer.

III

The Coercion of the Parental Non-Consumer

The Newcastle Commissioners had drawn the comforting conclusion that few children escaped the educational net completely. 'The name of almost every child is at some time or other on the books of some school at which it attends with more or less regularity.' An elaborate statistical exercise suggested that there were no more than 120,305 children unaccounted for amongst the 2,655,767 possible pupils in the three to fifteen-year age range. Once they had established to their own satisfaction that school attendance was almost the universally accepted norm of conduct, they had to account for the socially deviant absentees. Their explanation was they were either physically or mentally handicapped children, or were the victims of the personal and moral shortcomings of their parents, the offspring of 'out-door paupers or of parents viciously inclined'.[1]

During the course of the 1860s further investigations gradually undermined the credibility of the Newcastle Commissioners' findings. Shortly after the publication of their report, J. G. Gent, the secretary of the Ragged School Union, suggested to the Select Committee on the Education of Destitute Children that there could be as many as 100,000 children belonging to the 'ragged class' in London alone.[2] Two years later Robert Lowe exposed the untrustworthiness of the foundations on which the Commissioners had built their statistical edifice. He explained how they had calculated the number of unassisted schools to be 15,952. The religious societies had returned a total of 22,849 assisted and unassisted schools. 19,549 of them were stated to be in association with the Church of England. This figure was based on the

52

National Society's survey of 1847 which had produced a total of 17,015 schools. To this figure the National Society had added 2,534, the number of schools founded between 1847 and 1858. Yet, as Lowe pointed out, these figures included 3,222 dame schools. The Commissioners had then subtracted 6,897, the number of schools aided by the Education Department, from the inflated figure of 22,849 to arrive at a total of 15,952 unassisted schools. Lowe went on to compare the results of a survey he had asked HMI the Rev. J. P. Norris to make of the Anglican schools in Staffordshire with the figures in the *Newcastle Report.* Norris had counted 420 schools whereas the *Newcastle Report* showed 622. The latter figure included 19 grammar schools, 88 dame schools, 20 schools held in churches, 43 instances where more departments of boys, girls, or infants, had been enumerated than ought to have been, and one workhouse school. Lowe rightly concluded, 'it would be paying too great a compliment to those figures to base any calculation on them. The only conclusion we can come to on the subject is, that the whole basis of the calculation has failed, and that it affords no data as to the number of unassisted schools,' and, he might have added, of scholars.[3]

The Newcastle Commissioners had readily accepted the evidence of the very bodies whose activities they were supposed to be examining, the religious societies. They compounded their folly further by giving insufficient attention to those districts in which population growth had been most rapid and where the Church of England's provision was failing to meet the new demands made on it. In the London Metropolitan area two assistant commissioners examined the Unions of St Pancras, St George in the East, Chelsea, St George in Southwark, Newington, Wandsworth, and the Unions of St Olave and St Saviour, Southwark. Although this included some impoverished areas - the Medical Officer of Health for St George in the East had attributed over 120 deaths there to starvation in the first three months of 1868 - the Commissioners made no attempt to measure the extent of educational destitution in London as a whole. Although they had examined the port of Bristol, England's largest city except for London in 1760, apart from publishing a private survey they had ignored Liverpool whose population had exceeded that of Bristol by 1801. They had looked at the textile towns of Bradford and Rochdale, the pottery town of Stoke-on-Trent, and Merthyr Tydfil, but not at Birmingham, Leeds, Manchester, Newcastle, Sheffield, or Wolverhampton, all of which had populations in excess of Bradford's 106,218 by 1861. Lastly the Select

Committee on Destitute and Neglected Children had confined its attention almost entirely to Bristol and London where the ragged-school movement was strongest.

Private surveys in two of the omitted cities were made by the Manchester and Salford Education Aid Society, founded in 1864, and the Birmingham Education Aid Society, established three years later. Their findings that less than half of the children of school age were actually receiving some form of education were criticized by those who upheld the voluntary system. However, the publication of their reports together with the realization that some parents were too poor even to take advantage of the tickets for free education that were issued, helped to undermine confidence in the accuracy of the *Newcastle Report*. W. E. Forster, the Vice-President of the Committee of the Privy Council on Education in Gladstone's first administration, accordingly appointed two inspectors to survey the great cities of Liverpool, Leeds, Manchester, and Birmingham, all of which had been the subjects of recent private enquiries that had produced results at variance with those of the Newcastle Commissioners. These investigations, together with those conducted by the Society of Arts in parts of London and its environs,[4] underlined the lesson that could have been learnt from the evidence submitted to the Select Committee on Manchester and Salford Education in 1852. The greatest failure of the voluntary schools was with those who needed help most. In contrast, the artisan and lower-middle classes had taken advantage of the elementary schools to a far greater extent than any other social group.

HMI the Rev. D. R. Fearon's report on Manchester and Liverpool reinforced this conclusion. He saw that there were three main social categories for whom the elementary schools ought to have been making provision, the pauper and criminal classes, the very poor who were mainly unskilled casual labourers, and the skilled workmen. The very poor were the group amongst whom

the greatest amount of educational destitution exists, which has hitherto received the least amount of educational recognition and help from the nation, and for whose educational improvement the existing means are the most inadequate and defective. If a labourer of this class rises into the ranks of foremen, or obtains steady employment and good wages, he will find excellent schools . . . .

If that man, Fearon continued,

54

falls into the pauper or criminal class, here again the state will come to the assistance of his children . . . . But as long as he remains in the section which is neither wholly independent, nor yet quite pauper, he finds the provision made . . . is quite insufficient.

In common with other observers of the time Fearon found that the government-inspected schools were mainly patronized by the children of the skilled workmen and their social equals, the smallest shop-keepers. He then pointed to one problem that the inauguration of a policy of compulsory school attendance would create. The existing government-aided schools did not accept the children of the lowest labouring class. If they were to do so, the children of the more respectable working classes would leave. The skilled man did not want his children to 'associate with the lowest children of the town, whose habits and language are sometimes filthy, and whose bodies are almost always dirty and often diseased.'[5]

Table 3 shows the provision of elementary education in the four cities surveyed by HMIs J. G. Fitch and Fearon. The most reliable of the figures are those relating to the examination of the children under the Revised Code. Even if one allows for the unreality of expecting

TABLE 3   *The provision of education in four major cities*

	Birmingham	Leeds	Liverpool	Manchester
Number of children aged 3 to 15	97,736	68,556	137,851	100,457
Average attendance in inspected schools	16,053	12,422	25,083	21,437
Average attendance in uninspected schools	10,783[a]	8,593[a]	13,530[b]	4,678[b]
Presented for examination under the Revised Code	9,923	7,643	15,967	14,360
Standards I to III	8,047	6,054	12,736	11,431
Standards IV to VI	1,876	1,589	3,231	2,020
Presented in Standard VI	256	274	515	437
Passed in Standard VI	?	?	211	340

Source: Return, Confined to the Municipal Boroughs of Birmingham, Leeds, Liverpool, and Manchester, of all schools for the poorer classes of children, Parliamentary Papers, 1870, LIV, pp.30–1, 167 (302–3, 439).

[a] D. R. Fearon is rightly sceptical of the accuracy of these figures. See pp.24 and 43 of his *Report*.

[b] 'Actual attendance'. For purposes of comparison with average attendance, the number of scholars in 'actual attendance' in inspected schools in Liverpool was 28,882.

every child between the ages of 3 and 15 to be in school, it is clear that the schools both quantitatively and qualitatively were failing to provide an education that met the criteria enunciated by Bishop Fraser. In 1869 slightly over one half, 38,268 out of 74,995, of the children normally attending the inspected schools had been examined in the first three standards of the Revised Code. If the national average provides a reliable guide, two-thirds of them passed in all three subjects. Yet Standard III stipulated no more than arithmetic up to and including simple division, the reading of a short paragraph from an elementary reading book used in the school and the writing from dictation of a sentence from the same paragraph. In regard to the last two tests it should be remembered that the usual criticism of the Revised Code is that the children spent the whole year on one reading book, a consideration that makes the examination results look even less reassuring. Moreover, few emerged triumphantly at Standard VI, the highest level of an elementary school education. In the four cities no more than 1,482 tried to surmount this hurdle.

Table 4 shows the limited extent to which the state was making effective provision for the children of the pauper, near-pauper, and near-criminal classes in these cities. Children from this social level had been the losers throughout the nineteenth century. In one respect Joseph Lancaster had introduced the monitorial system with the best of intentions. He wanted to reduce the running costs of schools sufficiently to enable him to dispense with fees. However, both the British and Foreign School Society and the National Society soon decided it was necessary and desirable to charge them, thereby depriving the poorest children even of this limited succour. Ragged schools, whose origins date from the establishment of the London City Mission in 1835, if not earlier, tried to fill the breach. The Ragged School Union, founded in 1844 as a co-ordinating body, reached its apogee by the late 1860s when it assisted nearly 200 schools claiming an average attendance of 20,000 pupils. With the advent of the board schools the numbers attending ragged schools gradually declined. As well as giving very elementary education, the ragged schools engaged in a wide variety of social-welfare activities such as running Penny Banks, Clothing Clubs, Bands of Hope, and Soup Kitchens. One institution that combined many of the aims of the Ragged Schools, industrial training, the eradication of pauperism, and the inculcation of the doctrine of self-help was the Boys' Shoeblack Brigade. Founded in 1851, to provide a service for visitors to London for the Great

TABLE 4   *Extent of compulsory education in Birmingham and Leeds in 1869*

Agency	Birmingham	Leeds
Reformatory and Industrial Schools Act	192	126
In workhouse and Union schools	571	312
Paid for under Denison's Act	287	420
Paid for and sent by Education Aid Society	1,973	—
Half-timers under Factory Acts	315[a]	1,212[a]
Half-timers under Workshops Act	—[b]	—[b]

Source: J. G. Fitch, *Report on Schools for the Poorer Classes in Birmingham and Leeds*, Parliamentary Papers, 1870, LIV, p.120 (388).

[a] Most of the following acts applied to Leeds:- The Factory Acts, 1833, 1834, 1864 and 1867; Print Works Act, 1845; Bleach and Dye Works Act, 1860; Lace Factories' Act, 1861. The only one to affect Birmingham industries was the Factory Act, 1867.

[b] Both cities were theoretically affected by the recently passed Workshops' Regulation Act, 1867. In Leeds where the Town Council had decided to enforce the Act, employers had begun to discharge their juvenile employees. It was thought that prosecutions under the Act would lead to the wholesale dismissal of children in employment. The Birmingham Town Council had decided to defer action on the Act until after June 1870.

Exhibition that year, it outlived the ragged schools and was still flourishing at the end of the century.[6]

The Education Department offered ragged schools grants for industrial work only. As a consequence of this restriction Gent, the secretary of the Ragged School Union, believed that no more than 800 pupils out of a possible 25,000 in the London area qualified. The Select Committee listened with sympathy to evidence from the RSU, dominated by the evangelical Lord Shaftesbury, that government aid would interfere with the religious and missionary character of their work. They heard with horror the story of a schoolmaster who had misappropriated an order for paper costing £1,000 for a school making paper-bags. They recommended the withdrawal of the government grant. With the cessation of this grant, the ragged schools looked to certification under the Industrial Schools Act as a means of obtaining government assistance, a procedure that emphasised their custodial role.[7]

To justify their action the Select Committee cited the provision recently made by the granting of new powers to the Poor Law Guardians and the setting up of industrial schools. However, a brief examination of both these innovations shows that neither filled the gap. The Education of Children in Receipt of Outdoor Relief (Denison's) Act of 1855 allowed poor law guardians to pay the school fees of pauper and destitute children. A return made the following year shows how reluctant the guardians were to use their newly-acquired permissive powers. The guardians were paying the fees of less than 4 per cent, 3,986 out of 102,086, of the children chargeable to the poor rate but not residing in a workhouse. In many rural areas the Act was almost a dead letter. In 18 counties the guardians paid for the education of 23 children between them. In contrast, the industrialized areas of Lancashire and the West Riding of Yorkshire cared for 1,011 and 534 respectively. In his evidence to the Newcastle Commissioners John Snell, schoolmaster of East Coker, near Yeovil, illustrated the reluctance of rural boards of guardians to pay for education at the expense of the rates and thereby deprive the farming community of cheap labour. When a person applied for relief, the guardians insisted that the children left school to work in the fields. The 1856 return substantiates his statement. The Yeovil Union was one of 13 in Somerset where no fees were charged to the rates. A further *Return* of 1870 shows that some limited progress had been made. 9·5 per cent of the intended beneficiaries, 22,033 out of 233,036, had their fees paid for them. In the counties of Cornwall, Dorset, Cardigan, and Denbigh, the guardians had yet to operate the Act. A solitary child in Anglesey and three in Northamptonshire kept it alive in their respective counties. Even in Birmingham, the Midlands exemplar of municipal reform and platform for the cause of free education, voluntary effort outstripped local government provision. In 1869, the guardians were paying the fees of 287 children but the Education Aid Society had paid for 1,793.[8]

Children whose parents eked out a precarious livelihood learnt to depend on their wits and a life of begging and petty crime in the urban jungles of mid-Victorian England. In such a situation where 'the only crime was being found out', those who were unlucky enough to be caught by the police had their education provided by the Reformatory and Industrial Schools. The Reformatory Schools Act, 1854, dealt with children below the age of 16 who had been sentenced to fourteen days' – ten days' from 1855 – or more imprisonment. On the expiry of their sentence they could be sent to a reformatory school for a period varying between two and five years. Further acts passed in 1857 and

1861 allowed magistrates to send unconvicted children below the age of 14 to a certified industrial school. These schools took in children found begging or wandering without visible means of subsistence, those whose parents were dead or in prison, and those who frequented the company of reputed thieves. Thus by 1870 compulsory education of a punitive and reformative nature was provided for those street arabs unfortunate enough to attract the attention of the police. The rest were free to wander at will untroubled by the schoolmaster's demands on their time.

One of the main purposes of the Elementary Education Act of 1870 was to bring the social and the educational outcasts of the nation into the schools. During the first reading of the bill W. E. Forster had attempted to forestall criticism by emphasising that he was taking 'the utmost endeavour not to injure existing and efficient schools'. The purpose of his bill, he explained, was 'to fill up gaps'. Articles and theses essentially local in character written on the school board, that administrative innovation of the 1870 Act, have led commentators to think of the gaps largely in geographical terms. This has been partly the consequence of the manner in which the elementary schools had been established in the first place. As the initiative in providing schools had come from local enthusiasts and philanthropists the elementary-school system had not been a system at all. It had been a geographical and pedagogic mosaic, the uncoordinated creation of countless individuals, albeit with some central encouragement from the National Society and other concerned bodies. It had never been an ordered pattern, the product of a tidy-minded bureaucracy implementing a policy for the nation as a whole. In contrast to the emphasis that thesis writers have put on the spatial nature of these gaps, contemporaries were acutely aware of the social gaps that had to be filled by providing schools for those whom poverty had previously debarred from the classroom. To some extent the two views are reconcilable. There is evidence to suggest that residential areas of higher rateable value had a better *pre capita* provision of school accommodation than did areas of lower rateable values. Moreover it seems that school boards built and opened schools in the poorest areas first. However, the whole question of relating school provision to social class before 1870, as well as after, requires the educational historian to make greater use of the techniques of the urban geographer and historian than hitherto. In this way he will be able to explore more precisely than before the interconnexion between educational and socio-economic deprivation.

Contemporaries had none of these scholarly doubts about the nature of the problem that faced them. The same night that Forster introduced his bill 'to plug the gaps' Francis Adams, the secretary of the National Education League, explained what these gaps were to an audience at Huntingdon. With pardonable exaggeration he told them that the most momentous question that had ever come before the country and the House of Commons was 'how and where shall the children of the masses be trained in streets, gutters, kennels, and hovels, encompassed by misery, vice, dirt, poverty, and crime, . . . or in properly appointed and conducted schools.'[9] The need to build schools for the kind of children Adams had described was probably the one issue on which both the Birmingham-based National Education League, committed to free, compulsory, nonsectarian, if not secular education, and the National Education Union, the Manchester-based protagonists of the existing voluntary system, were in agreement. George Dixon, chairman of the first meeting of the NEL held in October 1869 declared, 'The new schools would be mainly, if not entirely, erected in those districts which are now destitute of them – that is in those districts where, by reason of poverty, free schools are most needed.' It was for children attending these schools, Dixon ingenuously reassured the supporters of voluntary schools, that their subscriptions and donations would still be needed. This money would no longer go 'to the building and maintenance of schools for the higher class of working men, some, if not all of whom are able to pay the entire cost of the education of their children.' Instead the new beneficiaries of the charity of the wealthy would be the destitute who were unable to attend any school at all because of their rags. Dixon, a member of the earlier Birmingham Education Society, knew full well from personal experience that many of his city's children had been unable to take advantage of free education because they just did not possess suitable clothes and shoes.[10]

A few days later at Manchester Earl Harrowby, the president of the NEU meeting, showed that despite his disagreement with Dixon over the means he agreed over the ends. The more respectable members of the working classes, he stated, 'are making sacrifices already; and are sending their children to school. You are first of all to deal with those who do not get education now, and those are the most ignorant and poorest.' For these children the NEU was prepared to countenance assistance from the rates together with a limited use of compulsion through the extension of existing administrative machinery. Its members wanted the permissive powers in earlier legislation, the acts of 1844 and 1848 relating to indoor pauper children and Denison's Act of 1855 providing for outdoor pauper children, together with powers conferred by the Industrial Schools Acts of 1857 and 1861, made into duties. By making the enforcement of these acts mandatory 'the education of this dependent class of children would be admirably provided for. Thus while we deprecate as strongly as possible, *rate aid* and *compulsion* for children of our independent labourers, we would apply both to the "dangerous classes" below them.'[11] These proposals were remarkably similar to those put forward by W. L. Sargant, chairman of Birmingham's first school board from 1870 to 1873, in his paper 'On the Progress of Elementary Education', which he had read to the Statistical Society in London in 1867. In his concern to minimise the extent of state interference at the local level he had harked back to the precedent of the unsuccessful Manchester and Salford Bills of 1852 by suggesting, 'It is from Manchester that the cry for compulsory education has come . . . it should be ascertained whether the Manchester case is peculiar . . . if it is peculiar, then a local bill is what is needed.'[12] The great attraction of limited programmes such as these was that they helped to obviate the risk of setting up popularly elected boards on any large scale, for extension of the principle of compulsory universal education to the children of the independent working classes put the unrepresentative and constitutionally irresponsible voluntary-school system in jeopardy. Parents who had won the vote in 1867 understandably wanted the schools in which their children were going to be educated brought under a semblance of popular control. The reform of the nation's schools was a political issue in which there were legitimate differences of opinion about how it was to be achieved as much as it was an educational one.

Many of the leaders of the working-class movement shared these views. The reform of education was a political issue that offered radically-minded politically conscious working men the opportunity of breaching, if not eliminating, the Church of England's influence. Hence the TUC conference resolution of 27 August 1868 that 'this Congress believes that nothing short of a system of free, national, unsectarian, and compulsory education will satisfy the requirements of the people in the United Kingdom' was as much about religion and politics as it was about education.[13] Moreover the conference had lasted the whole week from the Monday to the Saturday inclusive but the debate on education had occupied only part of a Friday session. The main concerns of delegates were working conditions and the status of trade unions.

There was also a tendency for the skilled working man to share the middle-class attitude that compulsory education was for somebody else's children. Skilled men were law-abiding respectable parents who already sent their children to school and kept them out of mischief without the intervention of any outside coercive agency interfering in their daily lives. Hence the *Bee-Hive*'s initial response to the idea of compulsory education was a muted one. In 1867 it had approved the education clauses in the Factory Act because they, 'if earnestly and fully administered will bring us soon far along the road to complete education without that compulsory education which meddles in house-hold business, its necessities and wants.' Similarly a few days before Forster introduced his bill in 1870 it spoke of compulsory education in a guarded way, 'a qualified meaning of the word, not using it in its positive, absolute, imperative, harsh sense . . . .'[14] Somewhat in this vein Robert Applegarth, the secretary of the Society of Carpenters and Joiners, pointed to the gulf between the skilled men who were 'beginning to see that they must have education to bring them to compete in the race of industry with the workmen of other countries' and the unskilled man against whom in his speech to the NEL on 13 October 1869 he took a hard line.

There is the careless and indifferent man, who has been so long neglected and degraded that he does not understand the value of education; and him the other class, the better class of working men have to carry on their backs. Those men who do not understand the value of education must be made to understand it.

He also admitted that the demand for the provision of education came from the better paid and more skilled workers and, by implication, not from the unskilled men. As a member of the NEL delegation to Gladstone in April 1870 he informed the prime minister, 'I say that the miners up to the most skilled artisans of the country, they have all declared in favour of compulsory education,' a remark in which the occupational groups Applegarth omitted are as significant as those he included. The skilled man's advocacy of compulsory education was partly a matter of enlightened self-interest. 'Those outside our unions', he wrote, 'appeal to us for advice when they are in difficulties, and to our accumulated funds for assistance in their misfortunes . . . .' Greater issues than the protection of trade union funds were at stake. Since it could be argued that the incidence of taxation fell more heavily on the working man than on the wealthier classes, the trade unionist had a particular interest both in reducing the total tax burden and in seeing that the money was spent in a way that met with his approval. There was 'an intimate and melancholy connection', Applegarth wrote, between the sum in excess of £10,000,000 spent from taxes in 1867 'to punish crime and perpetuate pauperism' and the two million children receiving no education. 'Since competent authorities tell us that "the taxation of the workman is double that of their richer neighbours" it is our duty to wage war against ignorance which taxes us so severely.' The artisan had the right to demand that his 'taxes should be expended on schools instead of on prisons and workhouses.' As Sir James Kay-Shuttleworth had written nearly forty years earlier, 'The preservation of *internal peace*, not less than the improvement of our national institutions, depends on the education of the working classes.' Although Applegarth at times assumed the mantle of the classical economists, while campaigning for a seat on the London School Board he struck a nobler note.[15]

The children of the poor must be placed on a footing of equality with those of the rich, in having access to the various Educational institutions for which their capacities may fit them, from our National Infant Schools to what ought to be our National Universities.

When looking at the evidence put forward by workers' leaders in any one industry or craft, it has to be remembered that these spokesmen were atypical figures. They owed their standing with their fellows, amongst other factors, to the extraordinary tenacity with which they had educated themselves under adverse conditions. The same energy and determination had brought them to the commanding heights in their labour movements. Conscious of what education had done for them they wanted their fellows to enjoy the same advantages for the common benefit of all. For without education the working-class movement could not prosper. Such a man was Will Thorne who was sent to work at the age of six. Still illiterate at the age of twenty-two in 1879, he had to make his mark in the marriage register. Taught to read and write by Eleanor Marx Aveling, Karl Marx's daughter, he became the secretary of a local branch of the Social and Democratic Federation in the mid-1880s and the founder of the Gasworkers' Union in 1889, which he eventually built into the General and Municipal Workers' Union. His early struggles left him with an abiding belief in the value of education ' "which is one of the greatest blessings a man can possess" for when "men are better educated they become sensible of the manner in which they have been deprived of the results of their labour".[16] Another was Alexander MacDonald, who after going down the pit at the age of eight, eventually saved enough money to go to Glasgow University. After running a school at Airdrie from 1851 to 1855, he devoted his time to the formation of the Miners' National Union and became its secretary from 1863 to 1881, the year of his death. As the earlier evidence of the miners' leaders indicates, men such as these were aware of the cultural and economic gulf that existed between themselves and the rank and file of the working classes. With the greater vision of an emancipated, prosperous working class in mind they could afford to take the wider view. Their followers, with immediately pressing household demands to meet, were often unable to defer present expenditure in the form of their children's earnings for the long-term ultimate good. Altruism on behalf of the working-class cause was a luxury they could not afford.

One must also remember that the more prosperous members of the working classes were in many instances socially displaced persons whose attitudes to elementary education reflect their incongruent status. Their sense of duty and obligation to their less fortunate fellows identifies them with the class from which they had sprung. Their belief that education would preserve social order and reduce crime and pauperism identifies them with the middle classes whose acceptance and membership some of them sought. A series of articles written by Edward Brotherton, albeit a middle-class industrialist, reflects many of these characteristics. Writing in the *Co-operator* in the autumn of 1865 he attributed the failure of the Co-operative Movement to win wider support to the lack of education among the working classes. If the masses 'were well disciplined, trained to habits of obedience and order, and made to see the use and necessity of discipline . . . almost every man would become a capitalist, by becoming the owner of Co-operative shares.' In a world made safe for working-class capitalists, Brotherton looked to every £1,000 spent on education producing a saving of £2,000,000 to £3,000,000 in the cost of dealing with crime and pauperism. Co-operators had, in addition, a duty to those who had not yet left behind them 'the old world of bondage and misery'. Accordingly, 'Every noblest and best impulse in the human bosom requires them to cry aloud that the slaves of ignorance . . . shall be freed from their Egyptian bondage, and enter into the land flowing with milk and honey.' Just how far some of them had left the old world behind is demonstrated in their journal in 1866 which advocated the extension of the savings-bank franchise qualification, proposed in Gladstone's Reform Bill, to include holdings of Co-operative shares. The *Co-operator* also gave details of the Rochdale's branch reading room and library. The society subscribed to nearly 200 newspapers and magazines a week. The library contained 4,000 books on religion, politics and social economy as well as such equipment as a pair of globes, a telescope, a microscope, and marine glasses.[17] Well-read men such as the users of this and other libraries wanted something more than the limited elementary education offered in most schools for their children. They saw the value of technical education which, unlike the unskilled labourer, who could hardly afford to send his children to school at all, they wanted for their own children to enable them to enter the better paid trades and occupations.

The prominence that has been given at times to Applegarth's activities on the NEL has tended to obscure the League's essentially middle-class nature. Although W. R. Cremer, George J. Holyoake, George Howell of the Operative Bricklayers' Society, George Odger, and Robert Applegarth were members of the League's Council, they were swamped by the remaining three hundred members. Applegarth, Cremer, Holyoake, Howell, Lloyd Jones, and Green the Chairman of the Birmingham Trades' Council spoke at the inaugural meeting of the League held in Birmingham on 12 and 13 October 1869. The major speeches, made by such influential Birmingham members as George Dixon and Joseph Chamberlain received wide publicity. In contrast *The Times* gave Applegarth and him alone of the trade-union representatives, one inch in its two-column report. In the 237-page verbatim report published by the NEL on the two days' proceedings, the contributions of the working-class leaders occupy no more than twenty pages. Although Cremer seconded a motion proposed by Joseph Chamberlain, the presence of these spokesmen seems to have been suffered rather than actively welcomed. At the Town Hall on 13 October the sheep were divided from the goats. 'The side galleries were occupied by ladies and gentlemen for whom seats had been reserved. The floor was filled (for the most part) by an audience consisting of working men, of which class there was a considerable number in the great gallery also.'[18]

As in the Town Hall of Birmingham so in the country at large separate provision was made for trade unionists. By August 1870 there were 140 branches of the NEL in the towns of England and Wales. These local organizations usually had the mayor and other civic dignitaries as their leading officials. In addition there were 20 Trades' Societies' branches listed separately in the League's literature. These branches had been affiliated in response to the TUC conference's motion passed in Birmingham in 1869 calling on trade unionists to support the NEL and its programme. As might be expected Applegarth's union, the Amalgamated Society of Carpenters and Joiners, was the most active. The Union joined *per se* as did its London branches in Borough, Islington, and King's Cross. Outside London the Branches in Birmingham, Bristol, Plymouth, and Trowbridge followed suit. The ASC and J was the only London-based trade society to follow the TUC's lead. In Birmingham, the home town of the NEL, there was predictably a better response from the Flint Glass Makers' Union, the Operative House Painters' Society and the Carpenters' General Union. Elsewhere support was sporadic, and largely, it seems, the result of an individual's initiative and enthusiasm in societies composed of small groups of skilled men such as the Scissor Grinders' Sick Society and the Wool Shear Forgers' Society, both of Sheffield, and the United Core Makers' Protection Society of Bradford. Three branches of the Amalgamated Cordwainers Society in Manchester, Nottingham and Tunbridge Wells, together with the Boatmakers' Society of Manchester, the North Shields branch of the Boat Builders' Association, and the Sheffield Operative Bricklayers' Society make up the score. If affiliation to the NEL is a reliable index of trade-union enthusiasm for the cause of education, that enthusiasm was slight.

Although the NEL courted the support of working men because of their sheer weight of numbers it kept them at arm's length, as the separate listing of the trade societies illustrates. Similarly, the practice of publishing detailed contribution lists helped to maintain, albeit unintentionally, the great social divide between the middle-class leadership and the working-class rank and file. Thomas Burt's contribution of half-a-crown was small beer compared with the magnums of seventeen promises of £1,000 made by January 1870.[19]

The composition of the NEL's delegation to W. E. Gladstone on 9 March, 'the most numerous and powerful delegation ever known to have visited Downing Street', is further evidence of the lowly status accorded working-class representatives. Out of a delegation of nearly 500 only Applegarth, T. J. Wilkinson, the secretary of the Birmingham Glass Makers' Society, W. R. Cremer, Daniel Guile, G. J. Holyoake, T. Mottershead, a silk-weaver, George Odger, and Benjamin Lucraft can be readily identified as members of the labour movement. In many

66

cases the deputations from the towns that participated were led by their mayors. It is not surprising that working men chose on occasion to work independently of the League. On 16 June 1870 Dr Spurgeon presided over a meeting of working men in Exeter Hall, London. Cremer, Guile, Mottershead, participants in the delegation to Gladstone, and Savage a die-sinker, moved a resolution for free, compulsory, and non-sectarian education. The respectability of the audience is attested by the fate of a motion moved by Daniel Chatterton, 'a man of very unkempt appearance', in favour of secular education. He had only twenty supporters. After the meeting Cremer took a delegation to meet W. E. Forster on 25 June. The list in *The Times* includes the well-known Osborn, plasterer, and Lucraft, chairmaker. Obscurer members were Britten, shoemaker, Trant, warehouseman, Savage, die-sinker, Mottershead, silk-weaver, Mineard, joiner, Evans, clerk, Knowles, turner, Skinner, labourer, Nieass, plasterer, Mullens, gold-chaser, Stafford, carpenter, Linn, shoemaker, Patterson, cabinet-maker, Souter, packing-case maker, Babbs, paint colourer, Stainsby, tailor, Sinclair, joiner, Chantil, ivory turner, Eglin, fishmonger, and Pratt, saddler and harness-maker.[20] As this list shows members of this delegation with one exception enjoyed the status and esteem of the skilled and semi-skilled artisan class.

The demand of the politically conscious working class was not just for education but for a particular form of education, nonsectarian education, a demand that involved the ending of the near monopoly of the Church of England. The extension of the franchise had made the retention of the control of the nation's schools in the hands of a constitutionally irresponsible and unrepresentative body a political anachronism. A Liberal victory in the general election of 1868 fought mainly over the issue of the disestablishment of the Irish Church that gave Gladstone a majority of over 110, the largest of any government since Sir Robert Peel's of 1841, made the creation of a national education system at last a political possibility. In one sense Lowe had been right. Reform in 1867 made a national system of education a necessity not because his future masters had to be educated but because they wanted the same semblance of control over the nation's schools that they now had over parliament. Lowe was also right in the long term. The introduction of the householder franchise had conceded the principle of equality in the boroughs. More perceptive than those who relied on the mystique of a deferential society, Lowe saw the electoral consequences. The Elementary Education Act of 1870 ensured that the 'future masters' of 1918 had learnt their letters. In this respect the legislation was a response to a much more primitive emotion, the fear of the mob, a fear that extended back through the memory of the propertied classes to the sturdy beggar of Tudor England and earlier. Industrialization and urbanization in the nineteenth had created a new mob, the 'residuum' of the slums and rookeries of England's towns and cities. The Reform Act of 1867 had taken the franchise a stage nearer this class. It had given the vote to those thought to be susceptible to the new demagogue of the 1860s, the trade unionist leader held responsible for the Sheffield outrages. The old order of society seemed doubly threatened.[21]

The masses will certainly use their power in the great changes which are rapidly coming upon the country, and unless intelligence guides their energy and strength, the results may be disastrous to the nation at large, as well as to class interests and privileged orders.

Yet as the newly enfranchised 'masses' were already sending their children to school just as they in turn had been sent earlier in the century, fears based on these grounds were baseless and exaggerated. The radical weekly, *Reynold's Newspaper*, argued that the real threat to the propertied classes was not that of an uneducated electorate but of an educated one. Quoting from J. M. Ludlow and L. Jones, *Progress of the Working Classes, 1832–1867* (1867) it reminded its readers that nearly £700,000 a year was spent by the state on furthering the education of the classes who were able to contribute something themselves for the purpose and frequented the National, British, and other assisted schools. Consequently,

the enfranchised operative of 1867 was a far more enlightened and much better educated person than the working man of 1832, who obtained the franchise by the Reform Bill of that period . . . . It is that knowledge which makes them [the aristocracy] quake for the safety of those privileges and power they have so long enjoyed.

The editorial comments in *Reynold's Newspaper* on the speech from the throne of February 1870 follow the same theme. There were different reforms for different classes. For the middle classes there was the promise of reform of the universities, the judiciary, and the rating system. For the working classes there was the prospect of trade union legislation. 'Then what do the poor get? A Bill for national education, given after all the funds left by pious donors have been embezzled by the upper classes, or by misappropriations too shameful for history to

68

record.' Finally, a comment made by T. P. Allen, the headmaster of a British school, who had carried out a survey for the Society of Arts aptly epitomizes contemporary social attitudes. The operatives in the workshops 'had reflected but little upon the great measure intended principally for the amelioration of their condition.' In contrast the overlookers who 'in many cases had read works on philosophy or political economy; who could discuss questions relating to capital and labour . . . were generally in favour of the changes, except as to secularism . . . .' They were ready, he averred, to bear the burden for the education of all. The small shopkeepers were also generally in favour. Resistance came, however, from 'the highest class of tradesmen, professional men, and parish officials' who were concerned about the effect of the Act on the rates.[22]

Within a short time of the passing of the 1870 Act comment on the changing social composition of the classroom suggests that the new Act was beginning to achieve one of its objectives. C. H. Parez, who inspected schools in Cumberland, Westmorland, and the Furness and Cartmel district of Lancashire, welcomed the 'large influx of rough and ragged children; and in those bare feet and tattered clothes', he exulted, 'one cannot but hail with inward rejoicing the first unmistakable signs of the great moral good which the recent Act is calculated to do for the poor neglected children, that swarm about the lanes and alleys . . . .' E. P. Arnold, whose allocation of Devonshire schools kept him as removed as Parez from the problems of the great industrial areas found, 'Compulsion is reaching the very class which it was intended to reach . . . . Already I recognize in some of the street arabs, selling pipelights under the railway arches and at the corner of streets boys who have passed a successful examination in two or three subjects at some recent inspection . . . . They cannot but be better for habits of cleanliness and discipline, to say nothing of the instruction which they receive, which there, and only there, are enforced upon them.'[23]

The presence of such children in the classroom, the social moraine of an uncontrolled economy, raised problems for their more successful social superiors, be they school managers, school masters, or more affluent members of the working classes. An acute moral and economic problem faced the Established Church whose traditional pastoral duty was the education of its poor parishioners. The Church did not have the resources necessary for building the requisite schools. In addition school managers saw that the admission of the children of the streets would offend many of the fee-paying parents whose offspring were the life-blood of the voluntary schools. The Rev. R. Gregory, Dean of St Paul's showed schools managers the way to an easy conscience. The problem facing them in the towns, he wrote, was whether the Church should educate the children of the higher artisans, the small tradespeople, and the steady, sober, diligent, fairly paid labourers or those of the ill paid, whose work was uncertain, and who were unthrifty or unsteady. Although he acknowledged the Church's obligation to the latter, he argued that a large proportion of them were in their unhappy condition through their own moral shortcomings. 'They were slothful or indifferent workmen, or ill-tempered, or drunken.' This absolved the Church from its duty, for 'the religious ground must seem to be very doubtful'. It was therefore 'wisest and best to instruct that class which will value the education offered and which will be the most likely to profit by it.' He warned his readers against 'being carried away by unthinking generosity' and admitting the children of the near-pauper classes. Such a policy would only 'throw most of the better home-trained children into the rate-founded schools . . . .' He concluded by laying the moral blame at the door of the State. Since the 1870 Act had not provided schooling for all out of the rates – a policy that the Church had opposed – education could be regarded in the same light as poor relief. 'With such a possibility before us, it would certainly seem to be desirable to provide voluntary schools for the education of the upper portions, whilst those who have sunk lowest are delegated to the schools furnished by the rates. Let it not be thought', he concluded, 'that in making these suggestions we part with the very poor and the outcast, the children of thriftless, drunken, wicked parents, without the deepest regret . . . . The loss they will endure, in being deprived of definite dogmatic religious teaching, will be great; . . . but it is not we who condemn them to rate board schools, it is not we who deprive them of creeds and formularies. That the State has done.'[24]

Schoolmasters, confronted with the task of teaching the unwilling conscripts of the 1870 Act, felt the need for enforcing firm discipline. They resisted the steps taken by the London School Board and others to limit the right to inflict corporal punishment to the head teacher. At a time when they were anxious about the social and professional status of their occupation, they saw such a restriction as a reflection on their expertise and judgement. In more practical terms they believed it made their job harder. The *Schoolmaster*, the journal of the recently established National Union of Elementary Teachers, came to their defence. 'The class of children who for some years are likely to form the majority in board schools are those who have hitherto been neglected, and whose everyday life is in the presence of moral laxity.' Teaching in board schools, the editorial article continued, would be a daunting task during 'the younger years of school-board life, while the unbroken youth of our country are being raked in from the gutter, the dunghill, and the hedgerow.'[25]

Working-class parents were also concerned about the future. When Mrs Georgina Grey, an unsuccessful candidate at the 1870 London School Board election, addressed a working-class audience she was at pains to allay their fears of an influx of dirty and verminous children into the schools attended by their well-kempt children. She suggested a three-tier system to separate the washed from the unwashed. The lowest establishment, to replace the ragged school, was to be 'for the unhappy children picked up in the gutter whom no respectable working man would like to see sitting on the same bench with his children, with all the dirt, moral and physical, belonging to them.' Once 'cleansed of their dirt', the children would be given the elements of education in the next class. Those who could afford to stay the longest, that is the children of her rate-paying audience, would reach the highest class where they would be socially and academically insulated from the nomads of the street.[26]

Although the better paid working-class parents were understandably reluctant to send their children to the board schools in the early 1870s, attitudes gradually changed when it became apparent that the board schools could provide facilities superior to those of many of the voluntary and privately run schools. In the long term the fears of Mrs Grey's audience proved groundless. The London School Board developed a scheme of differential fees that allowed the artisan rate-paying father to send his child to school secure in the knowlege that he would not come home harbouring lice from the children of the residuum. By the end of the 1880s the London School Board with 110,000 school places at a $1d$ a week, 180,000 at $2d$, 100,000 at $3d$, and 60,000 at $4d$ or more, had produced a scholastic and social hierarchy capped by the higher grade schools. As Table 5 shows, the numbers of children paying these fees corresponds roughly with the numbers in the various social grades of schools devised by Mary Tabor in her survey for Charles Booth. In all she used six categories or classes of schools. Class I, quasi-moralistically described as 'accommodating the "poor" and "very poor" with a sprinkling of the lowest criminal class' contained 110,054 children, a figure remarkably close to the

TABLE 5   *Classification of children taught in London Board Schools*

Social category of school	Number of schools	Number of children in social class												
		A			B			C			D			E			F and above			Total	
		No.	%		No.	%		No.	%		No.	%		No.	%		No.	%		No.	%
I	99	4,234	3·9		30,392	27·6		36,765	33·4		25,214	22·9		11,597	10·5		1,852	1·7		110,054	100·0
II	68	1,564	2·2		11,366	15·9		19,210	26·9		20,685	28·9		14,871	20·8		3,588	5·3		71,284	100·0
III	106	1,202	0·9		13,948	10·8		27,682	21·4		37,766	29·1		37,029	28·6		11,973	9·2		129,600	100·0
IV	59	151	0·2		3,214	5·0		7,459	11·6		10,423	16·2		29,407	45·7		13,751	21·3		64,405	100·0
V	48	106	0·2		1,734	2·9		4,307	7·2		7,404	12·3		24,154	40·0		22,486	37·4		60,191	100·0
VI	8	9	0·1		16	0·3		163	2·7		215	3·5		555	9·1		5,117	84·3		6,075	100·0
—	388	7,266	1·6		60,670	13·7		95,586	21·6		101,707	23·2		117,613	26·6		58,767	13·3		441,609	100·0

Source: C. Booth, *Life and Labour of the People in London, First Series: Poverty III* (1902), p.197.

72

TABLE 6   Classification of children taught in Voluntary Elementary Schools

Social category of school	Number of schools	Number of children in social class											
		A		B		C and D		E		F and above		Total	
		No.	%	No.	%	No.	%	No.	%	No.	%	No.	%
I	33	931	8·9	5,508	52·4	3,425	32·6	569	5·4	70	0·7	10,503	100·0
II	98	428	1·4	4,327	13·7	14,283	45·3	9,959	31·6	2,523	8·0	31,520	100·0
III	178	461	0·7	5,834	8·7	22,802	33·9	27,678	41·2	10,446	15·5	67.221	100·0
IV	134	262	0·5	1,264	2·3	7,632	13·7	31,366	56·4	15,094	27·1	55,618	100·0
V	102	10	—	76	0·2	1,117	3·2	9,493	27·2	24,164	69·4	34,860	100·0
VI	46	—	—	—	—	—	—	541	6·6	7,679	93·4	8,220	100·0
—	591	2,092	1·0	17,009	8·2	49,259	23·7	79,606	38·3	59,976	28·8	207,942	100·0

Source: C. Booth, Life and Labour of the People in London, First Series: Poverty III (1902), p.198.

110,000 school places available at 1d a week. Class V and VI schools, catering for the fairly-well-to-do held 66,266 pupils, slightly more than the 60,000 places provided at 4d or more a week. The Table also shows that slum children went to slum schools and that better-off children did not have to mix with them. Thus Class I schools, roughly those charging a penny a week, drew no more than 1·7 per cent of their children from Booth's top social categories. Similarly only 3·5 of the children from the bottom two social categories attended the most expensive schools. Table 6, which provides a similar analysis for the London voluntary schools, shows how faithfully they had followed Canon Gregory's advice to concentrate their energies on the education of the children of the more prosperous working-class parent. Whereas they drew 9·2 per cent of their children from Booth's two bottom social categories, they took 28·8 per cent, more than double the London School Board's figure of 13·3 per cent, from the top groups.

Whatever may have been the general expectation in 1870, the school board system in London soon became one of considerable variety, even within a particular neighbourhood.

In Southwark at one extreme the Orange Street Board School, where the children came from such poor families that it was amongst one of the first to provide free dinners, charged the parents a penny a week if they could find it. At the other end of the scale was Monnow Road Board School where fourpence a week gave a boy 'not only careful and efficient instruction in a well-ventilated room, but also the use of a liberal supply of school books and materials, all the copy books and home task books he needs, and even the paper and compasses he employs in drawing.' Recent research has revealed a similar diversity in the schools of Bootle, Lancashire.[27] Further investigations, using the techniques of the urban geographer, will doubtless enable us to extend our understanding of the social diversity of the late-Victorian elementary school and the extent to which it reflected the social gradations within the working classes themselves.

IV

◆◆

School Boards for All

◆◆

In 1870 the school boards created under the Elementary Education Act were the most democratically constituted of all elected bodies of local government. Members, who sat for three years, required neither a property nor a residential qualification. Although voters had to be rate-payers, they were all treated equally. Each had as many votes as there were seats on the board. Outside London, where special arrangements had to be made because of the size of the Metropolis, numbers varied between five in a small parish and fifteen in a large town. A voter could use all his votes for one candidate, a device known as plumping, thereby making possible the representation of minority interests. In addition the House of Commons after an all-night sitting, an occurrence so rare that it led *The Times* to protest that it could not meet its deadline for the country editions and fulfil its duty of informing the public, accepted the principle of the secret ballot for the School Board of London area outside the City of London. The City, clinging resolutely to its ancient traditions, resisted both the secret ballot and the extension of the franchise to women who were ratepayers in their own right.[1]

These arrangements marked a substantial advance on Forster's original proposals that the councils in the boroughs and the vestries in the parishes should choose the members of the school boards. Non-conformists feared that this method of indirect election would have left the Church of England the dominant influence in town and country alike. Moreover Forster proposed that these boards should be able to assist voluntary schools from the rates. A system whereby Anglican dominated boards would have been able to subsidize a predominantly Anglican voluntary school system seemed little more than the

75

resurrection of the compulsory church rate abolished only two years earlier. Nonconformists who had preferred to suffer the distraint of their possessions rather than pay the rate felt betrayed. The 1870 debate was not predominantly an educational one about the need to extend the existing provision of elementary schooling, on that point there was by now a substantial consensus of opinion; it was a political one about how this extension should be made, the extent to which the schools should be under popular control, and how they should be financed. Essentially it was a conflict between protagonists of differing visions of society, for whosoever controlled the schools could influence the education of the rising generations in a state that was moving slowly, albeit possibly unwittingly, towards parliamentary democracy.[2]

Furthermore, the extension of the franchise in 1867 made the retention of the running of the elementary schools in the hands of constitutionally irresponsible managers, who gave the Anglican Church an influence out of all proportion to the number of its active adherents, more and more of an anachronism. To the newly enfranchised non-conformist the next bastion of privilege to storm was the voluntary school, for until the nation's schools were answerable in some sense to the nation at large, the idea of representative government remained attenuated. With the controversy over the second Reform Act settled, the *Bee-Hive* pointed the way forward. 'The next great agitation of the working classes of Great Britain must be for a state education – entirely free, direct and indirect, from the influence of the clergy.' Jesse Collings told the new electors at a meeting of the Birmingham Trades' Council where their duty lay: 'They should make it a crucial question with every candidate whether he would, as soon as possible, vote for a national system of compulsory education.' *Reynold's Newspaper* also voiced the expectations that the recent electoral reform had raised 'Free schools, the ballot, equal voting, and school boards chosen by the people would give us a real system of national education.' By the beginning of 1870 the *Bee-Hive* was making the wish father to the thought when it proclaimed 'The tide of opinion sets strongly in favour of completely national education, on the basis of free schools, unsectarian instruction, and obligatory attendance.' A month later it professed 'The people, we believe, have made up their minds for a comprehensive scheme, unsectarian, free, and compulsory.' In contrast to the journal's equivocal attitude to 'naked compulsion' which it saw as 'but a clumsy and uncertain answer' it had no doubts about the desirability of nonsectarianism, 'a system wholly removed from every form of formally religious interference'.[3]

Thus the new Reform Act enabled the National Education League to mobilize grassroots support from the twin forces of the newly enfranchised and the dissenting congregations that had helped Gladstone to win a decisive victory in the general election of 1868. The idea, now within the realm of practical politics, that the schools of the nation's children should be under popular control, was not new. It had its origins in earlier social movements and aspirations, in particular those of Owenism and Chartism. Professor T. W. Laqueur's recent study, *Religion and Respectability: Sunday Schools and Working Class Culture, 1780–1850* (Yale University Press, 1976) shows the extent to which the early Sunday schools were the product of the cultural and educational aspirations of the working-class communities they were designed to serve. Education remained a plank in the Chartist platform during the whole of the movement's lifetime. As late as 1851 a Chartist convention proclaimed that 'as every man has a right to the means of mental activity . . . . Education should, therefore, be national, universal, gratuitous and, to a certain extent, compulsory.' When J. Winder visited Bradford on behalf of the Newcastle Commissioners in 1859 he found these ideas still discussed by the working men of a city in which Chartism had once been an active force.[4]

The extension of the franchise in the nineteenth century and the creation of elected units of local government had made self-government valued as an end in itself as well as a means of obtaining more efficient administration. In the particular case of education, the creation of a civic body to control the elementary schools had an added attraction for nonconformists. It provided an outlet for the provincial nonconformist, proud of his city's development, to satisfy his sense of mission. George Dawson, nonconformist minister, lecturer, and advocate of popular education, had voiced this mixture of proselytizing zeal and civic pride when he opened the free reference library in Birmingham, the future birthplace of the NEL, in October 1866. The 'glorious library' was 'the first fruits of a clear understanding that a great town exists to discharge towards the people of that town the duties that a great nation exists to discharge towards the people of that nation. A great town is a solemn organization through which should flow, and in which should be shaped, all the highest, loftiest and truest ends of man's intellectual and moral nature.' Dawson, reared on what John Vincent has described as a nonconformist 'view or recollection of English history', knew full well the second-class status that Anglicans accorded the dissenter. At the first meeting of the NEL he related how a High Churchman had told him that since he had been married by a nonconformist, he was not married at all, 'only joined together,' to which he had replied, 'Well', I said, 'as a practical man, for me that will do.'[5]

Joseph Chamberlain, addressing the same meeting of the NEL specified the issue at stake.

The real reason why our opponents support the denominational system is, not because they believe it to be the best means of securing the education of the people, but because they believe it to be the only means by which they can maintain a monopoly of instruction. Our choice is between the education of the people, and the interests of Church.

George Dixon, sometime mayor of Birmingham, chairman of the NEL and of Birmingham School Board, and MP for the Edgbaston division of Birmingham, reached the heart of the issue when he said, 'We are not here to patch the existing system - to patch the garment of semi-charity and semi-ecclesiasticism . . . . Looking over the Church flock we find a sheep that belongs to us, and that is education, the primary education of the nation. It does not belong to the Church in any sense - it belongs to the whole nation.' Ratepayer control, he assured the meeting, would ensure that the schools belonged to the people, and that the schools would be paid for and managed by the people. This was the antithesis of the policy adopted by Sir James Kay-Shuttleworth. He had valued the contributions of the wealthy as a way of ensuring that the schools remained 'to a great extent under the influence of the superior classes of society'. By preventing the parents of the children from becoming the sole paymasters of the schoolmaster he hoped to safeguard the teacher from the 'caprices of the least intelligent class'.[6] Despite Dixon's expectations, the Kay-Shuttleworth tradition survived with remarkable tenacity. Board schools and council schools kept parents at arm's length as successfully as did the voluntary schools.

A few days after the meeting in Birmingham the supporters of the voluntary schools launched their counter attack at the National Education Union conference in Manchester. HMI the Rev. W. J. Kennedy, enjoying a freedom of public debate denied civil servants today, questioned the competence of local authorities to administer education. He stigmatized the proposed Education Act as 'An Act for the ejectment of the present good men and true from all future management of schools'. In default of a logical argument he took recourse in appealing to his audience's veneration for the established order and the norms of a traditional society. He maintained that the successful running of schools required a particular mystique denied ordinary men. 'You know the qualifications we need in the managers of our schools. In order to find them do your minds instinctively turn to Town Councillors?', a group on whom he had poured ridicule earlier in his speech. The Rt Hon. W. F. Cowper was another speaker who thought that elected representatives would lack the necessary qualifications and experience for managing schools. 'This business of education is of a peculiar character; it requires for its performance a special knowledge and an interest in the intellectual and moral improvement of the children.' Where reverence for tradition was at a premium, reverence for the spirit of the constitution was at a discount. Cowper, doubtless with the county rate in mind, denied that if local rates were levied for education, it necessarily or logically followed that schools then had to be administered by local authorities. 'There was no such maxim in our constitution as that payment of rates was necessarily connected with the administration of those rates.' Yet another speaker, HMI the Rev. C. Sewell, making a bid for the retention of the control of education in the hands of the territorial aristocracy suggested the creation of a body similar in composition to that of the local commissioners of Inland Revenue, 'men of local knowledge and authority' who would be able to 'determine the wants of a locality, levy rates where necessary'.[7]

These disputes were part of a greater whole. The nonconformist's greatest grievance, as Dixon's speech shows, was Forster's commitment to maintain the voluntary system unimpaired as far as he could. Board schools were to supplement the existing church ones, not to replace them. With these great issues at stake, the passage of the Elementary Education Bill through parliament was perforce acrimonious and the months following the first reading a period of great political excitement. The index to the *Report from the Select Committee of the House of Commons on Public Petitions* for the 1869—70 session lists 7,428 petitions bearing over three-quarters of a million signatures that were presented to the House of Commons. Since many of these petitions were under a single signature the total of 768,343 gives an inadequate indication of the extent to which popular feeling was aroused. For instance the petition of the nonconformists of Bradford (No. 10,385) bore only one signature as did that of the inhabitants of Sheffield in meeting assembled (No. 10,395). Similarly nonconformist ministers frequently forwarded a petition on behalf of their congregations. In comparison the controversy surrounding the disestablishment of the Church in Ireland had aroused little popular concern. This contentious issue produced no more than 500 petitions backed by 177,952 signatures. Yet unlike the question of elementary education it had been the main electoral topic of 1868. Similarly the Education Bill, introduced by the Duke of Marlborough in March 1868 and abandoned two months later, had been almost ignored. It attracted seven hostile petitions and three in favour, two of which came from the same deanery, Culham, in the diocese of Oxford.

In organizing the petitions of 1870 the NEL tried to exploit the dissenter conscience to the full. Its *Monthly Paper* which published a pro forma petition calling for changes to the Bill in its March issue, urged an all-out effort before 14 March, the day set aside for the second reading. In the seven days, 8–14 March, 852 petitions were presented. In all 1,726 petitions with 199,935 signatures following the NEL's pro forma reached the House of Commons by 5 April. The genesis of the NEL's petitioning movement lay apparently with Joseph Chamberlain's realization of the ease with which the nonconformists could be roused through their ministers. A meeting of nonconformists which Chamberlain described as 'large, influential, and determined' had been held in Birmingham on 2 March to protest against Forster's draft bill. In a letter to George Dixon Chamberlain described the NEL's plans to mobilize the dissenter sense of betrayal.[8]

Very strong feeling was expressed against Mr. Forster, who was accused of gross ingratitude to the Dissenters who assisted so greatly in securing the present Government majority, and it was asserted amidst cheers that the present Education Bill was a distinct betrayal and contradiction of the principles involved in the Irish Church Bill . . . . If you see Mr. Forster you may safely tell him that he has succeeded in raising the whole of the Dissenters against him and if he thinks little of our power we will teach him his mistake.
Letters go out tonight to every dissenting minister (Independent, Baptist, Unitarian, and Wesleyan) in the country and you can rest assured that 'all the fat is in the fire'.

Although the Elementary Education Act did not give radical working men all they had wanted, it had provided the secret ballot in the London School Board area, outside the City of London, and had given both women and working men the chance to vote and sit on the new boards. The secret ballot which soon became the rule in both general elections and those for the school boards, was a comparative novelty in 1870. Its use had been made possible as long ago as the Select Vestries (Hobhouse's) Act of 1831, but in 1870 Forster did not know of a single rural parish where it had been put into effect. In London the secret ballot had been introduced under the Metropolitan Management Act, 1855, which created the Metropolitan Board of Works. The role that women could play in local government in 1870 was almost equally limited. Along with the secret ballot their right to vote had first been established under Hobhouse's Act. Their claim to the franchise in the election of poor law guardians was recognized four years later. Although they began to be returned as guardians from 1875 onwards, their eligibility for this office was not finally established until the passing of the Local Government Act, 1894. Apart from the extension of the vote to women ratepayers in municipal corporations in 1869, the only other opportunity they had of playing a part in local government was provided by the elections for the office of inspector of a highways board.[9]

In the particular case of the Metropolis the projected London School Board attracted wide interest for a number of reasons. Unlike the Metropolitan Board of Works, whose members were elected indirectly by the members of the vestries, it was the first directly elected body created to tackle a major social and administrative problem of the London area on a common basis. Moreover, through a rate that was uniform throughout the Metropolis the wealthier districts would succour the poorer. This collectivist principle had been first enunciated under the Metropolitan Poor Act, 1867, which had established the Metropolitan Common Poor Fund to provide medical services for the poor. *The Times* welcomed the prospect of the new board with great enthusiasm.

London is for the first time offered an opportunity of electing a real Metropolitan parliament . . . . The clergy are active because they see a promise of being heard at the Board. The working men are active because they see their way to a direct representation of their interests. We are . . . presented with something like a revival of that political energy which had been supposed to be extinct.

To *The Times* the means was more important than the ends. 'Education, the object to which it is directed, although of vast importance is yet comparatively subordinate. Any other branch of government would have aroused attention almost as great, and in some cases, perhaps, greater. Under cover of the Education Act the Legislature has made a step towards the resettlement of local self-government throughout the Empire.'[10] The election of Lord Lawrence, fresh from his viceroyalty of India, 1863–9, as the first chairman of the London School Board is an index of the high prestige it held in 1870.

Given the seemingly democratic nature of the school boards and the popular enthusiasm their genesis had aroused one might reasonably have expected to find that working men would have made their mark on them. Yet one of the most favourable estimates of the number that served on them at any one time is that of John Burns who thought that there were between 500 and 600 on them in 1896, or around 3 per cent of the total membership.[11] There were a number of reasons why the expectations of 1870 were never realized.

The rank and file of the Liberal party and the dissenting congregations did not speak for the whole of the working classes, nor was their campaign a purely educational one. In Wales, for instance, school boards formed with great political enthusiasm to oust the influence of the English landowning classes and the Anglican church quickly lapsed into educational apathy in many villages. In England, for reasons to be discussed later, there was a strong undercurrent of opposition to school boards from the poorer members of the working classes. In 1876 Robert Baker, an inspector of factories, gave a number of instances in which working people, who must have known him to have been a government official nevertheless spoke with remarkable forcefulness.[12]

'Nice fools the working men were', said a parent to me, 'riding about in carriages and voting for a school board; they did not know what they were doing, or they ought to have been shot first'. A woman said, 'Is this your skule board? I wish my maister had dropped down dead before he'd gone to vote for a skul board'. A man said, 'May my arms drop off if I ever vote at any kind of election again'. Another said 'If I ever go to vote again, I hope I may have my bl---y hands chopped off; talk about England being a free country when a man can't do as he's a mind wi' his own children'.

In the boroughs the working classes were not consulted on whether or not they wanted a school board. Borough councils, who did not want to wait until the Education Department used their compulsory powers to form a board, set the machinery in motion by passing a resolution in favour of one. In the countryside it was possible to sound local opinion by holding a poll of ratepayers on whether or not to have a school board in a particular parish. Although a thoroughgoing study of these polls is still lacking, the evidence of two such episodes is suggestive. In Luton the proponents of the voluntary system won a temporary victory thanks to their unholy alliance with the illiterates, those unable to sign a polling card, of the town. Anglican opponents of a school board played on parental fears of losing the children's wages in the straw-hat industry. Warnings that the manufacturers would not make good the earnings lost through attendance at school were taken to heart. The illiterates of Luton voted solidly against a school board and its attendant threat of compulsory education. 548 put a cross instead of their names on the voting papers. Of these only 40 voted for a board. In all 1,796 of whom 508 were illiterate, had voted against a board and 493 in favour.[13]

In Berkhamsted the illiterate voter provided an important proportion of the total opposition to a school board, 65 out of 194 votes cast against a board were unsigned.[14] Yet Berkhamsted had been a town of great religious and political excitement. In 1867 its leading Baptists had made it one of the centres of protest against the payment of compulsory church rates. The town was also up in arms against the local landowner, Lord Brownlow, who had attempted to enclose a substantial part of the common. The demand for a school board, in a town already well supplied with school places was essentially a bid to throw off the control of the Anglican church and local landowner influence. Yet the campaign leaders, the local business men and dissenting ministers, were unable to carry the poorer ratepayers who were more concerned about the possible loss of their children's earnings than about abstract religious and political issues. In Berkhamsted and Luton those who voted against a school board were not the poorest citizens, they were all ratepayers. The polls do not reveal the views of those who were too poor to be ratepayers and whose opposition may have been even stronger.

When a school board had been constituted, working men found that a series of obstacles prevented them both from voting and sitting on the boards. The short hours during which the polling booths were open proved a major stumbling block for many. Outside London, where voting took place continuously between 8.00 a.m. and 8.00 p.m., the booths had to be open for seven hours within the same limits. The usual choice was 9.00 a.m. to 4.00 p.m., hours that made it impossible for a working man who started his daily task early and ended it late to vote. Attempts to have the hours changed were frequently unsuccessful. The working men of Sheffield failed in this aim in 1870 as did those of Birmingham in 1873, where a demand for an eight o'clock closure was rejected on the grounds that 'the elections are held in the short days of the year, and it is important that the polling should take place during the hours of daylight.' Not only were the borough authorities concerned about the size of their gas bills if they held elections after dark but they feared the risk of impersonation in poor light by fraudulent voters. The lot of the working-class voter remained a difficult one until a year after the passage of the Third Reform Bill when the hours for parliamentary, municipal, and most school board elections were fixed at twelve, 8.00 a.m. to 8.00 p.m.[15]

Men who voted before 1885 often had to sacrifice part or all their day's pay to do so. Not only was 4.00 p.m. well before the time at which they normally stopped work, but working men frequently had long distances to walk home to the local polling station. Although the plight of the London working man who had to work long distances to and from his work before the days of cheap urban transport is well known, that of his provincial fellow has attracted less sympathy. The Sheffield School Board for instance, covered an area with a maximum length of eleven miles and width of seven. Here and in other towns men could often face a four-mile walk to and from work and the prospect of losing up to 2s in wages, a considerable sacrifice if they were in a seasonal trade such as building. Although it is impossible to isolate the single factor of a change in hours, a comparison of two elections in Leeds is suggestive. In 1873, when the hours, 1.00 p.m. to 8.00 p.m., suited working men, some 30,000 voted. In 1876, when the hours were changed to 9.00 a.m. to 4.00 p.m. thereby effectively disfranchising many workers, the total vote was 24,000, a drop of 6,000.[16] As school board elections were politically small beer, few men were prepared to follow the example of the miners of Morpeth who stayed out of the pits on the day of election in 1874 to return Thomas Burt as their member of parliament. In the coal-mining industry colliers had no option but to sacrifice a whole day's pay for engine-winders, working the cages, were wont to refuse to bring them to the surface at election time before their shift ended.[17]

Even in London, where the booths were open for twelve hours, working men still faced considerable difficulties. For many the daily round began so early that in the late 1870s the Metropolitan Railway, which began running workmen's trains from 5.00 a.m. onwards, was petitioned to start them even earlier. These early morning passengers, building workers expected to be at work at 8.00 a.m. in the winter and 6.00 a.m. in the summer, clerks required to be in their shipping houses and warehouses by 8.00 a.m., could not possibly vote before they started work. Those who had to work until 7.30 p.m. arrived home after the booths had closed. Although a few firms such as the East and West India Dock Co. gave men time off at a general election, none seems to have followed the example of the Royal Arsenal at Woolwich which allowed men to vote at school board elections as well. Thus although London working men had received special treatment from the Education Department to enable them to vote on the way home from work, many were never able to do so.[18]

Unfortunately the organizers of the first London School Board elections did not foresee the consequences of the Education Department's decision to make it possible for the London working man to exercise his franchise after the day's work. In 1870 a last-minute rush swamped a number of stations. The polling officials at Marylebone and Chelsea, for instance, sent men home without voting because they could not cope with the numbers. The returning officer at Stockwell found the pressure so overwhelming that he gave up all pretence of running the station in an orderly fashion and stood on a table giving out voting papers indiscriminately. At Lambeth the returning officer bent the law to accommodate those electors who arrived by 8.00 p.m. by remaining open for another forty minutes to allow them to vote. The *Bee-Hive* alleged a wilful delay in registering votes at Horseferry Road, Westminster, a 'thorough breakdown of the poll' at the Church-ward station, Chelsea, and that the supply of voting papers was exhausted before the Tower Hamlets station closed. The *Bee-Hive* was particularly concerned about the station in Horseferry Road as it was in the division of the London School Board for which George Potter, the founder-editor of the journal was standing. Two witnesses attested that only seven votes were recorded in the last seventy-five minutes and that for forty-five of them the doors had been closed. The presiding officer 'said he had had enough – and on its being pointed out to him that several hundreds were waiting to poll, he said he did not care – he was sick of it.'[19]

Some of the delay at the polls was the result of the novelty of the procedure for school board elections. In this respect artisans seem to have given a good account of themselves. *The Times* reported 'It is . . . stated that the professional classes require more assistance and instruction as to how they should vote than most of the working men who tender for themselves.' A few years later a vestry clerk complained, 'Ladies vote at the school board elections, and they come up in shoals and ask a great many questions . . .', a comment prompted possibly as much by male chauvinism as by the novelty of the woman voter. Other causes of delay included the need for the presiding officer to read the list of candidates to illiterate voters and help them to complete their forms and, where the landlord paid the rates, for the voter to produce his rent book or receipts for rents to prove his identity. Although the polling stations at Southwark and Greenwich did not cope satisfactorily in 1873 incidents such as those that had marred the 1870 election became rarer as officials gained more experience. However, the difficulties facing a working-class electorate in reaching the polls remained. As late as 1894 deputations to the London School Board sought a change in the election day from Thursday to Saturday to enable men to vote on their half day-off. Their request enjoyed wide support from organizations representing the aspirations of the politically conscious working man. Graham Wallas spoke on behalf of the Fabian Society, a second spokesman appeared for the Metropolitan Radical Federation, and a third for a widely drawn miscellany of institutions, 'the Working Mens Club and Institution Union, the London Trades' Council, the London Building Trades Federation, the unions of women workers of the Metropolis, and various temperance and co-operative societies'. As for the London School Board, memories of the Eatanswill election prevailed. Since working men were paid on a Saturday, 'it was not a desirable day on which to introduce all the excitement of a political election.'[20]

In 1870 the lead in attempting to obtain direct representation of the working-class interest was taken in London. Although at least twelve working men were nominated as candidates for the election, a number withdrew and only one, George Potter, the founder-editor of the *Bee-Hive* and a former carpenter who had been the secretary of the Building Trades Conference in 1860, was successful. Potter, however, had not put his trust in working men alone. He had actively courted middle-class support. A letter signed by five MPs, backing his candidature and the inclusion of working men on school boards, was read at his adoption meeting. To underline the social *entente* he sought, Potter declared 'the higher classes of society were fraternizing with the workmen and saying to them "If you select your man, we will help you to secure his election".' He continued in the same vein by drawing the conclusion, flattering to any middle-class voters in the audience, that since Westminster was 'remarkable for the social eminence of many of its inhabitants, . . . the greater, therefore, would be the honour of being chosen one of its representatives.' Another but unsuccessful candidate to look for middle-class assistance was Randel Cremer, a founder-member of the International Working Men's Association and the Reform League. Cremer appeared on the same platform as Professor Thomas Huxley in the Marylebone contest. *The Times*'s explanation of his defeat reveals the extent to which he became popularly identified with Huxley and Elizabeth Garrett, both of whom were successful. Working men, the paper commented, had failed to divide their votes equally between the three.[21]

Outside London those working men who attempted either to work with the existing parties or tried to go it alone met the opposition of those who wished to preserve their middle-class monopoly of local government bodies. In Birmingham, although the leading members of the Liberal Association and the NEL had been happy to court trade-union support, they had no intention of sharing office with working men. Naturally enough the faithful NCOs of the movement hoped that their earlier devotion to the cause would be rewarded by nomination as candidates for the Birmingham School Board. The local branch of the Labour Representation League submitted three names to the Liberal Association who in turn included only one, William Radford, a clerk and Wesleyan, on their final list of fifteen candidates. Joseph Chamberlain and Jesse Collings addressed a meeting of the LRL to dissuade its members from running their own additional candidates. After Chamberlain had made an appeal to them not to split the vote in this way, one speaker complained bitterly that the onus of damaging the Liberal interest was being put on the working man. At an adjourned meeting Jesse Collings flatly rejected the argument that just because the new act had been passed for the benefit of working men, the working classes were the proper persons to manage it. Although the LRL and the Working Men's Auxiliary of Birmingham reluctantly acquiesced with the Liberal Association's demands, yet another meeting of working men made a further and unsuccessful approach to the Liberal Association. The proposed nominee was David Kirkwood, a gun-action filer and president of the Birmingham Secular Society. At the subsequent poll neither Radford, whose occupation as clerk made his claim to working-class status dubious, nor Kirkwood, who had had to stand independently, was elected.[22]

In 1873 the opponents of the Established Church made common cause to reverse their defeat of 1870. The working men of Birmingham held a torchlight procession to celebrate the subsequent victory of the

Liberal Eight. Their sense of euphoria soon evaporated. In a bitterly contested by-election in 1875 they put forward their own candidate in opposition to the Liberal Association's Rev. E. F. M. MacCarthy, the second master at King Edward VI's School. W. J. Davis, founder and secretary of the Birmingham Brassworker's Association enjoyed wide support from the trade union movement. His sponsor and seconder were C. Bowkett, a house painter and president of the Birmingham Trades' Council, and S. Mills, a gun-action filer and member of the Liberal Association. Unions that endorsed the LRL's objective of securing 'direct representation of Labour . . . on all constituent bodies, boards of guardians, municipal corporations, school boards and the Imperial Parliament', included the local Operative House Painters Association, the Clickers Trade Association, the Operative Stone Masons and the boot and shoe makers of Birmingham. Shortly before polling day Davis held a public meeting in the Town Hall which was filled to overflowing with an unknown number of would-be supporters denied admission. Benjamin Lucraft and George Potter, both of whom were now on the London School Board, and Henry Broadhurst, secretary of the Labour Representation League and unsuccessful contestant for the London School Board in 1873, came from London to speak on his behalf. Middle-class Liberals opposed him. The Liberal *Birmingham Daily Post* advised its readers to give both their votes to MacCarthy. Jacob Bright wrote, 'I object to having him thrust upon the party merely because he is a working man. The policy now recommended to working men in regard to this matter is as fatal to unity, as it is to an honest representation of all classes and interests.' With a poll held on a Tuesday between 9.00 a.m. and 4.00 p.m., working men had only their lunch hour in which to vote. Although Davis with 9,951 votes was defeated, he was only 588 votes behind Burges, the Anglican contender for the second vacancy on the Birmingham Board. His defeat was even narrower than these figures suggest, for some 2,000 papers were rejected.[23]

For the 'Liberal Eight' the writing was on the wall. Not only had Davis nearly defeated the Liberal candidate but it is unlikely that Mills, his seconder, was the only defector from the Liberal Association. As *The Times* pointed out, 'the majority by which the Labour representative was defeated was so small as to make the return of one or more working men's candidates at the next election a foregone conclusion.' From 1876 onwards the 'Liberal Eight' always included at least one working man. Their first choice, T. Beston, a tinplate worker nominated by Joseph Chamberlain, was cautious enough. Beston had voted against the principle of direct representation of labour at the 1876 TUC conference held at Newcastle. By 1885 two working men were regularly nominated. The Church party, egged on possibly by the appearance of two Socialist candidates in 1888, followed suit in 1891. They also made their first choice with care. Their working-class frontman was J. W. Clarke, a carpenter, whose employment by another member of the 'Bible Eight' was a guarantee of his good conduct on the Birmingham School Board to which he was elected that year.[24]

In many instances the leading members of the main religious and political groupings attempted to settle the membership of the new school boards amongst themselves. Thereby they hoped to save themselves the cost of an election. In Leeds and Bradford initial attempts were made to settle the matter without recourse to an election in 1870. In both instances the objections of working-class organizations were one factor that made elections necessary. When the working men of Leeds objected to their exclusion from the party lists the *Yorkshire Post and Leeds Intelligencer* commented,

The clamorous 'working man', or rather those who volunteer to speak in his name, may probably have his or their irresponsibility appeased by such a modification of the original list as will admit the substitution of one – if not more – of their 'representative' men for the name of one of the gentlemen at present on the list. This sacrifice will ensure a peaceful solution of the present perplexity and confusion.

The *Leeds Mercury* had been slightly more sympathetic. Although it urged that the working classes should be represented on the Leeds Board, it argued that such men lacked the necessary time, knowledge, and experience. 'We suppose, therefore', the editorial continued, 'the working classes themselves would desire to see these onerous duties in the hands of men who have experience, knowledge, command of their own time, and only to have a fair representation of their own body on the School Boards.' On balance these editorial expectations were met. None of the candidates at Leeds claiming support as direct representatives of the working classes was elected. The Liberal party list which was eventually jointly negotiated by the Leeds Liberal Registration Association and the Leeds Reform League included W. Becksworth, a tanner and leather cutter who became the sole representative of Primitive Methodism on the 1870 Board. Furthermore, working men still identified their interests with those of their employers. W. J. Armitage, ironmaster, and Sir A. Fairbairn, engineer, were put near the top of the poll with the aid of the heavy support they received in the wards in which their works were situated. Those who had voted for their masters still saw society divided vertically into interest groups and not yet horizontally on a class basis.[25]

Again at Bradford, where the mayor had called a meeting of local influential people to draw up a list of fifteen members of the Board, artisans tried to break the middle-class monopoly of power. Working men held a meeting in the Mechanics' Institute to put forward their own candidates on the grounds that they, not the wealthy, would be sending their children to the rate-aided schools. Their list included James Hanson, a printer. Further meetings took place at which the original list of forty-six nominees was eventually reduced to sixteen. Pressure was then put on Hanson to withdraw to save the cost of an election. In situations such as this where the trade-unionist candidate, and later the Socialist, was the odd man out and refused to withdraw at the behest of his social superiors, he bore the blame for causing the ratepayers the cost of an election.[26] This was essentially a blackmailing tactic that his opponents hoped would lead to his failure at the polls. In this particular instance another candidate obliged. Hanson, who had had to start work at the age of eight, served on the Bradford Board for the next twenty-five years during which time he gave evidence to the Cross Commission on Elementary Education in 1888 on Bradford's higher elementary schools.[27]

At Nottingham, a city that had returned Feargus O'Connor as the first Chartist member of parliament in 1847, trade unionists served on the School Board from the start. The *Nottingham and Midland Counties Express* claimed that E. Smith, a lace-maker, was the first working man to be elected to a school board. He had been put there with 'the undivided support of the Liberal party'. Three years later, W. Hemm 'the working-man's candidate nominated by the numerous organized bodies of artisans in the towns, received the votes of the Liberal party and was placed fourth on the poll.' Throughout the life of the Nottingham Board the Liberals continued the tradition of having a working man as one of their group. The Church party does not seem to have followed the Liberal example until 1892 when their list included H. J. G. Collier, a joiner and builder's foreman, who came third on the poll. The Church's bid for the working-class vote came three years after the first appearance of candidates under a socialist or labour ticket.[28]

The advent of candidates standing for the Independent Labour Party and the Social Democratic Federation in the mid-1880s was as unacceptable to trade-unionist Liberals as their own arrival had been to the middle-class Liberal leadership in the 1870s. Even that normally progressive newspaper of a traditionally radical city, the *Nottingham Daily Express* opposed the appearance of Labour and Socialist candidates in 1892. The editorial condemned the innovation.[29]

What reason is there, . . . , why Labour as Labour should be represented on the Board? It is only represented because other 'interests' are represented. In the very nature of things a Labour candidate cannot spend much time on School Board work. There are no distinctive Labour problems to solve. It would be just as reasonable or unreasonable for teetotallers or publicans to be represented as such. The point is that they ought to be chosen because of personal fitness, and not because of their association with a particular interest.

The Leeds election of 1891, fought against a background of local industrial unrest, illustrates the antipathy that could exist between the skilled worker and the unskilled. Here the party leaders had hoped to settle the composition without recourse to an election but the appearance of five independent candidates frustrated their scheme. Both main parties had already included a working man on their lists following the narrow defeat of a candidate sponsored by the Leeds Trades' Council at the recent municipal elections. J. L. Mahon, secretary of the Gas Workers and General Labourers Union in Leeds, nominated by a number of gas stokers and labourers, stood as a representative of the unskilled worker. The Leeds Trades' Council promptly repudiated his candidature. They pointed out that they were likely to secure two members on the School Board to represent trade union interests as a whole, but Mahon stood for one union only. 'We appeal to all those who favour a Labour party, with the Trades' and Labour Council as its mouthpiece, to show their non-approval of his candidature by voting against him, and thus defeat the attempt made to divide and undermine the interests of labour.' The editorial of the *Leeds Mercury* endorsing this thesis, denied the validity of Mahon's claim to 'assert Labour's right to govern'. Since he represented only one union, 'He cannot, therefore, be recognized by the ratepayers as a properly accredited representative of "Labour" in Leeds.' Mutual recrimination continued. Mahon denounced the Trades' Council for colluding with the Tories and Liberals. The Leeds Trades' Council carried a resolution which unanimously condemned 'the action of Mr. J. L. Mahon in contesting for a seat on the School Board as a Labour candidate', and denigrated his supporters as 'the unskilled labour party'.

Meanwhile a section of the unskilled labour party in Leeds was attempting to improve its working conditions without any assistance from the local labouring aristocracy. The same night that the Trades' Council opened its offensive on Mahon, the Leeds tram and bus men attended a meeting to form a union. This meeting, addressed by Fred Hammill, the president of the London Amalgamated Omnibus and Tramworkers Union, was one of several attempts made by men in this trade to improve their conditions in the years immediately following the 1888 Dock Strike. Although the Leeds men, in common with transport workers elsewhere, enjoyed job security their conditions of employment were poor. They worked fourteen hours a day, seven days a week, for a wage that averaged 2½d to 4½d an hour. Ruefully the men compared their lot with that of the London omnibus horses who worked two and a half hours a day, six days a week. The results of the School Board election did not show any great upsurge of sympathy for the unskilled man. While both the Leeds Trades' Council's nominees in the Church party and the Liberal party were elected – the latter was rather improbably designated a gentleman – Mahon's poll of 10,934 put him well below the 24,288 votes secured by the fifteenth successful candidate. Mahon, whose expenses had been less than £10, lacked the facilities available to those who sheltered beneath the financial umbrella of an organized party machine or could dig deep into their own pockets.[30] E. N. Buxton, for example, spent £700 an election when fighting the Tower Hamlets division of the London School Board. As a general rule the local Liberal party supported the Board School party, or whatever name the opponents of the voluntary schools used, and the Conservative party assisted the Church party. Help included the holding of public meetings in their rooms, advertising, canvassing, and the provision of carriages on election day. Yet at times working men could achieve striking successes without any of this material assistance. The same year that Mahon was elected at Leeds after spending less than £10, W. H. Drew, an ILP candidate, got in at Bradford. However he had never held a meeting because he had not even been able to afford the fee for hiring a hall. In addition some forms of publicity were quite cheap. In 1876 a Mrs Surr and Benjamin Lucraft were elected to the London School Board with the assistance of shoeblacks who carried the legend 'Plump for Mrs Scurr' in their caps and 'clean-faced boys' who bore banners saying 'Vote for Lucraft the children's friend'.[31]

Generally speaking the instances in which working men saw themselves as a conflict group were confined to the larger cities and the industrial towns and villages of the latter years of the century. The spread of socialist thought, the growth of the Independent Labour Party and the Social Democratic Federation encouraged men to see the earlier policy of including a few of their fellows, on a grace and favour basis, in the established parties as a political sham. Earlier working men had seen themselves as an interest group. Their children were attending the board schools and those men in steady and better paid jobs sought opportunities of post-elementary education in higher grade schools for their offspring. In addition men frequently had a specific sectarian interest that competed with, or even dominated, their economic interests. In the early elections nonconformists were usually more concerned about the representation of a particular sect than of a secular interest group. In the large cities the pro-board school party was a coalition formed from a wide spectrum of dissenting sects. The published results gave details of the candidate's religious affiliation. In this context the fact that a Primitive Methodist was also an artisan was incidental. R. M. Mair, *The School Boards: Our Educational Parliaments* (1872) gives the names of some twenty nonconformists and secularists, following humble occupations, who were elected to school boards in rural areas and small towns. In small communities, where a sense of working-class corporateness had yet to grow, the reference group was the religious rather than the economic one. Although men had been attracted by the social and political teachings of a particular sect, the secularization of social protest was by no means complete. Even in Leicester, a town of nearly 100,000 by 1871, a framework knitter elected that year, was not described as a working man. The first member to receive that designation was not elected for another six years. The importance of the sectarian issue lived on. As late as 1889 J. Peacock, the socialist candidate for Nottingham who had previously been returned as an independent radical, found himself involved in a public correspondence on the relative importance of the socialist cause and the nonsectarian issue. By this time the dissenters, sinking their sectarian differences, had usually rallied under a broad banner as the School Board party, the Liberal party, or the Progressives, in opposition to the Voluntarists or the Church party. Both groups, with the Church party showing less willingness, were including trade unionists, but not socialists or Labour candidates, amongst their sponsored candidates.[32]

The presence of a strong Roman Catholic community tended to

delay the secularization of school-board elections and the success of working-class candidates. The allegiance of Roman Catholic voters was to their Church rather than to their social class. In Manchester, a city with a considerable Roman Catholic Irish immigrant community, the Unsectarian party made little attempt to include working-class representatives within its fold. As the use of the term 'unsectarian' in preference to 'Liberal' indicates, elections were fought on a religious rather than a political basis. Labour candidates sponsored by the Manchester and Salford and Trades Council did not appear until 1891, when the Unsectarian party was renamed the Free School Board party. Relabelled the Progressives in 1894, it combined with the Labour and Trade Union candidates as the United Education party in 1900, some twenty-four years after the Liberals of Birmingham had sponsored their first trade-union candidate in response to pressure from below.[33]

In Liverpool school-board elections were fought by Roman Catholics at one end of the religious spectrum and Orangemen at the other. Orange riots in 1835 and 1852 on the anniversary of the battle of the Boyne bore witness to the intensity of religious feuds in that city. Apart from the uncontested election of 1870 when Thomas Pritchard, a Baptist and an honorary member of the Amalgamated Society of Carpenters and Joiners became a member of the Board, working-class representatives fared badly. When Labour and Socialist candidates appeared alongside Orangemen in 1891 the *Liverpool Mercury* thought that they stood little chance of success. 'Present circumstances do not favour the candidature of their [working men's] nominees, as sectarian interests enter so largely into the composition of the Board.' The editor looked to the time when working men would succeed 'but for the moment there is a much stronger inclination among working men to vote on sectarian grounds than those affecting their social position.' The newspaper returned to the theme after the defeat of the candidates of the left was announced with a more traditional explanation. 'It was felt, however, that a very large proportion of working men now appeared to distrust their fellows, and to prefer as representatives men whom they considered better qualified by education and leisure to look after their interests.' In Liverpool the sectarian card remained the ace of trumps right to the end of the School Board's history. In 1900 George Wise, the author of an anti-ritualist pamphlet in which he demanded the building of board schools to replace those Church ones under the control of 'advanced ritualist priests' headed the poll in 1900 thanks to the Orange vote. S. Reeves, a Labour candidate who had fought the previous three elections unsuccessfully, suffered his fourth defeat.[34]

94

A further problem facing working-class groups seeking representation on school boards was that the plumping system, whereby voters could give all their votes to one candidate, spelt disaster for the incautious or politically inexperienced party manager. The failure of Birmingham's politically sophisticated Liberal Association to win the 1870 election provides the classic case of hubris. Overestimating the strength of its support, the Association instructed its followers to give one vote to each of the fifteen candidates it had nominated, a tactic that was expected to carry the day. Instead the Church party swept the polls with Joseph Chamberlain scrambling home an ignominious thirteenth. The lesson was soon learned. In 1873 the Liberal Association fielded the Liberal Eight, gave its supporters careful instructions on a ward-to-ward basis on how to allocate their votes amongst the candidates, and won control of the School Board.

For a minority party the penalty of nominating too many candidates could be complete disaster as the Manchester election of 1894 shows. On this occasion the three ILP candidates, one of whom was Mrs Emmeline Pankhurst, polled just under 66,000 votes between them. Although none was elected, collectively they had secured more than double the vote cast for the fifteenth successful candidate at the bottom of the list of those elected.[35] Although further research would be required to substantiate the assertion, Roman Catholics and small nonconformist sects had the best chance of working the system successfully. With a well defined and organized membership it was possible to calculate the size of the potential vote accurately and, more importantly, use moral pressure to ensure a high turnout on election day.

Once elected to a board a working man might well have thought that all his troubles were over. This was not so. Membership of a local government board was, and largely still is, an occupation suited to a person of independent means or one with sufficient job autonomy to choose when he will work. School boards normally met during most people's working hours. The demands made on a member of a large board were considerable. For instance the chairman of the Birmingham School Board was summoned to 128 meetings in 1875, nine other members had a commitment of more than 70 meetings that year alone. At Newcastle the chairman averaged over 120 meetings a year during the triennium, 1873–6, his vice-chairman 115, and the other members 60 a year. Moreover elected members of boards had to perform many duties that today would be delegated to paid officials. The first task of the Bradford School Board, for instance, was to visit over 100 schools to compile an educational census. Once the boards were established, a member keen to make his influence felt was morally obliged to sit on one of the many committees the board spawned to deal with such issues as truancy or the non-payment of school fees, matters in which working-class members had a strong interest. Yet working men who undertook this work did so at the sacrifice of their wages and earned few thanks from their workmates. This was true even of a craft union such as the Vellum (Account Book) Binders' Trade Society, whose members one might have expected to have had some regard for learning for its own sake. One of its members who had his wages stopped for attending school board meetings narrated 'in the eyes of my comrades I was rather a fool'.[36]

Existing members of boards were not necessarily ready to help their new working-class colleagues as James Ingham, a railway worker and secretary of the Brighton Trades and Labour Council, discovered when he was elected in 1893. Ingham, who lost half a day's pay whenever he attended a meeting, managed to have the time changed to Saturday afternoon. His success was short-lived. The other members, who saw no reason why they should be inconvenienced for the sake of one, had the old time restored after a month. Although three years later Ingham headed the poll, his motion to the new board to change the time of the meetings was once again lost. To his great credit Ingham stuck it out to the end of the life of the Brighton Board, being returned in 1899 with a poll of over 10,000, nearly 4,000 ahead of his nearest rival. Ingham's perseverance and self-sacrifice were exceptional. The more normal practice was to nominate a different trade union or socialist candidate for each triennium, an arrangement that sacrificed any continuity of the respresentation of a distinctive working-class interest. Even then, despite the concession that a member could be absent for six months before his seat was deemed vacant, working men did not always stay the course.[37]

Finally in this discussion of working-class participation in school board affairs one group moving socially upwards, the teachers, deserves special consideration. The 1875 Revised Code banned teachers from sitting on school boards, a restriction that the National Union of Elementary Teachers accepted with remarkable quiescence. Consequently those teachers who did sit on boards were drawn from private schools, women who had given up teaching on marriage, ex-teachers and those subsidized by their local associations. Teachers, enjoying the backing of their colleagues in the classroom, usually did well at election time. For instance John Cryer of Bradford came top, fourteenth, top, and second in the four elections after 1891. In Birmingham W. Ansell, holding out the inducement of higher salaries for teachers, headed the list in 1894. He had another, possibly greater, asset. He was the 'well-known honorary secretary of Warwickshire Cricket Club'.[38]

The NUT - it dropped 'Elementary' from its title in 1889 in the course of its upward social climb - did not show great interest in sponsoring candidates. Its journal, the *Schoolmaster*, reported the electoral successes only spasmodically. For instance in 1893 it published the names of twelve teachers on school boards but added there were 'probably others about whom we shall be glad to have particulars'. The journal's failure to print any further details in the immediately subsequent issues is a measure of the lack of concern that the NUT showed in this matter.[39]

Women were another politically underprivileged group to whom the new Education Act offered wider opportunities both as electors and as members of boards. Of the ten boards formed in 1870 representing the largest populations - London, Bolton, Bradford, Brighton, Leeds, Liverpool, Manchester, Nottingham, Salford and Sheffield - only two had women members. Emily Davies and Elizabeth Garrett sat for London and Lydia Becker, sometime secretary of the Manchester Women's Suffrage Committee and editor of the *Women's Suffrage Journal*, for Manchester. By 1879 Lydia Becker was able to list twenty-five women who had sat on urban boards and a further forty-three on rural ones. In 1885 London with three, Sheffield with two, and Bradford and Nottingham with one women member each, were the only major boards formed in 1870 to have women members. By 1900 only Brighton was missing. London had eight out of a total of fifty-five members, Bradford three, Birmingham, Leeds, Manchester, and Nottingham, two each, and Bolton, Salford and Sheffield one each. This gave women twenty-three of 190 places, or 12 per cent. By 1903, the year of the demise of the school boards, there were an estimated 370 women sitting, a total that was slightly more than half the number of working men John Burns believed to have been on school boards nearly a decade earlier. A comparison with women's performance as rural district councillors helps to put the matter into perspective. In 1907 there were 146 women amongst the 16,001 serving the rural district councils of England and Wales.[40]

Apart from the presence of such exceptional women as Helen

Taylor on the London Board and Lydia Becker (1870–90) and Emmeline Pankhurst (1900 to dissolution) at Manchester, there is little to suggest that the feminist issue ever played a major role in elections. Such tactics could have been unwise as there were few women voters and an appeal to women's rights might have been counterproductive amongst a predominantly male electorate. In the rural areas where there was difficulty in finding sufficient educated and caring people to sit on the school boards, some of the women were the wives of other members, sitting not so much in their own right as to make up the numbers. In these and other instances the sex of the candidate may have been no more than an incidental factor.

School-board elections were multi-faceted affairs. Competing with such issues as the status of women, a matter that concerned few at this time, or the representation of a distinctive working-class interest, were those sectarian differences, that some saw as transcending all human affairs. Despite the social and political divisions that the labels concealed, for those who believed revealed religion to provide the basis of all morality the conflict remained ostensibly one between secularism, dissent, and the Established Church.[41]

Part Two

◆◆◆

The Schools and the
Social Services

◆◆◆

V

♦♦♦

After Bread, Education

♦♦♦

'After bread,' said Danton, 'education is the first need of the people.'[1] Unfortunately thousands of schoolchildren found that Forster's Act gave them education but no bread. Indeed the Elementary Education Act, 1873, specifically limited expenditure from the rates to the promotion of elementary education, a restriction that ruled out of court any attempt to feed the children at public expense. From 1870 until the start of the next century the state's role was essentially coercive and punitive. It possessed powers, albeit seldom used, to bring criminal charges against those who failed to feed their children. It did little to ease the child's path into the classroom; until 1891 parents could not even demand free education as a right. The fees charged for compulsory schooling were a form of poll tax from which relief was granted on only a small scale. Moreover the state did nothing specifically to help those families that now suffered a loss of income because the children had to go to school. Such action would only have been seen to undermine parental responsibility and destroy the fabric of society. Even when rate-assisted school meals and medical inspection began, they were too grudgingly administered at the local level to solve the social problems of juvenile England. How much still remained to be done middle-class householders discovered on the outbreak of the Second World War when they received children into their homes evacuated from the slums of our great cities.

The greater concern for the welfare of children that was reflected in the legislation of the first decade of the twentieth century was part of a long-term trend, a movement dating at least from the solicitude shown by the Evangelical philanthropists of the late eighteenth century. The long series of Factory Acts passed from 1802 onwards is partly in this tradition. They combined humanitarianism with enlightened self-interest. At the end of their Fifth Report the Commissioners on Children's Employment hoped for an extension of the protection these acts gave to the very young and those of the tenderer sex of Her Majesty's subjects, whereby they would be relieved of the totally unnecessary burden of overtime and night work which depressed their vigour and shortened their lives. With such legislation children would

be under the obligation while between the years of eight and thirteen of combining a certain and very useful amount of school instruction with wages – yielding employment, and thus benefiting themselves and their country by reaching, as may be hoped, when they grow up, a higher standard of morals and intelligence.[2]

However it was not until near the end of Queen Victoria's reign that the physical condition of the great mass of schoolchildren became a widely debated issue and remedial action seen as a matter of national advantage, if not national necessity.

In contrast teachers had realized much earlier that children needed feeding and delousing. During the 1860s, for instance, teachers in Horncastle, Lincolnshire, were already waging their campaigns against children who came to school with verminous heads. It is difficult to assess how widespread were these practices. The evidence is fragmentary, its discovery largely a matter of serendipity. Before the influx of the poorest children into the urban schools it is possible that dirty heads posed a greater problem in country schools than in town ones. A survey made in Stroud Union in 1904 shows an infestation rate that rose from 16·85 per cent for urban children to 29·36 per cent for country ones. The presence of such children in large numbers in the school must have inhibited teachers from going near them to help them individually. The sulphur bags that women teachers wore in the hems of their long dresses may have given them some protection but they constituted an easily breached cordon sanitaire.[3]

The underfed child was a comparative stranger to the classroom before 1870 appearing mainly in those schools that made a special effort to seek out the poorest. In the 1860s Roman Catholic schools in the most destitute parts of London and some ragged schools were feeding their pupils. One of the earliest recorded societies, the Destitute Children's Dinner Society founded by Lord Shaftesbury gave dinners to children at a ragged school in Westminster from 1864 onwards. For the next forty to fifty years the seeming incongruity of the propinquity of abject poverty to the Imperial legislature troubled the consciences of reformers and provided them with ready-made arguments to use against their opponents.[4]

Immediately after 1870 the presence of underfed – the contemporary euphemism for near-starving – children in the classroom made perceptive commentators realize that it was not enough just to sweep the street arabs from the courts and rookeries into the classroom. The *School Board Chronicle*, that journalistic progeny of the 1870 Act, was swift to point out that the fidgety child could be suffering from some form of skin disease such as 'itch, or ringworm or lice, or it may be that his skin is irritable from mere want of washing or a warm bath.' Yet a warm bath was an amenity that many parents could not provide. Unable to afford fuel for heating their rooms, parents often sewed their children's clothes up for the winter. When Dr James Kerr, England's first school medical officer, made his first examination of Bradford children in 1894, he found that a third of the 300 he inspected had not taken their clothes off for at least six months. School medical authorities had to struggle, not just against 'indifferent' parents, but against poor housing conditions until after the Second World War. In 1939 large areas of slum property were still without baths. In Stepney, London, 90 per cent of the houses were without them as were 40 per cent in Hull and Bootle. In 1973 there were still 8 per cent of heads of households without access to a bath or shower.[5]

With the passing of the 1870 Act some school inspectors became aware of the contemporary social problems. 'Education will not do all things,' one HMI admitted, 'young Lancashire like young England in general, needs to be housed, fed, clothed, and educated.' Another saw that in poor schools 'the inefficiency proceeds, not from the educational defect, but from our social evils.' His remedy was the educationalist's millennium. 'Give us better homes, better dwellings, better streets, better habits, better social life among the poor, and better food, and then we shall have better schools everywhere.'[6] The humanitarian impulses of all those who wished to remedy the situation had to struggle against the orthodoxy of the canons of established social practice. As late as 1904 *The Times* dismissed the pleas of would-be reformers with a callous indifference buttressed by a blind belief in the innate strength of the British economy.[7]

We do not forget those 122,000 children in London going to school underfed . . . . But, after all, are they any worse off going to school unfed than if they remained at home unfed? They are only brought

103

more into evidence, and the spectacle seems to throw some off our economic balance altogether. But the resources of civilization founded upon economic competition are surely not exhausted.

Not everyone shared this cosy view of the United Kingdom's place in the world. The New Imperialism of 1880s and 1890s which reached its climax at the time of the outbreak of war in South Africa in 1899 was an aggressive manifestation of this uncertainty. For two decades Germany had been regarded with a mixture of fear and envy that is substantially documented in the serious periodicals. So well established was this sentiment that Robson used the German example to persuade the House of Commons to accept his bill extending the age of compulsory education to twelve in March 1899, some six months before the outbreak of war that year. The German states, he maintained, 'guarded the physical and intellectual development even of their poorest people'. The great secret of Germany's success in recent years had been 'the fact that she had begun this policy earlier and she had pursued it more strenuously than any other country in the world'. In the autumn of 1899 a committee of the London School Board produced a controversial report recommending the use of public money for the provision of school dinners. Commenting on this report one month before the British army received some of its worst reverses, but after German sympathies for the Boers had become voiced, the *Schoolmaster* developed a theme that became commonplace a few years later. 'The more one studies the stupendous responsibilities of the British people the more one is impressed with the virtual necessity to breed and train the best human material possible. The danger to the British Empire lies within the Homeland. The wastrel, the ne'er-do-well, the rickety, and the criminal; *these*, and not the Krupp gun or continental jealousy are the real danger.'[8] The events of the next few years, the Black Week of December 1899, the high rate of rejection of volunteers for the army, the eventual deployment of an army more than five times the size of the farming community it was fighting, added to the popular anxiety and provided a receptive readership for such works as C. F. G. Masterman (ed.), *The Heart of the Empire* (1901) and A. White, *Efficiency and Empire* (1901).

It is easy to exaggerate the importance of these events. As Bentley B. Gilbert has shown the legislation for the provision of school meals and the medical inspection and treatment of children was never an integral part of the Liberal government's programme. It would be equally misleading to portray all those who supported these services as the founding fathers of the Welfare State. The predominant fear throughout the period under survey was that too lavish a provision of food would pauperize the parent. The boy receiving free dinners while his brother was being treated by the doctor for overeating was part of the mythology of the social worker. Again in a part of Bermondsey described by Charles Booth as one of the most poverty stricken in London, the local Charity Organization Society man clung to the axiom that every meal given to a child meant another half pint of beer to a dissolute parent.[9]

However difficult the Bermondsey boy may have found it to obtain a meal, he had one advantage over the rural lad. School feeding agencies were mainly urban institutions, 55 of the 71 county boroughs and 22 of the large urban authorities controlling elementary education had some means of feeding children by 1905. Outside these areas there were at least another 55 feeding schemes, most of which were in the smaller urban authorities. Yet the children of rural England had probably as good a claim as any other to the generosity of the charitable. In the West Country, for instance, children were said to live on tea-kettle broth, a concoction of bread, dripping, and hot water. At midday they had a little weak tea, margarine, and a piece of bread. Many rural children had little milk to drink. Farmers preferred to send their milk to the towns where they obtained a better price than to sell it to their labourers. Others were reluctant to sell even their skimmed milk to their hands as they wanted to feed it to their cattle.[10]

In bad weather the undernourished country child arrived at school with his clothes drenched and his bundle of food sodden, after walking up to three miles along paths and unmade roads. Those who possessed outer clothes were the lucky ones. They were spared the misery of having to sit all day in their wet clothes. At dinner time the child found that the school normally offered him no more than cold water. In summer, when the storage tanks ran low, even water was in short supply. There was usually no means of providing hot meals. The penny dinners at Sir Henry Peek's school at Rousdon, Devonshire, much applauded in the literature of the day, were exceptional. The 1905 Inter-Departmental Committee on the Medical Inspection and Feeding of Children, hard pressed to find examples of feeding schemes in rural areas, devoted a disproportionate amount of space to describing the efforts of one schoolmaster. For a charge of 1d a week this man provided each child with a daily cup of cocoa. At his own expense, for the school managers had given no help, he had bought a large urn which he filled daily with water and put on top of the school stove to boil. At midday he added a pint of milk and some sugar and cocoa and shared the resultant brew with his fifty to sixty pupils. Unattractive though the drink may have been, the Committee applauded the 'zealous care' this Gloucestershire man had shown in the 'inception and successful' conduct of this good work.[11] Although the information the 1905 Committee received about feeding schemes in rural schools was incomplete, it is probable that few schools gave their children more than cocoa. Soup, being more expensive, was seldom offered.

In contrast, in urban England, soup was the mainstay of the voluntary feeding schemes. It had the advantage of being easy to produce without elaborate kitchen equipment, a large copper and a means of heating sufficed. It was easily divisible into equal portions. Its consumption did not require the use of any cutlery if drunk straight from the bowl. Last, a meal of soup and bread was a sufficiently unattractive proposition to deter all except the most needy.

One of the first teachers to concern herself about the increasing numbers of underfed children that came to school after 1870 was Mrs E. M. Burgwin, who became headmistress of Orange Street Board School, Southwark, in 1874. Fresh from a school in a more prosperous part of Chelsea she was disconcerted by the pallid appearance of the children she now had to teach. She consulted a medical friend who told her they were starving. She and her staff began giving milk drinks to the most needy. George Sims of the *Referee* newspaper, author of the sensational tract, *How the Poor Live*, based on the people of the district, visited her. Together they launched the *Referee* Children's Free Breakfast and Dinner Fund in 1880. By the turn of the century with an income of £4,000 a year, it had become the largest and best known of the London societies for providing children with school meals.[12]

During the early years of the *Referee* Fund's existence the problem of the underfed schoolchild received much wider publicity than Sims alone would ever have been able to give. In 1884 Dr Crichton-Browne published his report to the Education Department on the alleged overpressure of work in the public elementary schools. At first the discussion on overpressure had been confined to the effects of cramming on middle-class children. A letter from Dr Sophia Jex-Blake to *The Times* on 15 April 1880, in which she blamed the Revised Code for causing over pressure, extended the debate to board-school children. 'A great many doctors practising amongst the poor must be aware that a state of things is growing up that threatens real peril to the future brain power, if not to the physical health, of a very large section of the rising generation.' However medically inept some of the statements subsequently made may seem today,[13] the controversy had the merit of drawing public attention to the living conditions of the poor. During the next five or six years an ill-assorted field rallied to the cry of over-pressure. It provided apparent justification for all who fundamentally opposed the idea of educating working-class children to attack the extensions made to the Revised Code in 1879 and 1880. Children above Standard I were now allowed to study one or two 'subjects of instruction (e.g. geography, natural history, physical geography, natural philosophy, social economy, etc.) . . . illustrated if necessary by maps, diagrams, specimens, & etc.' These attempts to make reading and other lessons more interesting met with the objection, 'It must take several generations of evolutionary progress in the development of the average cerebral organism to produce brains which can be safely as well as successfully crammed as the empiricists of the Education Department would have the brains of millions crammed . . . .' More sinister was the charge, 'We have grounds for believing that certain well-known depravities which progress *pari passu* with cerebral exhaustion are on the increase amongst those overworked children.'[14]

Others pointed to the problems confronting working-class children. 'If there be any overstrain or overpressure of education in the London elementary schools', wrote one of the School Board's inspectors, 'it is mainly, though indirectly, due to the overpressure of poverty and drink', a comment that held the balance nicely between concern and censure. In the writer's division of Finsbury there were 10,490 families consisting of 41,044 persons living in one room, readers of *The Times* learned, and a further 17,210 families of 82,215 persons living in two rooms. In some of the Finsbury schools, 60 to 80 per cent of the children came from homes of one room only. Recent clearances for such improvements as the erection of the Peabody buildings had made matters worse, for those who could not afford the high rents had had to squeeze even more tightly into the remaining accommodation. The Peabody trustees had over 200 policemen as tenants, the writer con-cluded, who 'are probably employed in keeping [in] order in the over-crowded courts . . . the people who have been driven out of their homes to make room for them.' Given these housing conditions it is hard to blame the fathers of Finsbury for resorting to the public houses that outnumbered the schools by nine to one.[15]

Crichton-Browne's Report, published in September 1884, drew

attention to the presence of half-starved children in the schools. He publicized the fact that a mother would send her child to school without breakfast because she had no money, go out and earn some by scrubbing steps or selling flowers, and later appear at the school with some food. Other children had to forage the best they could and turned up at school eating rotten fruit discarded by costermongers. 'These children want blood, and we offer them a little brain-polish; they ask for bread and receive a problem; and for milk, the tonic sol-fa system is introduced to them', a comment to which *The Times* posed the question 'But would they be better fed if they were worse educated?' Crichton-Browne pointed out that 'The dinners of soup and bread, or of coffee or bread . . . are only palliative . . . . They do not offer that reasonable assurance of sustenance which is needful to healthy and happy childlife.' Consequently 'Liberal and regular feeding is necessary in order that a child may be prepared to profit by education.' This statement together with his speculation about the value of giving children two pints of new milk a day must have contributed to the Education Department's reluctance to publish the Report without the addition of a dissenting memorandum from their chief inspector, J. G. Fitch. 'A school is established', Fitch wrote, 'for the purpose of instruction, and not for the purpose of dispensing new milk.' In his opinion the Elementary Education Act had already done 'a little to diminish the sense of parental responsibility.' In the spirit of the Classical Economists he was ready to accept this as the state now demanded more education than the parent could afford. However, he drew the line at providing for the health and feeding of children. Such responsibilities clearly belonged to the parent.[16] Thus by giving wide publicity to the fact that some children went to school undernourished, the Report raised a series of issues that continued to be debated well after the Education (Provision of Meals) Act received the Royal Assent. What were the respective limits of the responsibility of the state and the parent? Were children underfed because of poverty or because of parental indifference and irresponsibility? How was one to distinguish the various categories, and how was one to feed any children without encouraging them to look to the state for help all their lives and without discouraging parents from maintaining their independence? On the one hand the propertied classes showed some concern for the children of the poor, on the other they feared the consequences of helping them too much. In the words of Octavia Hill 'Whatever is done towards supplying the necessities of life on any other footing [than a self-supporting one] will be distinctly a step in the wrong direction', for 'There are various things the poor might do to raise themselves from the verge of pauperism . . .; let us not stand in the way of their doing these by offering miserable doles'.[17]

Opponents of school-dinner schemes argued that the giving of free meals was not in what they deemed to be the best interests of the working classes. Free meals far from conferring a boon were a positive disservice. 'Feeding by the State in any form', predicted one member of the Charity Organization Society (COS), 'would lower the whole of the working classes to a state of serfdom instead of bringing them up as citizens.' The winner of a prize essay competition sponsored by the Central Council for Promoting School Dinners, a co-ordinating body formed in London in December 1884, developed a neo-Malthusianism that the judges must have found acceptable. 'If every child whose parent neglected to feed it had its free dinner, where would be the inducement for poor parents to feed their children, and where the check on over-population?' The effect of the working of free market forces would be such that:

If the maintenance of poor children were undertaken by the state, the wages of the lowest class of labour would be depressed a little more, for an expenditure hitherto necessary would be saved and thus there would be labourers able and willing to work for a little less. And the thought which may occasionally prevent an improvident marriage – that the children will suffer – would no longer have effect.

Twenty years later witnesses to the 1905 Inter-Departmental Committee on the Medical Inspection and Feeding of Children still shared these forebodings. One, for instance, raised the spectre of the Speenhamland system and warned that 'if the guardians and charitable people are both giving out-relief, we are gradually approaching the state of things that existed before the present poor law commenced. It must inevitably have the result of lowering wages, because it will be taken into consideration.'[18]

The COS, dismayed at the growth of yet further bodies offering relief to the poor saw a conflict of interest between themselves and the schools. School managers and others concerned to secure the attention of children in school, were ready to give boots, clothes and food, to secure what was primarily an educational end. In the eyes of the COS, such gifts were no more than a form of temporary relief that did not tackle the basic cause of a family's destitution. They were palliatives that encouraged fecklessness. At the Society's annual meeting held in 1891 Octavia Hill denounced what she thought to be indiscriminate charity. 'I can imagine no course so sure to increase the number of underfed children in London as the wholesale feeding of them by charity. I myself know family after family where the diminution of distinct responsibility increased drunkenness and neglect, where steady work is neglected and lost, training for work abandoned, house duties omitted . . . .' The COS saw the school board authorities, newcomers to relief activities, as unqualified amateurs, ill-equipped to do the job as they could not test effectively for need. Furthermore they breached a major canon of the COS by treating children apart from the rest of the family. To further the COS's objective of curing the cause of destitution Sir Francis Peek of the London School Board offered £1,000 a year to assist cases of distress that become known to the School Board authorities 'if there were likelihood of temporary relief being of permanent benefit to the applicant'. The fund was to provide 'such assistance as it might be hoped would render the applicant independent of charitable aid in the future'. Thus the COS were prepared to grant a loan to a cabman to buy a new horse or to buy a new mangle for a widow to support herself by taking in washing. A mere gift of boots or school meals was not considered to be 'productive of permanent benefit'. Moreover there was always the suspicion that clothing would be pawned or food tickets exchanged for 'luxury' foods. Strict application of the rules under which Peek's fund was administered resulted in the expenditure of no more than £551 in 1881. School board visitors, more concerned with the day-to-day problem of keeping up the school-attendance rate, gradually stopped referring cases to the COS. They found that they could achieve their objective more easily by advertising for clothes and money in the press.[19]

The COS's criteria for determining eligibility for relief were essentially censorious. Respectable families who had temporarily fallen on hard times were seen as deserving cases. In contrast the unskilled casual labourer had little claim to respectability. In an example quoted in their guide, *The Better Way of Assisting School Children* (1893), they explained why a daughter of a builder's labourer was given a letter to enable her to obtain medical treatment at a hospital but refused free dinners. 'A builder's labourer is bound to lose some time; the more need for him to be careful and saving. In this instance there seemed reason to think that the man might have done better if he had really tried.' The permanently poor stood self-condemned. They were averse to steady work, self-indulgent, and lived in dirty homes in squalid surroundings. Whereas 'The ideal economic man . . . is remarkable for his foresight and self-control; in the Residuum these qualities are entirely absent.' Their children formed 'the troops of ragged, dirty, stunted little urchins, neglected and crippled in mind and body . . . the offspring of . . . reckless marriages.' Their mothers were 'worn-out drudges' or 'careless slatterns'. The fathers 'with all self-respect crushed out of them, . . . reduced to picking up odd jobs at the street-corner, and living more in the public house than in their wretched homes' were equally morally reprehensible.

Children such as these, whose parents were 'negligent, improvident, or of worthless or vicious character', were beyond the pale. The provision of meals would only 'remove the spur to exertion and self-restraint, which the spectacle of his children's hunger must be to any man in whom the feelings of natural kindness are not entirely dead.' When these feelings were dead and the parents seen as beyond redemption,[20]

it is better, in the interests of the community, to allow in such cases the sins of the parents to be visited on their children than to impair the solidarity [sic!] of the family and run the risk of permanently demoralizing large numbers of the population by the offer of free meals to their children.

There was a further objection. If free dinners were given, the plight of the children would not be exposed to public horror in those cases where parents had lost all moral claim to their custody. It was thought better to do this, both for the sake of the children and society at large, than to give the children free meals while allowing them to remain under the corrupting influence of their parents. A closely related group consisted of those in a chronic state of destitution. They were the proper concern of the Poor Law Guardians, not of the COS or any feeding agency. The exclusion of these two categories left only a small number that the COS considered to be deserving of free dinners. These were the children of parents temporarily unemployed through no fault of their own, the morally blameless victims of economic circumstance. Another worker in the field added a further test of moral probity. Parents had had to send their children regularly and punctually to school in the past.[21] The upshot of this policy was that those whose economic needs were the greatest received the least.

It is one matter to discuss the principles of the COS, it is another to assess their influence. Many shared the view of the London School Board visitors that their precepts were too restrictive. Headmasters and others granted free school meals on a scale that the COS considered unduly lavish. Thus one can point to wide variations in the practice of schools in roughly comparable areas. For instance the Chaucer Council School, Tabard School, Bermondsey, regularly fed over a half of its children, 863 out of 1,357, with a large number of the remainder being fed elsewhere. In comparison the Northey Street School, Limehouse, fed an average of only 14 in the winter of 1903–4 and 30 the following winter, out of over 700 on the roll. The modest increase was the result of a new headmaster who 'as with most new people . . . thought . . . the people very poor indeed'. At the same time the head of the girls' department had become antipathetically less liberal. With nearly equal numbers in the three departments, 262 boys, 251 girls, and 250 infants, the provision of meals varied. 329 were served to boys, 97 to girls, and 94 to infants. Over a period of 70 school days, a total of 520 *meals* was made to suffice for a school containing 763 children. Yet it was in a dockland area where casual labour predominated. The social worker connected with the school stigmatized the fathers as 'Almost always casual dockers, and always dirty and miserable. Every one of them if he did not drink and gamble would have money.'[22] Beatrice Webb's contribution, 'The Docks', to Charles Booth's *Life and Labour of the People in London*, might never have been written.

Equally deserving of sympathy were the children of Lisson Grove, London, where a Miss Kate Hart worked for the last thirty years of the century. In putting the case against giving children free meals to the London School Board enquiry of 1898–9 she showed little awareness of how the poor lived. Free meals would destroy 'the natural affection that is often only kept alive by the mutual pleasure of giving and receiving the necessary food. The poorer the family the more important it is', she declared, 'that this bond of affection should not be interfered with.' Yet these were the very families that might not have been able to afford the scraps of frozen meat that she stated could be bought late at night for a penny a pound. To say that 'sitting round a long table with a number of other children is a dull business compared with the meal shared with parents, babies, dogs and cats' conjured up a picture of middle-class domestic bliss that those who lacked proper furniture could never have known. Finally, as was so often the case, she resorted to the unprovable question-begging type of assertion. 'Free meals are unnecessary because the children already have enough to eat, except in a few cases that can be easily dealt with.'[23]

Two main arguments were used to rationalize opposition to the principle of feeding children gratuitously, a refusal to believe that there were people too poor to feed their children adequately and a virtual denial of the existence of undernourishment amongst schoolchildren. It was possible for an observer steeped in the conventional self-help ethos of the period to ignore the evidence in front of him every day of the week. In 1905 the headmaster of the Chaucer Council School, Bermondsey, was asked if he thought that parents could pay for a meal. He replied,

If they can get a thing for nothing, and have been taught to get it for nothing . . . it is rather difficult to unlearn it. When you ask would they pay, they would ultimately pay but not willingly. They would have something to unlearn. They are exceedingly poor.

Yet he had admitted earlier that Charles Booth had described the area as one of the blackest spots in London. Similarly the School Medical Officer for Erith had 'no hesitation in saying that the children who suffer from defective nourishment and from neglect of their clothes are not the children of poor people, but the children of people who live on beer chiefly as their diet.' Akin to this view was the belief 'that when children come to school without breakfast it is laziness rather than cruelty or lack of food, as a rule'. Frequently mentioned as ogres were the parents who fell asleep at night too drunk to arouse themselves in the morning to feed their children. Yet teachers in one of the poorest Church schools in Liverpool found a different explanation when they went to the children's homes as whippers-in of absentees as late as 1905. In the middle of the morning the children were still asleep in sacks in cellars destitute of all furniture waiting for their parents to earn money to pay for some food. The children followed the teachers to school in the rags in which they had slept for they had no other clothing. The effort of both children and teachers was wasted. Once at school the children were too faint from want of food to learn anything.[24] Another tactic was to argue that children were ill-fed rather than underfed. The 1904 Inter-Departmental Committee on Physical Deterioration found that one witness 'emphatically stated, with the support more or less marked of others, a large proportion of British housewives are tainted with incurable laziness and distaste for the obligations of domestic life.' The Committee thought the situation a deteriorating one. 'There is no lack of increasing carelessness and deficient sense of responsibility among the younger women of the present day.' Some witnesses showed a prejudice against jam, ready-baked bread, and tinned foods; the new convenience foods of an urban society that 'do not understand how to provide themselves with proper food. They may have plenty of food, but it is not proper food; it is tinned food, easily got, and badly prepared.'[25] Even Dr James Kerr, who by 1904 was the School Medical Officer for the London County Council, thought bad feeding in infancy a much more important cause of poor physique amongst children than underfeeding. In pursuance of the thesis that the puny appearance of children was the result of parental ignorance and indifference rather than of poverty, witnesses sought refuge in other explanations. They laid the blame for the children's pallid complexions on such factors as the common practice of keeping bedroom windows closed at night, the insanitary surroundings of the homes, the long hours children worked before and after school, or their habitual uncleanliness.[26] Hence many social workers discounted the validity of the teacher's assumption that a child's unhealthy appearance was the result of not having enough to eat. The forthrightness of a Leeds doctor who arranged meals for some slum children after he had diagnosed scurvy amongst them was rare. 'These children are evidently, to any medical expert, underfed. You have the ill-nourished skin, the ill-nourished hair, the stunted growth, the light weight.[27]

Consequently a significant proportion of those who decided which children were to have free meals before the 1906 Act and, a point that can be easily overlooked, after it as well were not convinced that there was a widespread social problem. Under the new Act school canteen committees were formed to carry on the investigative work that had already been conducted before. With the addition of medical inspection and treatment to the list of services available to children, these committees became Children's Care Committees. Whether as the result of action by a voluntary or statutory agency, working-class parents who wanted school dinners or some form of medical treatment for which they were unable to pay suffered the humiliation of an inquisitorial investigation from their social superiors. These caseworkers' assumptions about working-class behaviour and daily life were derived from a middle-class morality unsympathetic and alien to the suppliants' world.

The selection of children for free meals began in the classroom where the teacher picked out the most deserving cases. In some instances before 1906 this seems to have been the end of the affair. The child received a ticket and went off for his meal. Other schools and dinner agencies had a more elaborate system. The headmaster questioned the children, interviewed the parents at the school, obtained information about the family from the school attendance officer, or referred the case to a committee of school managers. The rigour with which these enquiries were conducted varied considerably. The headmaster of one board school in Walworth started a scheme for feeding children after he discovered that some of his pupils had not eaten for over twenty-four hours. He made sure that the children were telling the truth by sending to a baker's shop for 'some of the driest crusts he had on the premises'. The boys had eaten them ravenously. At this particular school children became eligible for meals if the family income did not allow the expenditure of three-farthings a meal a child, three times a day. This was less than the average of 1s 6d a week that the local Board of Guardians allowed for each child. At another school near Waterloo Station the headmaster watched to see which boys spent the dinner hour in the playground without anything to eat and followed others along the market stalls in The Cut to find out who scavenged for bits of discarded food. At yet another slum school near Waterloo Station the headmaster sent for 'careless' parents. 'I always tell the children and the parents themselves', he informed the 1905 Committee, 'that it is the father's duty to get the child a meal. That is the principle I go on.' At a school in the Seven Dials district, London, children's names were put on the list for free dinners for a fortnight after the home had been visited. Any extension required a further visit. Yet some of these homes were so unpleasant that the ladies of the committee refused to enter them. They sent the school attendance officer instead, an official that the parents saw as their persecutor. Such men, frequently at odds with the very parents whose need for meals they were required to assess, were not normally predisposed to treat them kindly. For instance the school attendance officer at Bolton, a former postman believing that school meals did more harm than good, won the approbation of his superiors by reducing the list of applicants by nearly two-thirds through the exercise of a rigour that would have delighted the COS.[28]

As applications for free meals could rebound in an unfortunate manner, parents had every reason to hesitate before asking. The Relief Committee of a Chelsea school tried to see the food the parents gave their children. If they disapproved of the way in which the home was run, they said so pointing out that more nourishing food could be obtained for the same money by making soup or porridge, advice that took no account of the monotony of the diet they proposed. This high-handed attitude kept the number of children given free meals down to 25 out of the 1,192 in the school. Even the 1905 Committee, despite their preoccupation with the amount of care with which children were selected for free dinners, were surprised at the amount of paperwork that investigations at this school had generated.[29] At a number of schools where the visitors thought parents neglectful they did not hesitate to call in the inspector of the Society for the Prevention of Cruelty to Children to initiate a prosecution or to refer the case to the Poor Law Guardians.

Stringent, but less capricious, were the poverty scales used in some areas. These involved the calculation of the total income of a household and made the unrealistic assumption that every penny earned went into the common purse. The Manchester School Board used a scale similar to the one they developed earlier for determining whether parents qualified for the remission of school fees. After the deduction of rent, it allowed a weekly income of 3s a head for a family of two, 2s 9d for three or four persons, and 2s 6d for five or more. The Board justified these gradations on the grounds that a larger family could live more cheaply than a smaller one. In Bradford the test was simpler, families with a *per capita* income of 3s after the payment of rent were eligible. In both instances the scales put the family below the poverty line devised by Seebohm Rowntree for his study of York. After the deduction of rent he calculated that a family of four, two adults and two children, required a weekly income of 3s 8½d each, a family of five needed 3s 6½d and ten needed 3s 2¼d. Moreover he based these budgets on a diet that excluded any butcher's meat and was less generous than that required in workhouses by the Local Government Board. Nevertheless the largest group of eligible children in Bradford, 247 out of 1,520, had fathers in full-time employment. 8 men on the railways, 10 cart drivers, 33 woolcombers and similar workers in a staple industry of low wages, 3 corporation employees, 14 outdoor labourers, 2 soldiers away from home, and 3 who were unclassified, made a total of 73 fathers with large families in occupations too poorly paid for them to feed their children sufficiently well to meet Rowntree's far from exacting standards.[30]

Further safeguards against the pauperization of the masses included attempts to charge the parents for the meals provided and a policy of making the food deliberately unattractive. The publicity that the

116

underfed child received as a result of the 'overpressure controversy' and the high rate of unemployment in the severe winter of 1885–6 brought a marked increase in the number of voluntary feeding agencies. Some provided self-supporting dinners, that is dinners for which the parents were expected to pay a considerable proportion of the cost. By December 1885 there were fifteen such centres in London alone. The penny charged covered the cost of the materials, labour, and occasionally the hire of the hall. Only the utensils came entirely from private donations. At a time when a substantial meal for a working man cost 5d or 6d, a penny meal was poor in size and quality. For instance 25 lb of pork at 6½d a pound, 112 lb of potatoes, and 3 pecks (6 gallons) of dried peas sufficed for 255 portions of boiled pork and pease pudding; 28 lb of meat, 6 lb of suet, four-shillingsworth of flour, and 120 lb of potatoes produced 270 portions of meat pudding and vegetables. Promoters soon found that the charge of a penny debarred the really poor. Yet *The Times* valued the principle that dinners should be self-supporting, 'They are designed to inculcate thrift, not to add another element of pauperization to those already existing.' It took comfort in the thought that there was 'no genuine case of destitution which could not be amply relieved if the funds of Charities were not so often mis-applied to the benefit of the improvident.' As for the 'children with pinched faces and ravenous eyes crowding round the school doors at the dinner-hour, and praying, crying to be fed', they could be referred to the parochial authorities and the clergy.[31] In practice the promoters of the penny dinners in London and elsewhere followed the lead of the London Board School Free Dinner Fund founded in 1882 and abandoned their attempts to put school meals on a self-supporting basis.

A provincial organization that found it had seriously underestimated the extent and reality of contemporary poverty was the Birmingham Schools Cheap Dinner Society formed in October 1884. At first this Society offered penny dinners only to find that most of those who could afford the cost of the meal preferred to go home. The Society's reduction of its charge to a halfpenny was equally unsuccessful. As HMI Dr O. Airy, a member of the Birmingham Society subsequently explained, 'Then came a revelation which was astounding to me', despite his eight years' experience of the city's schools, 'there were many hundreds of children, and even thousands, who could no more find a halfpenny for a dinner than they could find a half-sovereign.' Birmingham eventually achieved the curious distinction of serving some of the cheapest school dinners in the country, partly as a means of deterring the 'feckless' parent and partly out of financial necessity. A locally produced pamphlet, *Farthing Dinners*, showed the way. For a halfpenny – the other farthing met administrative costs including £150 a year for the manager's salary – it was possible to provide half-a-pint of soup and a tenth of a pound of bread spread with $\frac{1}{4}$ oz of jam bought in bulk at 24*s* a cwt. Given such fare, the advice 'If no gentleman can be present during dinner time, it is necessary to have a policeman', sounds prudent enough. F. H. Sargant, the author, provided a recipe for making soup at $1\frac{1}{2}d$ a gallon. For this he added 8 lb dried peas, 3 lb Indian meal, 6 oz dripping, 2 lb carrots and onions, 1 lb salt, $\frac{1}{2}$ oz pepper and 2 oz sugar to 10 gallons of water. Before cooking this gave each child less than one ounce of peas, the largest constituent in the recipe, in his helping of soup. The 'Irish Stew' was slightly more expensive. To every 6 gallons of water he added 36 lb potatoes, 4 lb rice, 4 lb carrots, 4 lb onions, 2 lb meat scraps and 1 lb salt. After simmering all night this reduced to 12 gallons of stew and gave each child before cooking, 3 oz potatoes, $\frac{1}{3}$ oz of the remaining vegetable and grain ingredients, and $\frac{1}{8}$ oz meat. As an alternative to bread, the Birmingham Society offered $\frac{1}{6}$ pint of cocoa made from $10\frac{1}{2}$ gallons of water, $5\frac{1}{2}$ oz cocoa, 1 lb tin of condensed milk, and $2\frac{3}{4}$ lb demerara sugar. A drink containing less than $\frac{1}{30}$ oz condensed milk, $\frac{1}{60}$ oz cocoa, and $\frac{1}{11}$ oz sugar must have deterred all except the most needy. Moreover the mass production of soup and cocoa was such a crude process that 'a starving child new to the Birmingham dietary, could not digest the soup'. More than thirty years later, the City's medical superintendent recommended that the sugar and cocoa should be made into a paste before they were added to the milk. 'This will make a more appetising concoction and one from which the cocoa will only separate slowly.'[32]

The circumstances under which the meals were served did nothing to mitigate their Spartan character. Dismayed at the sight of children tramping a mile or more through slush and snow the Society had provided canvas shelters in the playgrounds of the schools to which meals were brought from a central point. When asked by the Select Committee on the Education (Provision of Meals) Bill in 1906 if these shelters were cold, Airy replied 'Certainly it was cold. We did not propose to give every luxury or even comfort. We proposed only to do the best we could to keep these children alive.' When the children had drunk their soup under the canvas shelters they went out into the playground or the streets clutching their pieces of bread and jam. In Airy's words, 'The meal was reduced to the very bare necessities to such an extent that it did not tempt the vicious parent to try and impose on the Birmingham Society by planting his children on their charity.'[33] With the passing of the 1906 Act standards improved slowly but the hungry child could not yet afford to be a fastidious one. In 1910 the City's Schools Medical Officer welcomed the introduction of tables and seats, plates, forks, and knives. But as late as 1913 in at least one school the same mugs were used by two batches of children without being washed. Elsewhere 'The supply of utensils . . . was too small for the numbers fed . . . .'[34]

Although the Birmingham schoolchild received some of the cheapest meals ever served in schools, many of his contemporaries fared little better. In London the standard of meals had deteriorated by the mid-1890s, a policy that

may be ascribed partly to the fact that the need to attract children is not so pressing as it was when it was still hoped to establish the meals on a self-supporting basis and partly to the influence of the National Food Supply Association whose promoters desire to encourage the use of vegetable soup as well as to relieve distress.

Philanthropic agencies such as the London Vegetarian Society, the Bread and Food Reform Society, and the Women's Total Abstinence Union, had joined forces to provide strictly vegetarian soups made from lentils, haricot beans, dried peas, carrots and turnips, supplemented by wholemeal bread, a menu that could cause diarrhoea if indulged in for more than a few days. The addition of cheap and fatty cuts of meat elsewhere made little improvement. Sixpennyworth of bones in 50 gallons of soup did not make a feast when the other ingredients were 40 lb peas, 8 lb onions, 10 lb carrots, 4 lb pea flour, and 70 lb wheat flour. Even hungry children found the daily doles of soup so monotonous and poor in quality that they refused them at times, a point that unsympathetic observers seized on to argue that the children were not really hungry. Mrs Burgwin, one of London's pioneers of school dinners, found it impossible to give the children soup every day, 'as the stomach revolts against it, and a weak stomach cannot digest it, especially if it be of a fatty nature.' Even the preparation of the soup, a process that often involved boiling bones for a long period, Mrs Burgwin found so offensive that 'It is wonderful', she said 'how the teachers endure it.' Another witness to the London School Board's enquiry of 1895 added her complaints about the soup. It was 'made from greasy matter and from coarse vegetables, which kind of food is calculated to cause diarrhoea. I should expect', Honnor Morten a London School Board member for Hackney continued, 'many children would die from that complaint if fed daily on such a diet, which is almost devoid of nourishment.'[35]

Apart from their concern not to breed a nation of spongers, the financial stringency under which the feeding agencies worked helps to explain the poor quality of much of the food provided. The findings of the 1905 Inter-Departmental Committee that 'nearly all the witnesses stated that no difficulty has been experienced on the part of the voluntary agencies in raising the funds necessary for their operations' has to be seen in the context of the limited concept these bodies had of their work. With an annual income somewhat in excess of £30,000 for the winter 1904–5, there was enough money to give over 7,000,000 meals a year at a penny each. With one child in ten at school fed, there would have been meals for three weeks a year for the most needy. The one witness to admit that lack of means constituted a serious constraint was George Hookham of Birmingham who had started his own free breakfast scheme to supplement the efforts of the Birmingham Cheap Dinner Society. After enquiries in the schools there, he calculated that 4,500 children needed a free meal throughout the year. This would have cost £4,500, an amount the Inter-Departmental Committee felt 'many people might consider unnecessarily large'. This sum he held was impossible to raise. He pointed out that the City's Cheap Dinner Society's annual income was under £300 despite a contribution of £75 from the local branch of the NUT. Certainly the Society's practice of selling off the bones that had been boiled overnight for the children's soup suggests that charitable contributions were not easy to come by. Unfortunately boiled bones proved a declining asset, worth £7 8s 8d in 1888–9, their value slumped to 12s by 1896–7 when their sale was abandoned.[36]

It was a common complaint that money seldom reached the agencies until there was a severe frost or a heavy fall of snow. Similarly a premature spring could cause the flow of funds to dry up before the seasonal trades had fully revived. Hence the serving of meals was frequently limited to a period extending from Christmas to Easter at the latest. Although this fitted in well with the incidence of heavy unemployment in many trades, the plight of gas workers' children in the summer is a reminder that there were exceptions. Within the limited period during which meals were available, few organizations in

London offered them five days a week. Nearly every school avoided giving meals on Mondays for Sunday was the one day of the week when the poorer families, but possibly not the poorest, managed to have something approaching a decent meal cooked, if necessary, in the neighbouring bakehouse. During the winter of 1904–5 for example, 16 of the London County Council's schools gave one meal a week, 90 gave two, 61 gave three, and 41 provided four or five. As the number of tickets was limited, the same children were not fed every day. Thus neither parents nor children knew before setting off to school whether a meal would be forthcoming. To add to the uncertainties, the head-teachers of the separate boys', girls', and infants' departments seldom co-operated to treat each family alike. Hence families with a child in each department must have found the daily selection process baffling in its randomness. For instance during a week in February 1895, a tenth of the children on the rolls in the London School Board area, 51,897 out of 489,671, received a meal. With 122,605 meals served each of those children had an average of $2\frac{1}{3}$ meals that week when 'the frost having continued with great and increasing severity the figures actually represent a period of very marked distress.'[37]

Estimates of the number of children requiring meals varied. A London School Board sub-committee thought that during the year ending March 1889 some 43,888 children habitually attended school in want of food, less than a half of whom were ever fed. The remission of the fees of 110,759 children at some time during the same year gives an index of poverty in London at that time. Some fifteen years later Dr Eichholz estimated that the number of underfed children which he had first put at 60,000, was approximately 122,000, or 16 per cent of the elementary school population of London. This was the highest figure presented to the Inter-Departmental Committee on Physical Deterioration in 1904. The London School Board, at the other extreme, had put the number below 10,000. There was a similar conflict of evidence over the numbers of underfed children in Manchester. Eichholz consulted the City's School Medical Officer who put the figure at 15 per cent. On the other hand the vicar of Pendleton, Salford, assured the committee that no more than 2 per cent of the children of Manchester and Salford came to school underfed.[38]

Apart from any clinical problems of defining underfeeding, the attitudes of outside observers to the social questions of the day made agreement impossible. The well publicized visit of Sir John Gorst, Lady Warwick, Dr Hutchinson, a physician from the Children's Hospital,

Great Ormond Street, London, and Dr T. J. Macnamara, MP for Camberwell North, to the Johanna Street Council School, North Lambeth, in March 1905 shows how widely opinions could differ. In Standard I they found that 20 boys had been told not to come back home at dinner time as there was no food in their homes, but that there were tickets for only 16 dinners. The same story was repeated throughout the school. The headmistress had no more than 12 tickets for the 50 girls who had come to school breakfastless. In the following week the number of tickets available was expected to drop by almost 50 per cent because of falling subscriptions. Following the visit, the local Board of Guardians empowered the relieving officer to grant immediate relief. Only one family applied so great was the reluctance of working people to turn to the Guardians for help. When the relieving officer finally made his report the Board of Guardians resolved that the visiting deputation had overstated their case. Food tickets, they alleged, had been given away with little, if any, enquiry, and the children had obtained them merely to have a change of menu. Yet Gorst and his colleagues had thought that there were sixty cases of pressing destitution.[39] This was not the end of the affair. The protagonists of the conflicting social policies continued their debate in the House of Commons and before the Select Committee on Education (Provision of Meals) Bill, 1906, unable to agree as to what were the basic facts in a small case study.

The episode provided an unfortunate augury for the success of the Relief (School Children) Order published the following month, April 1905. The Order broke new ground by allowing Guardians in parishes where the Outdoor Relief Prohibitory Order was in force to grant relief to the child of an able-bodied man without requiring him to enter the workhouse or to perform the outdoor labour test. The Order encouraged co-operation between the Local Education Authorities and the Poor Law Unions by empowering employees of the former to refer children to the relieving officers. If the father of the child were deemed to be neglectful, such relief had to be given as a loan. In other cases the Guardians enjoyed discretion. When relief was granted as a loan, steps had to be taken to recover the amount expended. Whether or not the money was recovered the father was disfranchised. It thus became theoretically possible for a child to be given meals without the knowledge of his father who then found himself threatened with disfranchisement and the recovery of the cost of the meals through County Court action or by recourse to his employer. Parents naturally refused to allow their children to have meals on such terms. By an act of maladroit administration those that needed help the most, the children of absentee fathers or of widows, were specifically excluded from the Order. The official explanation was that the Guardians already possessed power to help them and that no further sanction was needed. However, this point was never fully explained and many local officials thought that there was no provision at all for these children.

Given the confusion over the scope of the Order, the unpopularity of the Guardians amongst the poor, and the Guardians' adhesion to their traditional function of deterrence rather than succour, it soon became a dead letter. To the credit of many local authorities and feeding agencies the Order was never implemented. In the few instances where Guardians and Local Education Authorities did co-operate, the number of meals provided declined sharply. In Birmingham the Free Dinner Society which had previously been providing 6,000 dinners a day, stopped work. The Guardians fed 400. In Bristol the Guardians decimated the 129 applicants by approving 12 cases only. Apart from the Guardians of Kettering who approved practically all the cases referred to them, the Commissioners on the Poor Laws were justified in their conclusion, 'It seems clear, from the small extent to which the Order has been put in force, that there is little desire amongst Local Authorities to make the feeding of children a charge on the rates.' Attempts to recover costs from the parents met with little success. The draftsmen of the Order would have done well to have pondered the earlier failure of the voluntary societies. In 1899–1900 the Birmingham Society, for example, had recovered no more than $7\frac{1}{2}d$, the cost of fifteen dinners, while it had served over 170,000 meals. The City of Bradford, where some of the most determined efforts were made to charge the parents, recouped £1 19s 3d by voluntary action and a further £1 by a Court Order, out of £1,323 14s 4d spent in the winter 1905–6. Coercion had failed to revive a moribund self-supporting system.[40]

Nevertheless the principle received a further lease of life in the Education (Provision of Meals) Act, 1906, a measure that has been hailed as marking the beginnings of the Welfare State. Although it is true that parents who could not afford to pay for their children's meals no longer faced the penalty of disfranchisement, the Act had not created a precedent. From 1876 parents had been able to obtain the payment of fees at voluntary schools from the Poor Law Guardians and patients had been allowed treatment in a poor law hospital since 1883 without losing their right to the vote. Of greater importance than these legal quibbles was the spirit of the law. The recommendations of the Select Committee which examined the bill set the scene. Their endorsement of the use of public money was cautious and tentative. Not only did they consider that such extra powers had to 'be most carefully safeguarded' but that no local authority should have recourse to such expenditure 'unless it were shown that neither the parents' resources nor voluntary funds were sufficient to cover such cost'. They stipulated that 'In the first instance the payment for the meals should be required from the parents' and that assistance from public funds was for supplementing rather than supplanting the contributions of the charitable. Furthermore legislative action was seen as a means of remedying some of the weaknesses of the voluntary system which had created 'an unofficial and defective system of outdoor relief attended with a certain amount of overlapping and abuse'; for 'voluntary efforts unarmed with statutory authority must fall short in efficiency of administration when contrasted with what would be expected of an organization regulated by Act of Parliament.' In particular the existing agencies had no means of forcing parents to pay who were able but unwilling to do so, nor could they punish neglectful parents except through the officials of the Society for the Prevention of Cruelty to Children. They accordingly recommended the formation of the committees first known as School Canteen Committees and later in London and certain other cities as Children's Care Committees. These committees were to be drawn from members of the local education authorities and the voluntary societies and supplemented, where desirable, by members of the Poor Law Guardians and the SPCC. In addition the committees were recommended to work with local headmasters, school attendance officers, and relieving officers. Whereas the COS had seen the school board visitors as amateurs in relief work, a generation later the Select Committee pronounced 'The duty of investigation and enquiry appears to be one peculiarly suitable for them to assume.'[41] In one sense the 1906 Act was an endorsement of the principles of the COS. Its concern was to prevent the indiscriminate granting of a particular form of relief. In another way it marked a step forward. The sins of the fathers were not to be visited upon the next generation. No child was to be refused a meal because it had not paid for it. However, as a survey of the working of the Act will reveal, there was a gap between the intent of the legislature and the implementation of the Act at the local level.

124

Appendix: A note on the nutritive value of some meals served to schoolchildren

It is difficult to find menus that describe accurately the contents of meals served to schoolchildren. It is even harder to measure their nutritive value. When prices are given for certain ingredients, it is not always clear whether they are wholesale or retail ones. If the price is retail one does not always know whether it refers to the price paid by a working-class customer in a street market or to that paid by a middle-class customer in a shop. Despite these uncertainties, P. M. Mumford of Queen Elizabeth College, London, has estimated the calorific and protein value of the meals mentioned in the preceding chapter. In each case it should be noted that today's recommended daily intake for children aged 5 to 12 is about 2,000 kilocaries and 50 grams of protein. As she points out, the following calculations reveal very clearly the value of pulses and bread as cheap sources of protein and calories. The soups are less useful. One unquantifiable feature is the importance of providing something hot at a time when many of the poorest did not possess any cooking facilities of their own. It was for this reason that soup was the basis of many of the charity meals served during cold weather.

The penny meals of 1885 (p. 117)	per serving	
	Kcals	*protein*
1 boiled pork	460	32g
2 meat pudding and vegetables	360	15g

F. H. Sargant's farthing dinners (p. 118)	per serving	
	Kcals	*protein*
1 soup		
soup	102	6g
bread	110	4g
jam	18	—
Total meal	230	10g
2 Irish stew	125	3g
3 cocoa served as an alternative to bread	14	< 1g

This compares with 100 Kcals and 3 g protein derived from 1½ oz bread.

Soup served in London in mid-1890s (p. 119)	*Kcals*	*protein*
Half-pint portion	200	8g

In addition to the above the *Report of the Inter-Department Committee on Medical Inspection and Feeding of Children attending Public Elementary Schools* gives the following menus.

At Dartford, Kent, the Wesleyan Mission provided 5,000 breakfasts a day consisting of 5,000 rolls at 23*s* 5*d* a thousand, 60 gallons of milk at 11½*d* a gallon, 64 lb of cheese at 6*d* per lb, 160 lb of sugar at 22*s* per cwt, 20 lb of coffee at 8½*d* per lb. In addition firing, lighting, and labour cost £1 17*s* 6*d*. The witness claimed that this worked out at exactly a penny a breakfast. As his figures stand the average cost is 0·7*d*. However, by doubling the quantities of milk, cheese, and sugar one reaches an average price of 0·98*d*.

		per serving	
		Kcals	*protein*
1	Taking the quantities as listed		
	a assuming 2 oz roll	224	6g
	b assuming 4 oz roll	364	10g
2	Doubling, milk, cheese, and sugar		
	a assuming 2 oz roll	310	8g
	b assuming 4 oz roll	450	12g

George Hookham of Birmingham gave a breakfast consisting of half a pint of cocoa made from skimmed milk, five ounces of bread known in the trade as seconds, cut into two slices, one covered with jam, the other with butter. His milk cost 32½*d* for every hundred children, his bread 28*d*, butter 12*d*, jam 11*d*, cocoa 5*d*, sugar 3*d*. In Birmingham market milk cost 3½*d* a quart. For this reason it is assumed that the milk given to the children was diluted with water, approximately two parts water, one part milk. With bread at 4*d* to 5½*d* for 4 lb the amount given may have been nearer 4 oz than the 5 oz he claimed. If one assumes: ½ pint of skimmed milk undiluted, ⅛ oz sugar, 5 oz bread, ⅙ oz butter, ⅙ oz jam, the value of each serving was 510 Kcals, 22 g of protein. If one assumes that the milk was diluted and that only 4 oz of bread were served the figures become per serving 375 Kcals,

12·9g of protein. In both calculations the amounts of butter and sugar assumed to have been served may have been slightly higher than those quoted above.

In Brighton the Free Meal Society gave children half a pint of hot milk and a 4 oz currant bun. Hungry children were allowed an extra half bun when available.

Estimates depend on whether the milk was whole or skimmed.

	per serving	
	Kcals	protein
½ pint of whole milk + 4 oz bun	470	16g
½ pint of whole milk + 6 oz bun	620	20g
½ pint of skimmed milk + 4 oz bun	380	17g
½ pint of skimmed milk + 6 oz bun	530	21g

Source: Report of the Inter-Departmental Committee on Medical Inspection and Feeding of Children attending Public Elementary Schools, Parliamentary Papers, 1906, XLVII, Qs. 1141, 1236–9; 2466; 5838–9.

VI

••

Cleansing the
Augean Classrooms

••

Some of the more progressive school boards began to appoint school medical officers nearly two decades before the passing of the Education (Administrative Provisions) Act, 1907. Such Boards had taken advantage of a legal loophole in Forster's Act of 1870 that allowed them to engage 'other necessary officers' or had extended the duties of doctors employed under the Elementary Education (Defective and Epileptic Children) Act of 1899. To start a school medical service and a school meal service school boards had strained the spirit, if not the letter, of the law. The London School Board had not only begun to provide some facilities such as the services of its caretakers, the building of special shelters and other accommodation for school meals from the 1880s onwards, it also appointed a medical officer as early as 1891. Although such expenditure was of doubtful legality the district auditors never surcharged the boards. Similarly the Report of the Inter-Departmental Committee on Medical Inspection carefully evaded any discussion of a possible misuse of the 1870 Act by commenting, 'It is not within the range of our inquiries to ascertain precisely what are the limits of this power.'

By 1905 there were 85 school medical officers all of whom, except for six employed by county councils, worked in predominantly urban areas. Most of these officials held part-time appointments. They were either local practitioners or medical officers for health who received a small additional salary, that could be as little as £10 10s a year. Only the School Boards London, Bradford, and Manchester, seem to have had full-time medical officers for their education services before 1908.

The duties of the doctors varied as much as their terms of service. Those on a small annual salary usually did little more than examine children alleged to be unfit to attend school and grant medical certificates where appropriate. By contrast the doctors in a few small towns, Keighley and Kidderminster are examples, looked at every school child. Such thoroughness was unusual for only a minority of the doctors ever entered the schools, let alone made an attempt to examine the children. Usually when they went to schools they seem to have been more concerned with the premises than with the children who were only inspected during outbreaks of infectious diseases.

A few authorities showed greater concern by instructing their teachers to refer children thought to be suffering from some physical defect. In reporting such cases women teachers were considered to be much more conscientious than their male colleagues. After dealing with these particular children, some doctors asked the whole class to file in front of them so that they could pick out those obviously requiring attention. Other doctors contented themselves with casting their eyes over a class sitting in their seats. Lastly, teachers in many districts carried out a rudimentary test for myopia, testing for hypermetropia was a luxury apparently confined to the children of Salford. These eyesight tests owed much to the initiative of the Board of Education who had issued a circular on the subject in 1901 following their investigations into the problem in the mid-1890s.

The giving of any form of medical treatment was a much rarer event than a medical examination. The LCC's service, the largest of all, was headed by Dr James Kerr, late of the Bradford School Board. His staff of one full-time assistant, 23 part-time assistants and 12 nurses examined the children but did not treat them. Kerr, who believed that free medical treatment tended to pauperize parents saw schools as places 'where children should be educated as much as possible and handled as little as possible'. Hence the LCC's nurses advised parents on treatment but never gave it. On hearing that some nurses had paid out of their own pockets for verminous children to have a haircut, Kerr expressly forbade them to do it again. In a few London schools nurses belonging to the Queen Victoria Jubilee Institute for Nurses, founded in 1887, gave treatment; but this work was financed by voluntary agencies independently of the LCC. In the provinces, these nurses gave some treatment with the help of voluntary funds in Birmingham and Liverpool. Children treated by these nurses were particularly fortunate. At a time when many nurses could not have passed the examination of the General Nursing Council, Queen's Nurses had to have undergone a year's training in a recognized school attached to a hospital, plus six months' district nursing.[1] Reading and Widnes, where the nurses cleaned dirty heads, seem to have been the only towns in which any treatment was provided at public expense.

There was a similar disparity between the provision made for diagnosing poor eyesight and the steps taken to remedy it. Unless parents had access to a local charity, the most help they received was through the development of hire-purchase schemes to enable them to buy spectacles for their children. Where such provision existed the local authority usually offered glasses at a cost of around 3s 6d, instead of the more normal 10s 6d and allowed parents to pay off their debt at a rate as low as a penny a week. In Salford where such a scheme operated, parents were not given the glasses until the total amount had been paid. Despite this lack of trust, Salford parents were amongst the lucky ones. Usually nothing was done beyond informing the parents that their child needed glasses. With even less attention being paid at this time to diseases of the ear and bad teeth, it is not surprising that no urban authority was spending more than the product of a 1/10d rate in 1905.[2]

A study of the children of Johanna Street Council School, Lambeth, shows how the social problems associated with poverty impeded the physical and scholastic development of the pupils. None of the fathers was in regular employment, the one possible claimant to that status being a father who whistled for cabs at Charing Cross. A third of the children required free meals for the six winter months of the year. The boys did not possess the stamina necessary for a full-length game of football. The girls could not cope with a full physical training syllabus. Their academic performance was similarly disappointing. 92 per cent of those in Standard I were above the correct age, as were 85 per cent in Standard II and 80 per cent in Standard III. None ever reached Standard VII, only 8 per cent achieved Standard V. The performance of the children at Honeywell Road Council School, Wandsworth, provides a striking contrast. Here the fathers were clerks and in other occupations well enough paid to enable them to afford rents of £30 to £45 a year. This school was reputed to enjoy a Continental reputation for the breadth of its curriculum, its girls a wide renown for their physique. At drill 'they bore themselves as well as German soldiers.'[3] Children from such a school stayed the academic course to win scholarships to secondary ones or to pass the examinations for the Civil Service.

The acts designed to alleviate the plight of the Johanna Street children ensured that the cornucopia of public largesse did not undermine parental responsibility. The first act, the Education (Provision of Meals) Act gave local authorities a power, that of spending a maximum of a halfpenny rate on subsidizing school meals. It also imposed a duty, that of recovering wherever possible the cost of the meals from the parents. The Board of Education advised that the safest way of doing this was to insist on pre-payment – from parents who could not afford to feed their children. The Education (Administrative Provisions) Act reflected a similar dualism. It required local authorities to conduct medical inspections and gave them the power of 'attending to the health and physical condition of children educated in public elementary schools'. To keep responsibility where it was seen to belong, parents were encouraged, if not expected, to attend the medical examination. This step was taken not out of any consideration for the feelings of either child or parent but to enable doctors to point out the type of treatment required and to impress on the parents their duty to obtain it. The Children Act of 1908, the Childrens' Charter, liberated the child at the expense of the parent. Under this Act a local authority could prosecute a parent for failing to give his children adequate food, clothing, medical attention, or accommodation. Poverty was no excuse, for parents, unable to afford these essentials, faced prosecution if they did not apply to the poor law guardians for the necessary relief. Under another much used clause, local authorities could compulsorily cleanse the body and clothing of a verminous child. If that child then became reinfested, the local authority could take legal proceedings against the parent. Finally, the Local Education Authorities (Medical Treatment) Act, 1909, was cast in the same mould as the earlier Education (Provision of Meals) Act. This Act made it obligatory for local authorities to charge the cost of any medical treatment to the parent of the child except in those cases where they were satisfied that the parents could not pay. Under both acts outstanding debts could be recovered through the courts.

Thus the new legislation of these years brought the poorest and least articulate families into conflict with the state over several issues. Such families, suspicious of the motives of those in authority, had to deal with a host of officials that included hospital almoners, members of the Children's Care Committees, headteachers, school nurses and school attendance officers. In particular the drive local authorities made to rid children of vermin presented parents with many difficulties.

Even with the best will in the world many of the poorest families

131

were unable to rid their children of vermin, let alone keep them clean afterwards. To delouse clothes mothers had to boil them and press the seams with a hot iron. Yet many of the poorest families had no utensils for boiling water except a kettle and a small tin. They could not afford soap. Some did not even have a wash basin. Those who managed to boil the clothes did not always have facilities for drying them afterwards. Hence the children had to go to school the next day wearing clothes that were still wet. The means the London County Council and other authorities recommended for the treatment of verminous hair left much to be desired. They suggested either sassafras oil, too expensive for the poor to buy, or paraffin oil the danger and unpleasantness of using which they compounded by failing to tell the parents to wash their children's hair afterwards. As for the aesthetic problem, one medical officer wrote, 'If the people do not care for the smell of paraffin they must belong to a class which can afford to go to the doctor.'[4]

The disinfestation of individual children remained a Canute-like operation so long as parents and other members of the family remained untreated because local authorities lacked the facilities. In 1904 when the LCC began its campaign against the verminous schoolchild only half the metropolitan boroughs possessed the equipment necessary for treating the home. Even dealing with the family's living room was of little use if the rest of the building remained untouched and children could pick up lice in the streets. Worst off of all were the semi-nomadic families renting a room by the night, tramping the streets looking for shelter, or seeking the hospitality of a friend who would let them share a corner of his room. For children of such families the hot baths they received at the cleansing centres were their first experience of soap and hot water.

Once medical inspections were under way, local authorities showed greater concern for dealing with body lice and ringworm than with tackling any other complaint. A number of authorities treated every child who suffered from either condition. This showed good business sense for they stood to lose more from a cut in the annual grant because of absenteeism than the cost of treatment. In both instances local authorities used their legal powers under the compulsory attendance bye-laws and the Children Act to force the parents to have their children treated. The London schools, for instance, were thought to be losing £5,000 or £6,000 a year from their grants because children were away with ringworm. This was roughly double the cost of treating them at the expense of the authority. At the end of 1911 there were 2,458 children with ringworm in London, the successful treatment of which cost between 18*s* 4*d* and 21*s* 3*d* a case.[5] X-ray treatment counted for most of this sum. However this new but more expensive method had the great merit of reducing the time required for treatment, six to eighteen months, to a few weeks. The treatment of ringworm, a complaint associated popularly with poverty and dirt, must have caused the patient considerable embarrassment. Children under medication usually attended school segregated from the others either in a special class catering for all the infected children from a particular area or in a special part of their normal class. Forced to wear skull caps over their short-cropped hair they were unable to hide their shame. Kept apart from other children, leaving and arriving at different times to the rest of the school and using separate washing facilities, they led a pariah-like life. They had one consolation. The most extreme form of segregation was for favus, another scalp complaint. Virtually confined to children of the Russian Jewish refugees in the East End of London, who were thus doubly conspicuous, its sufferers attended a special favus school in Whitechapel.

Contemporary data do not show the full extent of the success of the school health service in dealing with verminous heads and ringworm before 1914. At first when children were easily seen to be verminous, the nurse's inspection was often no more than cursory. With the gradual elimination of 'the open unabashed condition of heads practically alive with lice', her inspection became more thorough. The lightly infested child, who had previously escaped notice, now began to receive attention. Despite the earlier underestimation of the gravity of the situation, the figures show a remarkable improvement. Whereas London nurses had found more than a third of the children verminous in December 1904, 23,573 out of 50,694 inspected, they found less than a twentieth, 23,573 out of 630,359, in this condition in 1912. In London the authorities owed much of their success to the vigour with which they used their statutory powers. They justified this policy on the grounds that parents saw a dirty head or a dose of ringworm as a ready-made excuse to keep their children off school for as long as possible. To prevent this the LCC decided in 1904 to exclude only the worst cases, that is those children who had lice falling out of their hair. As a rule they gave the parents three weeks' grace after which, if the children were still dirty, the school excluded them. This allowed the LCC to prosecute the parents for failing to send them. In 1904—5 the courts dealt with 21 such cases. The 1908 Act, which gave the LCC two legal sticks with which to beat the parents without having to resort to the previous cumbersome process under the attendance bye-laws, brought an increase in the number of prosecutions that reached a peak of 670 in 1913.[6]

At times the courts showed some sympathy for the plight of the parents. In 1912 the question arose as to whether illiterate parents understood their legal obligations. As a result the LCC henceforth had to send first the school attendance officer and, at a later stage, the school nurse to ensure that parents knew what was required of them. A further difficulty was that the LCC had to prove that they had cleaned the children properly when they sent them to the cleansing stations, otherwise they could not bring a successful charge against a parent for allowing his child to become reinfested. As far as the parents were concerned, this legal requirement initially designed to protect them, had a boomerang effect. On magisterial advice the nurses began cropping the children's hair. By 1915, when the legality of this action was questioned, the number of children so treated had risen to over 6,000. Understandably the LCC's campaign was unpopular with those facing genuine difficulties in keeping their children clean. In 1922, for instance, angry parents surrounded an ambulance in Stepney and prevented a nurse from taking some boys to a cleansing station.[7]

Although the worse conditions were gradually alleviated the incidence of pediculosis remained higher in the poorer, older and over-crowded parts of Great Britain until after the Second World War. Reception centres for ATS recruits found infestation rates of 20 per cent in 1942 and 1943 and 26 per cent by the end of the war. The rates varied between 60 per cent in Northern Ireland and 8 to 16 per cent in the more prosperous areas of the Eastern, Southern, and South-Eastern Commands. Amongst children evacuated from the Metropolitan boroughs of London in September 1939 the incidence ranged between 4 per cent and 45 per cent. In 1947 the Chief Medical Officer to the Ministry of Education admitted, 'Though a great reduction in the extent of this condition has been achieved year by year, some 10 per cent of the elementary school children are still found "unclean".' A recent survey estimates that there are still over 200,000 children with infested scalps. Likewise ringworm still awaits elimination. The conservative estimate of 2,458 cases in London in 1911 can be profitably compared with 3,056 for the whole of England and Wales in 1937 as a measure of progress achieved. During the Second World War a momentary upsurge of cases in certain areas delayed further improvement so that as recently as 1972 doctors found 840 children infected with ringworm.[8]

When one turns to other complaints such as decayed teeth, discharging ears, enlarged tonsils and adenoids, and eye complaints one finds a less satisfactory picture even in those areas where the authorities had pursued a vigorous campaign against vermin and ringworm. First, one cannot be sure that every child at an elementary school before 1918 received a medical inspection. In 1908 the Board of Education required local authorities to inspect children shortly after they began attending school and before they left it. In addition they recommended a third inspection mid-way through a child's school career. Many of the larger authorities carried out all three inspections as well as examining children referred to the doctor by the teacher or the school nurse. Where an authority was content to do no more than perform the statutory minimum the handicap of a child already in school in 1908, could escape attention for most of its school life. To close the gap the Board decided in 1913 to make the third mid-school inspection mandatory from April 1915. With the outbreak of hostilities and the enlistment of doctors in the armed forces the Board had to drop all compulsory examinations and instruct the remaining doctors to concentrate on 'ailing children'.[9] Consequently it was not until some time after 1918 that all children received their three inspections as a matter of routine.

A less serious lacuna was the exclusion of secondary school children from compulsory medical examinations. On balance the social assumptions that led to this omission were pragmatically, but not necessarily morally, justified. A return made of the physical condition of the scholarship winners to the Bradford Grammar Schools in 1913 is remarkable for the virtual absence of poverty associated diseases and complaints. None of the 520 children examined voluntarily by the Bradford Education Committee had unsatisfactory clothing, dirty bodies, ringworm or 'marked rickets'. Only one girl had unsatisfactory footwear, 10 girls had pediculi in their hair – the girls' long hair of the period made them readier hosts than boys – and 3 boys suffered from bad nutrition. The Board of Education thought this was typical of the physical condition of scholarship winners.[10] If this was so, the medical evidence confirms the view that the bottom rungs of the educational ladder set up from elementary school to university were beyond the reach of the slum child of Edwardian England.

The care with which medical examinations were conducted varied considerably. It is hard for instance to believe that in 1908 one Salford child in 162 suffered from ringworm while in neighbouring Manchester only one in 259 was similarly afflicted. Again the discrepancy between Bradford and Swansea, 1 in 82 and 1 in 955, was unlikely to have been entirely the result of environmental factors. To take another example, it is probable that three-quarters to four-fifths of all children needed dental treatment. Yet in 1913 the School Medical Officer for Preston claimed that 77·84 per cent of the entrants and 72·67 per cent of the school leavers had sound teeth. The Board of Education suspected the accuracy of even an estimate as high as 71·8 per cent, the figure returned for Surrey, as an understatement of the proportion requiring dental treatment, because the examinations were not made with a dentist's mirror and probe. Similarly it would be equally misleading to attribute today's standards of care to the pre-1914 years. Although over 40 per cent of the 200,000 London children examined in 1913 had carious teeth – surely a low estimate – only 16·8 per cent were recommended for treatment. Authorities showed a similar caution in providing glasses. The Board of Education's Chief Medical Officer quoted the opinion of the Medical Officer for Staffordshire.[11]

There is no doubt that many people suffer very little inconvenience from a defect of 6/12. On the other hand, 6/18 is a really high and disabling degree of defect. Defects of 6/18 always merit treatment, but defects of 6/12, if they do not cause headache or other complaint, may often be passed over.

In other words the child who could only read a test type at 6 metres that he ought to have been able to read at 12 did not necessarily qualify for glasses. Such a child would have found it hard to read the blackboard from the back of the classroom. Today's adolescent with 6/12 vision would just be able to read a vehicle licence plate to qualify for his driving licence. Despite the difficulties that most children with 6/12 vision had in the classroom, many authorities did nothing for them unless their eyesight was as defective as this or worse. Moreover, the glasses supplied usually contained spherical lenses that made no attempt to correct for astigmatism, the treatment of which was still comparatively rare.

As a general rule the rural child's chances of receiving the necessary medical treatment were less than his urban brother's. Most of the 300 or more clinics that had been established by the end of 1913 were in towns or cities. The high cost of providing facilities in thinly populated regions, where transport costs were a serious consideration, deterred most local authorities from providing them in the lowly-rated countryside. Occasionally the practitioner went to the country child as did the school dentist for Devonshire who took his equipment round with him in his car - an impossibility a decade or so earlier - and sent the other children out to play while he dealt with his patients in one-room rural schools. Over the country as a whole, the readiness of local authorities to spend money, the scale of charges they imposed on parents, the vigour with which Children's Care Committees 'followed up' the medical inspection, were some of the factors that influenced the individual child's chances of being relieved of his disability. The contrast between Breconshire, where 15 children out of 86 requiring treatment for their tonsils and adenoids obtained it, and Ashton-under-Lyme, where 37 out of 39 were treated in 1911, shows how misleading it is to think of a uniform standard of service at this time.[12]

The doctor's recommendation that a particular child be treated raised a series of problems for parents. Contemporaries, who complained of parental indifference, failed to realize how low were the standards of health the poor had for long accepted. Decayed teeth, poor eyesight, discharging ears, or body vermin were part and parcel of everyday life. The contact the poor had had with medical services had been minimal, frequently unpleasant, and usually confined to whatever the local poor law authorities offered. Hence the idea that childish complaints could be and should be cured was a novel one. The seemingly harsh judgment, 'Medical inspection in the elementary schools is necessary because the parents are ignorant. It is only a means to an end, and at present the end is the education of the people',[13] had some justification at a time when parents believed that body lice were a natural brood spontaneously generated from their own persons. Those who put their faith in such remedies as an infusion of roasted worms to cure discharging ears or a dose of live snails crushed in their shells and squeezed through muslim and brown sugar to revive a child laid out for dead were clear candidates for embourgeoisement by their social superiors.[14]

Before the establishment of school clinics parents had, in the main, three ways of obtaining treatment. They could go to a general practitioner if they could afford his fee, but they were unlikely to be able to afford any lengthy course of treatment for their children. The majority of doctors in poor areas were said to make no pretence to cure discharging ears, a process that required more than one visit. Even if a minor complaint required only one visit there was a limit to what a doctor would do for a fee of 1*s* 6*d* or so. Resort to the poor law dispensary or infirmary was a second possibility. However, definitions of destitution varied between union and union and had little to do with the medical needs of the patient. In addition Medical Orders were often issued by the relieving officer who had no medical knowledge. Applicants to the parish doctor could hope for little more than some medicine or a dressing. Poor law dispensaries, not possessing the facilities of an out-patients department of a hospital, did not offer any assistance for testing eyesight, nor did they make any provision for giving X-ray treatment for ringworm, dental treatment, or the daily syringing of discharging ears.

Finally parents could try the out-patients department of a large hospital. Since these were virtually confined to London and the major cities, many parents must have found them inaccessible. Even those who attended were not always adequately treated. Once medical inspections in schools began many hospitals found themselves overwhelmed by applicants and at loggerheads with the Local Education Authorities, despite the fact that less than half the children requiring treatment ever came. Visits to out-patients departments often involved long periods of waiting that could prove fruitless if the schools sent the children at the wrong time or to the wrong department. This was a serious matter for the accompanying mother or father who lost a day's wages needlessly. Not only were the voluntary hospitals ill-equipped to deal with the large numbers of children that presented themselves but the doctors objected to the volume of routine work entailed. Medical men, who regarded an honorary appointment at a voluntary hospital as a prestigious position, undertook the work involved without remuneration as a means of enhancing their professional expertise by working on medically interesting cases. They did not expect to have to spend their time dealing with batches of ringworm patients. At times their complaints were justified. After the teachers of the London School Board had examined the children's eyesight in the autumn of 1899, 800 children came in one week alone to the Royal Free Hospital. The staff were working up to 9.00 p.m. to cope with the numbers.[15]

Limitations of human and financial resources restricted the amount the voluntary hospitals could do. In many instances applicants for free or subsidized treatment had to obtain either a subscriber's letter of recommendation or a note from a charitable body. For instance parents taking their children to the Midland Eye Hospital, Birmingham, had to obtain one note for the opthalmic examination and then a further two to obtain the glasses prescribed. Parents had to tramp round the city visiting the agencies that issued the notes; in return for their subscriptions the hospitals allowed the charities to issue a quota of tickets. In collecting the necessary tickets the poorest, the least able to deal with officialdom and convince others of their bona fides, had the least success.[16]

The establishment of school clinics helped to remedy these deficiencies. On balance the better-off, more articulate and informed parents benefited most. They saw the value of treatment and did not regard bad health as their inevitable lot. Disqualified by their higher incomes from any form of financial assistance, they escaped the searching inquiries of the local Children's Care Committees whose responsibilities had grown considerably by 1910. By that year the duties of those in London and some of the major cities included the assessment of charges for school meals and medical treatment, the provision of play centres and other means of recreation during school holidays, the removal of neglected children from their homes, advising on the treatment of persistently verminous children and assistance with respect to the choice of suitable employment of boys and girls under the age of seventeen. Since these committees had grown out of the School Canteen Committees, the upshot of recent legislation had been to bring poorer parents and their children increasingly under the influence of social workers nurtured in the faith of the COS. In other words some of those who opposed, as a matter of principle, the use of public money for feeding children and curing their ailments were now determining which children should have what. The extent to which local persons frustrated the intent of the legislature cannot be estimated. However, there can be little doubt that some Care Committees took a censorious attitude and 'punished' the parents by withholding meals and other benefits from their children.

Finally, one has to remember that many parents and children must have preferred the disease to the remedy. No child could have regarded the prospect of either a tonsillectomy or the extraction of decayed teeth with any feeling except one of foreboding. Before 1914 dentists made sparing use of either general or local anaesthetics. For this reason the dental surgery in the LCC's clinics was 'always located in such a way as to enable children who have been treated to leave the centre without being seen by those awaiting treatment. Nothing demoralises', the LCC's dental officer explained, 'a room of waiting children more than the crying face of a child who has, perhaps, had some teeth extracted'. The use of any form of anaesthetic remained a luxury until after the First World War. A special report made to the Board of Education in 1919 recommended a 'general or local anaesthetic should, practically, always be used for the extract of permanent teeth; that for temporary teeth it is not generally necessary, unless several are to be extracted, when a general anaesthetic is very desirable; that local spray or other application is very useful for the extraction of loose or insignificant teeth or roots.' The same report condemned the giving of 'monetary bribes to children who silently endure painful extractions' as radically wrong. The infliction of unnecessary pain was anathematized as scientifically obsolete and deterrent of further treatment. The less drastic process of drilling a carious tooth could also be lengthy and painful when a foot-operated drill was used. Electrically driven dentist's drills, first introduced in 1908, were unlikely to have been widely used in school clinics until after 1918.[17]

The solving of the problem of preventing a haemorrhage during a tonsillectomy or adenoidectomy in the 1880s made surgeons readier to undertake these operations. In the early 1900s the enlargement of these organs was held responsible for mouth-breathing, a practice that contributed to stunted growth, stooping shoulders, and mental and physical sloth. The child with enlarged tonsils and adenoids was said to be two years behind the normal child in physique, health, weight, and mental activity.

The comparative novelty of the operation made parents and children face the prospect with apprehension. Those who went to the Charing Cross Hospital, London, where one would have expected high standards, had good grounds for their concern. In January 1911 the secretary of the Care Committee for St Peter's School, Holborn, complained to the LCC about its out-patients' department.

It appears that children are operated upon in that department in quite considerable numbers and are brought out of the operating room and laid on the floor of the ante-room in batches to recover consciousness, often with quite a considerable amount of blood on their garments, where they are seen by other children passing through to be operated on. The different mothers have to come in and take away their respective children. As may be imagined, several of the mothers have been very much upset, one or two fainting and going into hysterics, one woman going so far as to say that rather than go through the same experience again she would suffer whatever imprisonment would be the penalty of her refusal.

140

In reply the hospital admitted that children did lie on the floor after the operation, an arrangement they defended on the grounds of safety, and that blood escaping from the children's mouths soiled the garments they were wearing. They added that not only were the mothers not required to enter the recovery room but that the sister-in-charge had complained of 'the very great difficulty she has in keeping them out, especially the foreigners.' For a while parents apparently refused to send their children to the hospital until conditions improved.[18]

Children stayed only a short time in the hospital or school clinic in which the operation had taken place. At the Norwood School Treatment Centre patients were put in beds with hot water bottles for no more than two to three hours after the operation. It seems that the demand for the use of beds for other cases was too great to allow even a night's stay without a considerable expansion of existing resources. As Dr James Kerr explained, 'Whilst it may be expected that the retention by the hospital of every child operated on, for the night following the operation, would improve the results obtained, the improvement would be very costly.' Despite the cost involved the Board of Education encouraged Local Education Authorities to provide beds in their school clinics to allow the children to remain overnight after the operation. Authorities that kept the children for twenty-four hours, such as Southend-on-Sea and Birmingham, were singled out for praise. On discharge, parents were recommended to protect their children from dust and to give them cold soup and iced water, a diet that few could have provided. Such experiences did little to allay working-class fears of hospitals and operations under anaesthetic. As the outburst of the unknown mother at the Charing Cross Hospital suggests, Children's Care Committees put considerable moral pressure on parents to consent to the performance of a tonsillectomy. In extreme cases they prosecuted parents for refusing permission.[19]

Most of the work of the school medical service was curative, not preventive. The main exception to this rule was in the field of dentistry where teachers began to teach children to use toothbrushes. The recent war in South Africa had increased public concern about the dental health of the nation. The high casualty rate through sickness, said to be nearly double that of Prussian troops in the campaigns of 1870–1, led contemporaries to believe that the physical standards of the British army were deteriorating while those of our continental neighbours were improving. A proportion of the casualties were the result of gastric and intestinal complaints that were attributed, not so much to the climate, as to the soldier's inability to eat his rations properly. With a 'general absence of grinding teeth' men perforce had to swallow tough meat, often that of slaughtered trek-oxen, and hard biscuits without proper prior mastication. To cope with this problem one battalion had had to send to base for 'two large mincing machines', so serious was the matter. At the same time army medical officers were attaching more importance to the state of a volunteer's teeth. The rejection rate on this score had risen from 10·88 a thousand in 1891 to 63·26 a thousand by 1903. The army, which had sent four civilian dentists to the front in 1901, set an example by issuing the troops with toothbrushes. Unfortunately soldiers soon found, as have generations of barrack-room dwellers since, that one end of the brush provided an excellent means of cleaning brass buttons and the other a way of boning boots.

The 1904 Interdepartmental Committee mirroring this anxiety recommended the Board of Education to take steps to ensure that parents and teachers made children clean their teeth daily and that local education authorities instituted dental inspections. Amongst the first children to experience a daily toothbrush drill were those of the Hampstead, London, workhouse. In 1906 the London County Council decided to teach toothbrush drill to deaf children only 'it being looked upon in the light of an experiment'. The experiment was apparently successful for shortly afterwards LCC teachers began to form toothbrush clubs. Schools bought brushes wholesale at $2\frac{1}{4}d$ each and sold them at a profit of a farthing to provide free brushes for the poorest. Other children paid off their debts at a farthing or a halfpenny a week. They could also buy precipitated chalk in halfpenny lots. The poorer or more frugally minded used soot, a free but abrasive material. Schools also took care to ensure that the children actually used the brushes once they had been bought by keeping tooth-cleaning registers or having tooth-cleaning sessions as part of the daily timetable.

Before these initiatives were taken the toothbrush was virtually unknown in the homes of the poorest. One survey made in Swansea in 1906 of a school in a 'thickly populated working-class area' showed that 22 out of 150 children used a brush while in a 'better residential part of the town' 35 out of 150 did so. A year later a school medical officer of the LCC wrote 'among a thousand children I found two who used a toothbrush' while another reported 'A few older children take credit for using a toothbrush on Sundays.' Last, it was said of one school in Brixham that no child had cleaned its teeth until a club was formed in 1912; at the Church school in Totnes the proportion of children using brushes rose from 4 per cent to 75 per cent on the establishment of a toothbrush club the same year.[20]

By March 1914 the basic task of ensuring that local authorities had a scheme of medical inspection that met the requirements of the Board of Education was nearing completion. Every local education authority had a principal medical officer but 22 areas were still without approved schemes of inspection. Although the Board of Education's Chief Medical Officer had actively encouraged each authority to provide medical treatment, a number were content to do no more than meet their minimum obligation of inspecting the children. There were 127 areas that had not yet taken any steps to start a school clinic, 139 that operated one or more, while a further 51 had submitted schemes to the Board. The range of services offered varied. For instance, 13 clinics, including the only one in the County Borough of Lancashire, provided dental treatment only. At the same date 53 authorities, including some of those with clinics, were making contributions to hospitals for the treatment of children. Roughly a third of all authorities, 125 including 14 county councils, provided spectacles at low cost, when not free, to the parents. Lastly there were 84 authorities with dental clinics capable of treating an estimated 250,000 children a year. Some districts provided more than one of these services. On the debit side there were 77 authorities that had not yet done anything. During the First World War progress continued at a slower pace. By 1918, although the number of authorities providing clinics, spectacles, and making financial contributions to hospital had increased to 252, 110, and 235 respectively, 31 had remained resolutely inactive.[21]

In London, Bradford, Bristol, and a few other cities the Children's Care Committees supervised the task of 'following up' children after their medical examination and took over the task of selecting children for school meals. At the other extreme parents had to use whatever voluntary facilities, charities, and other services were available. Although there was no uniform means of dealing with the child needing medical treatment, all authorities using money from the rates to feed children had to have a supervisory body. These committees variously called School Canteen Committees, Children's Aid Committees, or the Children's Aid Association, differed in their composition from town to town. Whether or not they took on responsibility for a child's medical treatment as well, their major preoccupation was that of authorizing school meals for the individual child.

The prototype of these bodies had preceded the 1906 Act. Because of the scale of the social problems confronting the London schools, the London School Board had been the first authority to make a major effort to see that children did not abuse the good offices of the charitable. After rejection the recommendation made in 1899 that the rates should be used to help to provide school meals, the London School Board had appointed a Joint Committee on Underfed Children. This body, formed to demonstrate that voluntary subscriptions would be sufficient and that no demands needed to be made on the rates, looked to the day when it would have eliminated 'those not really in need of food' from the list of underfed children. To achieve this it set up sub-committees to supervise the schools and kept a close watch on the numbers fed. So careful was this supervision that individual head-masters had to account for any significant increase in the number of children fed in their schools. Some feeding agencies understandably objected to the interference of an outside body, an attitude that the Joint Committee condemned as mistaken. 'This feeling, that those who pay the piper may call the tune, . . . is opposed to the higher principle which looks upon the distribution of charity as a sacred trust to be executed with the utmost caution to avoid the demoralization of those who are relieved . . . .'[22]

In London caution prevailed. The Joint Committee's report for the winter of 1906–7 showed that the new legislation had not brought a change of heart.

We have felt grave anxiety lest the provisions of the Act should be so worked as to encourage the demand for meals by the too lavish supply, and lest the sense of parents towards their children should be weakened by this relief . . . . We have repeated in this *Report* what we have always maintained, . . . that all the relief required by necessitious children can be met from voluntary contributions, provided that the organization for enquiry into want, for collecting subscriptions, and for distributing food, is rendered effective,

sentiments that the Royal Commission on the Poor Laws endorsed. Despite these brave words, the Education Committee resolved in December 1909 to draw a maximum of £10,000 from the rates for school meals, a decision that caused *The Times* to comment,[23]

The Socialists are openly jubilant at the prospect of the breakdown of voluntary effort . . . . For the same reasons that recourse to the rates rejoices the Socialists it must be regarded as a contingency to be

144

deplored, and if possible averted, by those who take the opposite view of social well-being.

This same concern to ensure that the expenditure of public money on school meals was carefully scrutinized and that parents did not abandon their responsibilities to their children is a theme of both the majority and the minority reports of the Royal Commission on the Poor Laws. Both reports pointed to the undesirability of having two bodies, the local education authorities and the boards of guardians, providing relief for school children. The majority report, unlike the dissenting minor one, did not think the Local Education Authorities possessed the machinery necessary for supervising the home, 'an essential factor in the relief of children'. They accordingly wanted the Public Assistance Committees, bodies they proposed to create, to take over the provision of meals. In rejecting this suggestion, the authors of the minority report argued that the boards of guardians had failed in their duty of relieving distress amongst children. Not only was the provision of outdoor relief to feed the hungry insufficient and badly organized but medical relief, when granted, was given grudgingly. The guardians 'have been praised for deterring people from applying for medical orders by means of inquisitorial enquiries, . . . and even making it a condition of relief that the head of the family should enter a work-house when his child was ill.' Of equal concern to the dissenting four was other evidence of inefficiency. With two authorities in the field, families in receipt of outdoor relief could obtain free school meals for their children and thus be doubly relieved. For good measure the Distress Committee under the Unemployed Workmen Act might be giving relief work and wages to a father who obtained meals for his children at a school, clothing for them from a local police fund as well as other gifts from private charities. In conclusion they reported 'these competing systems of relieving child destitution by rival Local Authorities in the same town – in many cases simultaneously assisting the same children – without effective machinery for recovering the cost from parents able to pay, and for prosecuting neglectful parents, are undermining parental responsibility, whilst still leaving many thousands of children inadequately fed.' To end the 'wasteful and demoralizing overlapping' they wanted the local authority to be responsible for all the relief the state made available to school children. To demonstrate the suitability of the local education authority for this work, they argued that the LCC's campaign to cleanse dirty heads had 'actually a tendency to increase parental responsibility'. Through their readiness to use the final sanction of prosecuting neglectful mothers, the LCC had been able to reduce the number of verminous children in school. In this instance 'The expenditure from public funds, far from being "relief" to the parents, has actually been the means of compelling the less responsible among them to devote more time and money to their children's welfare.' Thus the Local Education Authorities, working through their Children's Care Committees, were well equipped to seek out and relieve child destitution and could ensure that parents did not shrug off their responsibilities. They could deal with the parent 'recalcitrant to moral persuasion' in one of two ways, either by prosecuting him under the Children Act, 1908, or by sending the child at the parent's expense to an industrial school. The latter action ensured the proper feeding of the child without relieving the 'careless or neglectful parent' of the cost and was thought to be as effective as invoking the Children Act for 'bringing to an end a large amount of wanton parental neglect to provide meals.' In conclusion, the legislation of the past few years now made possible the efficient discharge of the welfare task of 'searching out every child destitute of the necessities of life' and of enforcing parental responsibility, if necessary by punitive means, when moral persuasion failed.[24]

The assumption that the Children's Care Committees would seek out every undernourished child was misplaced. Better founded was their conviction that the committees would not allow a profligate expenditure of any public money entrusted them. It was a common criticism that the cost of the enquiries into the circumstances of applicants exceeded the amount recovered from them. Some saw this as money well spent for it had taught the parent a valuable lesson. To an extent impossible to measure, the school canteen committees contained members who had personal scruples about using public money to feed children gratuitously. They saw themselves as guardians of the public purse, as bastions against the onward march of socialist measures, rather than as diligent searchers of childish destitution. They thwarted the intent of the legislature to make food available to 'any of the children attending a public elementary school . . . unable by reason of lack of food to take full advantage of the education provided'.

The *Economic Review*, the journal of the Oxford University Branch of the Christian Social Union, published an account of such a committee in 1912. The chairman and author of the article was the Rev. H. Iselin, curate of St. George's in the East, London, 1898-1916, a firm advocate of the tenets of the COS. His committee worked on the basis that the nature of relief should not be superior to that which parents could provide in employment, according to the standard of life prevailing in the district. Yet his was a parish where 173 of the 189 claimant fathers had no skilled or regular occupation. They were labourers, carmen, or odd-job men who did 'anything'. For many the only regular employment was three six-week stints on the wool cargoes in the docks a year. Nearly three-quarters of the women bringing up children alone went out charring. Overall 91 per cent of the men and 77 per cent of the women wanting food for their children had no distinct calling. Yet Iselin castigated his parisioneers for having given no practical forethought to their problems and for having failed to make any provision for the loss of wages through sickness. He saw the Education (Provision of Meals) act as harmful to the morals of benefactor and recipient alike. It tempted the poor to 'sell their birthright of parental responsibility for a mess of pottage'. It detached the taint of pauperism from relief; beneficiaries felt no sense of gratitude nor did they feel any loss of prestige. The Act posed a temptation to the Care Committee for 'nothing is so popular as giving away other people's money'. By providing a breakfast of porridge and milk the Committee maintained its moral probity intact for 'This food was distributed at such an hour and was of such a character as to constitute in itself a definite test of need.' The net result of Iselin's activities was that the percentage of children fed by his committee was less than one half of that of the neighbouring schools. In this poverty stricken part of London he had fed 2·9 per cent of the school children in December 1910; the 6·6 per cent fed in other local schools could only have represented the fringe of the problem.[25]

However atypical Iselin's committee may have been, it was no more than an extreme example of the general parsimony with which local authorities implemented the Act. On no occasion did they ever regularly feed the 10 per cent of children the Board of Education had conservatively estimated to be undernourished. Despite the start of medical examinations it remains difficult to provide a more accurate estimate of the incidence of malnutrition from official sources as the data provided by medical officers varied so much. These differences, partly reflecting the social and economic circumstances of the localities, are further influenced by the dissimilarity of the criteria doctors adopted. Amongst the counties returning the highest figures were Bedforshire with 26·1 per cent, Durham, 24·1 per cent, Westmorland, 23·7 per cent, and Staffordshire 13·4 per cent. Towns high on the list include Bradford, 55·8 per cent, St Helens, 17·5 per cent, Tynemouth, 17·1 per cent, Todmorden, 28·5 per cent, Widnes, 19·7 per cent and Shipley, 24·3 per cent. When one considers the towns not appearing on the list in which social and economic conditions were similar to those picked out above, one realizes the importance of the social and political assumptions that underlay doctors' judgments about what constituted undernourishment.[26]

Symptomatic of the primacy of poor-relief considerations was the failure of committees to make the school doctor a key figure in the referral process. Although a few doctors recommended children for free dinners, such children were in the minority. In the few districts where doctors were consulted, they played a subordinate role. Children were referred to them by the Care Committees as a second filter in the selection process. This subordination of the doctor to the Care Committee was contrary to the wishes of the Board who wanted medical men to approve the dietary, supervise the cooking arrangements, and to select the children on medical criteria.

The fundamental problem was a confusion of purpose. It was all very well for Dr George Newman, the newly appointed Chief Medical Officer to the Board of Education, to see the purpose of the Act as primarily educational: the requirements of the Act and the general expectation of the period - for instance the minority report of the Royal Commission on the Poor Laws - made it a form of relief administered by a new agency. The Board of Education's Circular 552 of 1 January 1907 advocated that parents should be required to pay in advance, whenever possible, for school meals and reminded local authorities of their statutory duty to recover payment from all applicants according to their means. Local persons, whatever their views on the expediency of using public money to feed school children, perforce had recourse to explicit poverty tests based on enquiries into family income or implicit ones where individual cases were decided on their merits. These practices stamped the meals with the stigmata of pauperism and poor relief, especially when a local committee contained a poor law guardian. Not surprisingly parents, faced with a demand for prepayment, confused this new relief with the older outdoor relief. Knowing that committees sometimes approached employers for details of their wage packets some refused to allow their children to have school meals. Others, when required to appear before a committee, failed to attend. In Birmingham more than a fifth of all applicants, 4,700 out of 22,753, were turned down between 1909 and 1911 because no parent had kept his appointment. Apart from any feelings of diffidence and objections to the practice of making enquiries of employers, parents faced practical problems as well. To keep his appointment an unemployed man might have had to abandon his search for work and, as occasionally happened, pay tram fares to arrive on time to prove his inability to feed his children. Even if an applicant arrived on time there was no guarantee that he would receive prompt attention. A small-scale survey suggests that, contrary to expectation, the absentees were not the potential scroungers whom the appointments system was designed to deter. The home circumstances of the absentees were much the same as those of the families whose applications were granted. A working-class tradition of independence was as effective as any official machinery in making any applicant think twice about asking for what he saw as a barely disguised form of relief or charity.[27]

As before 1906, the provision of school meals remained an urban phenomenon. By 1914 nearly three-quarters of the county boroughs, about half the urban districts, but only one-sixth of the counties had used the Act at some time or another. The Board reported 'The counties, however, have only put the Act into force in a few scattered localities, and it is hardly too much to say that in practice the Act has been a dead letter over the whole rural area of England and Wales.' Some of the worst conditions under which meals were served were in the countryside. In one instance 'Children had spoons only, and being unable to attack the meat with those, they either left it, tore it to pieces with their fingers, or lifted it bodily out of the plates and chewed at it.' At another rural centre seventeen children used a table that seated seven in a shed approached through a yard containing fowls and the family washing. The ten who stood took their pastry in a piece of paper and then departed. Of the seven who could sit one had a knife and fork, the remaining six had spoons for the meat course. To put these accounts into some perspective one needs to know how familiar the various strata of the working classes were with the use of table cutlery at the end of the nineteenth century. For instance some contemporary observers reported that 'Many neglected children do not know how to use a knife or fork. They do not even know how to use a spoon.' It was also explained that some children bolted their food, not because their manners were consciously bad, but because they had never been taught to use cutlery and their teeth were bad. Finally one should remember that 'eating irons' were not issued to naval ratings

149

until after Sir John Fisher became First Sea Lord on Trafalgar Day 1904.[28]

The number of children fed by local authorities reached a peak in 1912, the year of the coal miners' and dockers' strikes. That year 137 authorities, the largest number to invoke the Act before the collapse of the post-war boom, fed 358,306 children at some time or other during the year. This total was markedly below the 550,000 or so that constituted 10 per cent of the elementary-school population. 1912, a year in which voluntary contributions totalled nearly £6,000 was the last one for which they exceeded £1,000. By 1918–19 they were under £1, having fallen steadily from £17,831, an incomplete figure for 1908–9. The rapid fall after 1912, reflecting the winding up of voluntary funds once local authorities began to use the rates, may have been accelerated by reactions to the labour disputes of that year. In London the dockers' strike caused some to question the desirability of spending either public or private funds on feeding the strikers' children. An attempt by the Education Committee of the LCC to use an act of 1887 to provide meals out of the rates for the children was defeated by one vote; the argument that the Committee was not justified in using ratepayers' money to feed the children of those who had unwisely thrown themselves out of work just carried the day. Similarly a fund opened in West Ham with an initial contribution of £2,000 attracted only another £362 for fear of prolonging the strike.[29]

Throughout the pre-war years the idea that a man's inability to feed his children was a temporary misfortune prevailed. Children were usually granted meals for a fortnight or a month at a time and then had their cases reviewed. Few authorities made any attempt to provide meals throughout the year. Hence the average number of meals given a child a year fluctuated between 60 and 65. In the year ending 31 March 1910, the six cities of Birmingham, Bradford, Bristol, Leeds, Manchester and Sheffield, fed no more than 17,701 for three months or longer out of the 38,943 for whom meals were provided at some time during the year.[30]

Despite earlier assumptions to the contrary, the Act did not allow the feeding of children at public expense during the school holidays or on Saturdays and Sundays. After some initial confusion over the matter the District Auditor disallowed West Ham's expenditure from the rates on school meals during the Christmas holiday of 1908. Some authorities then began to rely on voluntary contributions or, as happened at Bradford and elsewhere, other forms of revenue such as trading profits. During two special occasions, the school holidays for the king's coronation in 1911 and the miners' strike of the following year, the Local Government Board made special provision.[31] After a series of unsuccessful attempts by members of the Labour party to introduce private bills, the Education (Provision of Meals) Act of 1914, which received its third reading in the House of Commons the day war was declared on Germany, rectified the situation. It also removed the halfpenny limit on expenditure from the rates, a restriction that had particularly hit poor and lowly rated urban districts such as West Ham where local means were hard pressed to meet local needs. It had also adversely affected mining and industrial villages as the amount that could be used was restricted to the product of a halfpenny rate in the parishes served by the school, yet the rate was levied over the administrative county as a whole. Last, local authorities no longer had to obtain prior permission from the Board of Education before using public funds.

As a result of a temporary rise in unemployment in the early weeks of the war and the enlistment of men in the armed forces the number of children fed reached a wartime peak of 195,751 at the beginning of October. Once mothers began to receive their separation allowances and the economy revived, the numbers fed at public expense began to fall until they reached the low figure of 36,550 in the year ending March 1919. With more mothers working full-time during the war the number paying for their meals rose to 15,940. Whereas despite the efforts of the various Care Committees no more than £2,430 had been recovered from the parents in 1912–13, parents paid £21,985 in 1918–19. Lastly, the average cost of food for a meal varied between 1·27d in 1912–13 and 1·5d in 1914–15. By 1918–19 it reached 3·73d, an increase broadly in line with the rise in the cost of living over the same period.[32]

Throughout the inter-war years, the schools meals service remained an educational Cinderella despite the high level of unemployment. By 1933 nearly all the large industrial towns were providing meals, but some of the county authorities, the comparatively prosperous seaside towns, and small county towns were still doing nothing. During the school year, 1933–4, when over two million workers were registered as unemployed, 158,543 children received free school meals. They were also providing free milk to nearly a third of a million children. By the outbreak of the Second World War 15·5 per cent of all children in local authority schools were receiving some form of free sustenance (11·5 per cent free milk; 1·2 per cent free solid meals; 2·8 per cent free milk and solid meals). The 110,000 children having free meals usually took theirs at a feeding centre. Those 50,000 who paid for school dinners, mainly children living some distance from their schools, fed at school canteens, a form of social discrimination that did not end until the amalgamation of the facilities in December 1940. In the summer of that year, before the Battle of Britain had been fought and while invasion still seemed a real possibility, steps were taken to improve the scope and quality of the school meals service. By September 1941, against a background of the U-Boat campaign, the rationing of essential foods, and higher infant death and tuberculosis rates, a further expansion of the service took place.[33] Wartime exigencies helped to rid, but did not entirely eradicate, earlier opposition to feeding children at the expense of the ratepayer; thus the school meals service still arouses a political ardour that makes it a popular candidate for cuts in expenditure in times of financial stringency.

Part Three

In and Out of the School

VII

Schools, Parents and Children

In November 1875 *The Times* reported two cases involving the London School Board in adjoining columns thereby drawing attention to some of the less happy aspects of the new Education Act. One report dealt with the appearance in court of a father who was fined for failing to send his child to school. The defendant, an old soldier, substantiated his claim that he could not pay the school fee by pointing out that he could not afford to buy boots for his son. To corroborate his father's testimony the boy had come to court barefooted. In another court a school attendance officer of the same Board gave evidence against a boy who had assaulted him and abused him. 'A rough crowd assembled' and 'threatened to "do" him if he took out a summons.'[1]

These two reports suggest that the poorest were the first to feel the full impact of the new legislation. Unfortunately we lack analyses of the occupations of the parents whose children were being put on the school registers for the first time in the years immediately after 1870. We also know little about the social background of those who were brought before the courts because their children missed school once their names were on the rolls. Nevertheless there are good reasons for suggesting that the hard working respectable poor were the first to bear the full brunt of the ministrations of the school attendance officer and not the poorest, the group whom many saw as the target of the legislation of 1870.

Those parents who had already been sending their children to school before 1870, as and when family circumstances had permitted, were comparatively easy to trace. Visiting the schools to find out the names of irregular attenders, going to their homes to ask why they were not attending, were easier tasks for hard pressed officials than seeking out children hitherto unknown to the authorities. The children of the poorest, the social class for whom many saw the board schools as their proper destination, were the most elusive and evaded the effective working of the law the longest. The experience of a factory inspector, in pursuit of a boy illegally employed instead of attending school, provides a telling example. The official wanted to trace a boy known as Sam Collins. He discovered that this was the boy's nickname given him in allusion to a popular music hall singer of the period. After establishing the boy's real name, he went to the local police who found a 'woman who knew where the wife pawned'. By the time the inspector reached the boy's last known address the family had 'hand-moved'. Difficulties such as these, combined with the frequency with which families moved, made it virtually impossible for the school boards of large urban areas to keep their information up to date in their poorest districts, the very ones most needing supervision. In the 'lowest areas' of Birmingham the officials were constantly taking censuses at first; consequently in 1878 there were some districts that they had not been able to tackle for the last four years. In a plea of mitigation the Birmingham School Board pointed to Liverpool's experience where the Board had adopted an elaborate system of removable slips for their school visitors' books. Despite this archival flexibility the Liverpool authorities had not been able to keep up to date either. Some boards conducted raids of doubtful legality to round up the children and haul them off to school. In Manchester these sorties into the urban jungle had led to affrays when parents had tried to rescue the captives. Police then had to be summoned to rescue the would-be captors.[2]

So strong was the antipathy to the school-board officials that it was argued that parents were under no legal obligation to answer their questions. A handbill circulated in one part of London in 1874 advised them,

When you are asked any question about your children . . . give this answer 'I have nothing to say to you', and get rid of the inquisitor as soon as possible. There is no clause in the Elementary Education Act which compels any person to answer any question put by the School Board or their agents. Never let them come into your home, but speak to them outside. Some of them walk into your rooms, if they do so, order them out; and if they refuse to go after being told, put them out, if you are strong enough.

Strictly speaking this advice was sound enough; however, the parent who summarily ejected a school board visitor soon found out that officialdom had other powers at its disposal. The 1873 Act had given JPs the power to demand the production of a child before the bench. Moreover, if a child was apparently of school age the onus lay with the parent to prove otherwise and to show, if required, that the said child was attending school in accordance with the local bye-laws.[3]

Although parents had no means of making good the earnings lost when their children went to school, short of invoking the uncertain mercies of the relieving officer, the 1870 Act gave them two means of obtaining free education for their children. School boards could remit the fees charged at their own schools and pay those of children at voluntary schools. The latter power, denounced by nonconformists as a clandestine revival of the compulsory church rate under another name, became a matter of political and religious controversy out of all proportion to the amount spent. In 1874 it was £6,256. The Elementary Education Act of 1876 transferred power to the poor law guardians who already had been able for the previous three years to pay the fees of children whose parents were on outdoor relief. Last, outside the field of statutory provision, there was nothing to stop managers of voluntary schools from remitting fees in their own schools if they so desired.

The guardians used their powers sparingly. During the school year, 1875–6, they paid the fees of 57,196 children, of whom 12,625 attended board schools. By 1890–1, the school year before which free education became widely available, the figures had become 170,311 and 35,847 respectively, approximately 4 per cent of the 4,800,000 children on the registers. Parents seeking payment from the guardians were usually expected to appear before them, a requirement that could involve a considerable journey for those living in a rural area followed by a long wait, all for twopence or threepence a week. The majority report of the Cross Commission, published in 1888, quoted the testimony of one witness with approval.

'They feel the humiliation, not only of seeking relief at all, but of having to ask *in forma pauperis*; they have to go to the same office, and to the same officer, as if they were applying for outdoor relief, and the same time of attendance is generally appointed for them. They object to the exposure of their private family circumstances, and to the offensive examination subsequently by the relieving officer, who goes through the rooms of their homes, and makes inquiries at the workshops and works, and so on; and they also object to the harshness and oppressiveness of the guardians, who treat every applicant more or less as an impostor, or as being lazy or inebriate.' Similar objections are repeated over and over again.

The witness, a diocesan inspector of Roman Catholic schools for Westminster, instanced the parsimony of his local guardians. Out of 24,000 children, many of whom were 'exceedingly poor', the guardians had paid the fees of only 153 or 154 in 1886.[4] The voluntarist majority of the Cross Commission, anticipating the spirit of the minority report of the Poor Law Commissioners by nearly a generation, went on to recommend the transfer of the power of the poor law guardians to pay the fees of indigent children to the district councils proposed in the Local Government Bill then before parliament. To some extent the Commissioners, in their concern to save the poor from the indignity of being classified as paupers, were pleading their own case. The voluntary schools were the chief sufferers of the guardians' husbanding of the ratepayer's money.

As a general rule those parents who wanted board school fees remitted found officialdom only marginally more pleasant. During the school year, 1874–5, school boards remitted the fees of 1·89 per cent of the children in their schools. By the mid-1880s the proportion had reached 4·43 per cent over the country as a whole. There were wide variations. Birmingham, the home of the National Education League with its commitment to free education, made 33 per cent of its places free. Huddersfield gave free education to 6 per cent, London provided only 4 per cent of its places free.[5]

Voluntary school managers showed a similar variation in their readiness to remit fees. Roman Catholic schools, with a high proportion of very poor children in their classrooms for whom the faithful were prepared to make great sacrifices, made more than 10 per cent of their places free. With an average of 2 to 3 per cent of the places in Anglican schools free and a further 4 to 5 per cent in British schools, the proportion of free places in board and voluntary schools hovered around the 5 per cent mark throughout the two decades after 1870. With a further 4 per cent who had their fees paid by the poor law guardians the proportion of free places in all elementary schools was still under 10 per cent by 1890–1. School managers, whether of voluntary or board schools, had good reason to be chary of remitting fees. Such a practice reduced the school's local income, a figure that the Education Department did not allow the annual grant to exceed. This administrative legacy of the doctrine of local self-help was just one way in which a poor school became doubly disadvantaged.[6]

For the working classes as a whole the introduction of compulsory education imposed a considerable extra burden on the family budget until 1891. Weekly fees in voluntary schools rose from an average annual total of 8s 4¼d in 1870 to 11s 3½d by 1891. Board schools, non-existent in 1870, charged an average of 9s 1¼d by 1891. Average attendance more than trebled from 1,152,389 in 1870 to 3,749,956 by 1891. Total annual expenditure on school fees almost quadrupled from £502,023 in 1870 to £1,969,370 twenty years later. If 1850 is taken as the base year real income, not allowing for unemployment, rose from 118 in 1870 to 169 by 1890. Although this rise outstripped that of the fees in voluntary schools and board schools were slightly cheaper, one must remember that for many parents paying for schooling represented an entirely new financial burden. Moreover, the poorer families suffered a particular disadvantage. They probably had to keep their children longer at school than did more prosperous families, to enable them to qualify by reaching the Standards requisite for full- or part-time exemption from attendance.[7]

As the London School Board remitted the same proportion of school fees as the country as a whole until the mid-1880s, an examination of its policy is of wider interest. Initially it made a determined effort to see that parents paid the comparatively low fees it charged. During the first three years of its existence it paid the fees of only 254 children and remitted those of another 304. A debate on a motion to provide free education for a number of children in 1872 shows the strength of the Board's reluctance to be more generous. Typical of the cases considered was that of a widow with three children who never earned more than 9s a week. It was argued that if the Board paid the fees 'the number of applicants for free education would be multiplied indefinitely . . . and effect a revolution . . . for it would bring about free education generally'. Arguments based on this fear prevailed in a thinly attended meeting that rejected the motion by 15 votes to 9. To show the reverse side of the coin, parents granted remission the following February included a clerk with a terminal illness supporting a family of seven on 9s a week, a labourer earning 12s a week, and a shoemaker with a consumptive wife and ten children earning 16s a week.[8]

Ten years later George Sims gave some examples of parents who had been ordered to appear before the school managers to show cause why they should not be summonsed before a magistrate and fined for failing to send their children to school, a procedure that gave them a chance of pleading their poverty. One was a mother of seven children for each of whom she had to pay 2d a week. The total earnings of the family were 10s a week, of which 5s 6d went on rent. The father hawked fish and vegetables. The half-starved children ate the oranges that were too bad to sell. Another was a father with eight children of school age, with neither an income nor parish relief, about to pawn his last rags.[9]

The breakthrough for poor parents came after the judgment in *London School Board v. Wright*, following which the Board found it could no longer allow credit or collect arrears, for 'If a poor parent were allowed credit for the school fees with the consequent liability to be sued for arrears the burden might become intolerable'.[10] Although this might be seen as relieving the poor of a burden the first reaction of the Board was to make a determined effort to secure the prepayment of all fees. In the long term the Board was caught in an impasse. If a parent sent a child to school without his school pence the Board could prosecute him for failing to cause his child to attend school in accordance with its bye-laws. This course of action raised further problems. Until the case was heard the child was free to work illegally and earn more than enough money to pay the small fine that was eventually imposed. Thereby the Board earned the contempt of some and the hostility of others. If the Board admitted the child without his weekly pence, however, it forfeited all legal right to recover any arrears.

After rejecting a scheme sponsored by Helen Taylor, the stepdaughter of John Stuart Mill, and Benjamin Lucraft to remit school fees where the family *per capita* income, excluding rent did not exceed 6d a day, the London School Board produced its own plan. From the autumn of October 1886 children who came without their pence were to be sent home. Their parents, regardless of whether or not they were literate, were to be given a comprehensive questionnaire about their family circumstances to complete. The fifty or more Radical Clubs in the Metropolitan Radical Federation advised parents to stop paying school fees altogether and organized a rally to be held in Trafalgar Square on Sunday 3 October, the day before the new plan was due to start. The police, fearing a repetition of the disorders of the previous February when a march of the unemployed had caused damage in the West End, were out in force to control a meeting addressed by Bernard Shaw, William Morris, John Burns, H. H. Champion, and others. The Trafalgar Square demonstration was by no means the only occasion of popular protest against school fees. The working men of Norwich, a city with a long history of radical protest, had launched a similar campaign eight years earlier.[11] In London despite all the Federation's efforts there was no popular boycott of the Board's demands. *The Times* claimed that only one parent sent the questionnaire back commenting 'I claim the same right to have my children educated free as is now accorded to the aristocracy.' However, in the long run the Board had secured a Pyrrhic victory. At the Orange Street Board School, Southwark, for instance, where over 200 came without their money the new regulations produced an extra 10s 4d. School managers, who had the power to remit fees, found a multitude of cases in the poorer areas. Their attitude varied. In some cases parents had to wait until as late as 11 p.m. to see a school manager and claim twopence or so a week. On the other hand another manager was credited with remitting 4,000 cases in one division.[12]

Following this experience the proportion of free places in London board schools grew more rapidly than in the country at large until it reached 22·02 per cent in 1891. This did not relieve the poorest entirely. Two years earlier Charles Booth had estimated that 30·7 per cent of Londoners lived in poverty. The solution came in 1891 by which date *The Times* had discerned a change in public attitude. 'The great majority of the public . . . are clearly of the opinion that the enforcement of compulsory education upon the poor, at their own expense, was a grievance from which they might reasonably seek relief; and that '– here *The Times* re-echoed the arguments of the classical economists – 'if the education were given with a view to the benefit of the entire community, the community might fairly be asked to make the necessary provision.' The 1891 Act removed a more subtle barrier to working-class progress, the practice of charging higher fees in the upper standards to force cheap juvenile labour on to the market.[13]

The need to pay school fees had brought the parents one consolation, that of regarding themselves as the teacher's paymaster. The church schoolmaster was in a doubly dependent position. The subscriptions of local philanthropists that helped to provide the school with part of his salary made him their hireling; parents paying twopence or threepence a week saw him as their employee. Before 1870 parents had been able to act like any other purchaser of goods or services. If they had not liked what was on offer, they had been able to take their custom elsewhere. It was a common complaint that if teachers were too strict over punctuality, regularity of attendance, or in the view of the parents, punished children too frequently, the children were taken away. The more relaxed attitude of the private adventure school teacher accounts for much of the popularity of such schools. Moreover, working-class parents found such teachers, drawn from the same social milieu as themselves, more approachable than the managers and teachers

161

of a voluntary school. After 1870 as compulsory attendance at a school declared efficient by the Education Department, the local justices of the peace or the school board gradually became enforced, parents found their freedom of choice more and more circumscribed. Yet at the same time that the schoolmaster realized that he could demand higher standards of conduct and enforce a stricter discipline, the cash nexus continued to encourage parents to go on thinking that they were the teacher's clients if not his employers. Given parental resentment at having to submit to a new form of authority imposed on them by the state, such a confusion of roles bred further conflict especially when children were punished.

The educational journals regularly debated the efficacy or otherwise of the use of corporal punishment. At one extreme its supporters cited scriptural injunctions to justify their cause. One who did so proceeded to argue,

So far from doing away with corporal punishment, I would do away, if it were necessary, with all other punishment, for surely we cannot hope that our children will turn out holy men and women without the blessing of God; and how can we hope for a blessing if we dare resign the means ordained by God and substitute others in their place.

The argument that the only form of punishment should be corporal provoked correspondents to the *Monthly Paper of the National Society* in 1868 to point out that ultimately the running of their schools depended on parental consent. One contributor admitted that the plan 'might be adopted in country schools; but in our large towns, especially in London, I fear its introduction would cause a great outcry.' Another after advocating the merits of birching 'with due deliberation, and with all solemnity, in the hearing, though out of sight, of the school', saw a snag. 'How far would parents amongst the lower classes tolerate it? And if not, could they be gradually reconciled to it?'[14]

Parental attitudes to the physical punishment of their children varied considerably. Robert Roberts in *The Classic Slum* relates that parents in Salford, on hearing that their children had been beaten at school, gave them another thrashing at home.[15] Other parents saw the schoolmaster as a public flagellator who would punish their children if requested. This view received quasi-official endorsement. Children caught truanting by the school attendance officer, instead of being handed over to the courts, were sent to the schoolmaster for chastisement. Sometimes the courts themselves, rather than send a child to a reformatory or industrial school, secured parental consent and directed his school-master to flog him.[16] Although parents in such a case may have had little option but to acquiesce there were others who brought a charge of assault against the teacher concerned. Motives, according to cases reported in the *Schoolmaster* were mixed. Just as there were some with what appear to be justified grievances there were others who started proceedings as a blackmailing tactic to induce the teacher concerned to part with a sovereign as a consideration for dropping the case. Simi-larly, a summons could misfire if it came out in court that the child was more severely treated at home.

Generalizations about the magistracy are hard to make. However, the courts usually stood by the schoolmaster who had been assaulted by a parent irate at the detention of his child after school or because he had been beaten. Since schoolmasters had to be provided with police escort in extreme cases,[17] magistrates must have felt their natural inclination to support the pedagogic representatives of law and order amply justified.

The fate of the schoolmaster charged with assault was more problematic. In 1880 the *Schoolmaster* reported two cases where the magistrates fined the defendants either because of their own personal opposition to the use of corporal punishment or the vividness of their own schoolday recollections. In contrast, twenty years later the chair-man of another bench dismissed a case arguing that if the sons of gentlemen submitted to a birching that drew blood then the summons brought before him was ridiculous. In yet another case the chairman of the bench visited the school in question after dismissing a case brought against a mistress. He told the children that as he thought the cane exhibited in court the previous day was not strong enough, he was presenting the teacher with another he had bought specially for the purpose.

The magistracy, recognizing the clergy as their social equals, treated them with leniency despite the dubiousness of their right to share the schoolmaster's claim of acting *in loco parentis*. Two examples have the added interest of illustrating the kind of authority that the clergy had been able to wield in the countryside until their parishioners were brave enough to challenge it. In one case an incumbent was fined a shilling after beating a boy who had attended a special Wesleyan service on a Sunday. As it came out in evidence that the lad had been absent from school for several months on weekdays tending cows the punishment seemed to breach the spirit of the conscience clause of the 1870 Act.

Yet in imposing the fine the chairman of the bench expressed his regret that a gentleman to whom the parish owed so much should be put to such inconvenience. On another occasion an incumbent was fined the same sum for birching a boy. The defendant had forced his way into the boy's home and then dragged him off to school. In neither of these instances can one argue that the legal issue of assault was the crucial factor that had led parents to take out a summons.[18]

To say that the cane was used excessively in the elementary schools and that the magistracy was unsympathetic to the complaints is to judge the past too readily by the standards of the present. Public executions were not abolished until two years before Forster introduced his bill into the House of Commons and branding in the Army only a year afterwards. The abolition of flogging in the Army did not come until 1881, a year after the introduction of universal compulsory education. Although the humanitarian argument was not necessarily the prime cause of these reforms, they helped to produce a less cruel and violent society. The discussion on the birching of girls conducted in the *Englishwoman's Domestic Magazine* during 1870 reflects the same conflict between the old and the new. Those who advocated birching on the bare buttocks described it as 'birching in the old fashioned way', in other words they were supporting the perpetuation of what they saw as the normal practice of an earlier age. On the other hand approximately half the correspondents found the whole debate and practice distasteful, if not indecent. Yet it is clear that the daughters of some of the 'best connected families in the land' were still being birched at a time that Poor Law Board regulations theoretically safeguarded girls in workhouses from any form of physical punishment. Similarly birching was still a normal practice in the schools their brothers attended where indignation was directed, not against the barbarity of the punishment, but against the victim who failed to bear pain with fortitude. In public schools the practice died hard. Extensions made to Lancing College in 1877, for example, included the provision of a special birching room. If in addition one remembers the extent to which corporal punishment was a feature of the judicial system, one is more impressed by the minority of cases in which schoolmasters were found guilty of assault than by the majority in which they were exonerated.[19]

On balance the Education Department showed a greater humanity than did the schoolmaster. From the 1840s onwards school inspectors had protested against the excessive use of the cane in schools. During the 1880s the Department instructed its inspectors to dissuade teachers from its use. They recommended that corporal punishment should never be given by assistant teachers, pupil teachers, or school managers, but only by the head teacher who should make an appropriate entry in the school log-book. The Department dropped these regulations during the 1890s. Not until 1900, by which time it had been reformed as the Board of Education, did it require schools to keep a record of such cases. The following year Sir John Gorst announced the government's intention of laying down the principles that there should be no punishment that caused bodily pain in infants' schools, corporal punishment should be discouraged as an ordinary expedient in boys' schools, and not used in girls' schools. However, the caveat that the application of these principles was to be left to the discretion of the school managers and teachers greatly weakened the Board's chances of achieving its objective.[20]

This pronouncement came only a few years after the *Church Times* had reported its adherence to the view that corporal punishment was a manifestation of Divine Love. 'The Lord loveth whom He chastiseth, and scourgeth any Son whom He receiveth.' It set its face against the new humanitarianism. 'The Englishmen who won at Waterloo and Trafalgar were men, who, in their youth, were chastised when they deserved it. The flabby sentimentalism of Rousseau and his followers did not pervade Old England.' In its wider context the debate reflected changing attitudes towards childhood and the doctrine of original sin. If one believed that it was necessary to eradicate a boy's innate wickedness and accepted Thomas Arnold's dictum that one could make Christian gentlemen but not Christian boys then one could agree that 'No one who has had much to do with children can doubt that punishment is necessary to their proper discipline, or that sometimes it needs to be administered with considerable severity.'[21]

The very act of providing school buildings prejudiced poorer parents against the school board and its teachers from the start. There can be little doubt that sheer necessity to make good the deficiency of school accommodation in the great cities meant that boards had to use makeshift arrangements and rent such premises as they could find. In poor districts a Board's choice was restricted. For example Lant Street Board School, Southwark, began in some rooms rented from Pickfords. Children reached the classrooms by climbing up ladders direct from the street. The walls between the rooms were so thin that the boys made holes in them to go from one to another. Around the school were overcrowded dilapidated buildings that were liable to collapse and bury the inmates. A teacher recalled, 'John D had his name removed from the rolls in this way.' For the first week the only pupils were the unfortunate sons of the cleaner. During the next few months the hostility of the neighbourhood was such that the school had to rely on those children forced into it by the school attendance officer. In an area such as this, teachers were insulted on the way to and from school until after the start of the twentieth century.[22]

The building of new schools created further problems in those already overcrowded urban areas where street improvements and other rebuilding schemes had already deprived the poor of much existing accommodation in the neighbourhood. Although a school occupied less space than a railway goods yard the latter held out the consolation of future employment. A board school presaged the loss of juvenile employment, lower living standards, and trouble with authority. Local overcrowding increased because unskilled and irregularly employed men needed to be near their place of employment in case their services were suddenly required. The combined effect of the demolitions necessary for the erection of Peabody Buildings and a board school in the Covent Garden area was that workers in the market had to pay more for less accommodation. When a board school was one of a number of local building schemes, as happened in Ann Street, off the Gray's Inn Road, the increase in rents was thought to be as much as 50 per cent.

Statutory protection for tenants displaced by the preliminary clearing of a site for a board school outside London seems to have been non-existent. In the Metropolitan area the Education Department Provisional Order Confirmation Act (London) of 1895 came tardily and proved a broken reed. The Act required the Board to submit a scheme for rehousing members of the labouring classes when it wanted to demolish twenty or more houses on a given site. The safeguards of the Act, so far as the poor were concerned, proved almost illusory. Property acquired by auction lay outside the jurisdiction of the Act. The Board was also able to evade the intention of the Act by subdividing a site into parts containing less than twenty houses each and scheduling them in successive years. By 1899 the Board was already being accused of having done this in 'several cases'.

Prior to 1895 the only consolation for tenants of property about to be demolished was the prospect of a small sum of money, usually between 5s and £1, to induce them to move out. In this respect they fared better with the London School Board than they would have with the Metropolitan Railway Company, whose normal offer was 1s to 1s 6d. Railway companies had every reason to make these payments. If they could induce tenants to move out voluntarily, they were relieved of their legal responsibility of rehousing them. As the School Board was normally under no such obligation it seems that its officials made these payments to induce tenants to leave houses in districts that were already overcrowded so that they could get on with the job of building the schools quickly and without arousing undue local antagonism.[23]

In deciding to build a school the London School Board had also to contend with the opposition of the more articulate middle classes. Not only did the Board have to receive delegations of local residents, dismayed at the prospect of a board school in their district, but it had at times to defend its bills before the Private Bills Committee in parliament. The fact that the local landowners and residents were prepared to embark on the expensive procedure of briefing counsel to represent them for this purpose is an indication of the loss to property values that they thought was at stake. The 'daily influx of rough children' and the 'noise of the teaching' arising from the 'monotonous repetition from the classrooms' of information learnt by rote were feared by those who lived in 'desirable residences'.[24]

The rough child who, despite the opposition of his social superiors, eventually found his way to a board school built by one of the more progressive authorities was one of the lucky ones of his generation. By contrast the schoolroom, housing all the children from the age of three upwards within its four walls, was the norm for much of rural England. Such buildings, with a single undivided classroom, giving each child eight square feet of floorspace, were still being erected after 1870. As the overall size of the school was calculated by reference to the average annual attendance and as daily attendance fluctuated widely during the course of the year, there were times when the schoolroom was overcrowded. On such occasions it was impossible for the young ones to take part in those 'games . . . action songs, dances, and marching, and all the other cheerful methods', that by the late 1880s were 'recognized as essential for a good infant school'. The limited success enjoyed by the Education Department in the 1890s in improving the standards of the rural schools left an embarrassing legacy for the new authorities created in 1902. In 1908 the Board drew up a Black List to encourage the local education authorities to remedy the worst deficiencies, a process that was interrupted by the outbreak of the First World War, revived afterwards only to be further truncated by the economy cuts of the early 1930s.

The National Union of Teachers produced a pamphlet in 1897 describing some village schools chosen solely, it alleged, because they lay 'in the route of itineraries (made by two distinguished officials of the Union) in various parts of the country'. Be that as it may, the extracts provide a depressing picture of unhygienic and overcrowded classrooms or schoolrooms. Poorly paid teachers, who in church schools might be expected to teach in the Sunday school, play the organ, and train the choir as well, had to teach five or six standards at a time. The description of one such school, in which most of these faults existed, seems typical of those delineated. 'Seated on ten broken desks are sixty children, working as best they may. It is some time before one can see them clearly, so gloomy is the place. There is but one room, that formerly served as a stable . . . . In winter lamps are lit all day, so few and so small are the windows. Maps, blackboards, books and stationery are antiquated, dilapidated, or scarce. The playground is swimming in water, so is the approach to the latrines, which are never cleansed.' Possibly with a view to rebutting any charge of exaggeration the same issue of the *Schoolmaster* built up an account from inspectors' reports of one rural school where 'the offices are filthy unfloored, and draining into the open ditch. A covered shed connects the closets with the school, and childrens' dinner-bags hang there, with but the thickness of a brick between them and the hoarded filth. There is no water supply.' However, the financially hard-pressed clerical manager could always turn dross to gold. 'By making a free use of charcoal, all offensiveness is instantly and effectively removed, and a large quantity of valuable manure is secured without any of the usual disagreeable results.' The voluntary and board schools of rural England suffered alike if the local inhabitants were poor, indifferent or hostile to education. Where local enthusiasm flourished, however, conditions in a village school stood comparison with the best the urban boards could offer. The same pamphlet included such an example. This school had a well-fitted workshop and gymnasium for the boys whom the village doctor took to a nearby swimming bath each week. 'Rich maiden ladies' took an interest in the training and welfare of the girls. With a lengthy subscription list for the school the teachers had an ample supply of books, stationery, and apparatus for their pupils.[25]

Whatever shortcomings the solidly built board schools of the great cities may seem to possess today, they offered the child from the slum an amount of light, cleanliness, and warmth he could never have experienced at home. Moreover, the major boards were readier purchasers of such items as maps, books, scientific apparatus, cookery and other specialist equipment than the voluntary schools. A perusal of the advertisements of the educational literature of the period shows that Forster's Act had led to a new growth industry. One C. Kemp, for instance, who held the contract for supplying clocks to the London School Board, advertised his timepiece as being of the approved pattern with a twelve-inch dial (very bold), a perfect timekeeper for 50s. George M. Hammer, manufacturer of school furniture, so successfully cashed in on the new boom industry that he had moved from an obscure address to 370 Strand, next door to the Exeter Hall, by 1875. His most heavily promoted ware was Moss's Patent School Board desk, a marked improvement on the long bench-like type, made perhaps by the village carpenter or wheelwright for use in the voluntary schools. This double desk, a prototype of those still in use three-quarters of a century later, had a backrest and movable seat attached to the sloping front by an iron frame. To encourage sales the manufacturers devised a drill with seven stages of command by which the class put away their slates and books and marched out of the room in an orderly manner. Thus 'at the word "return" the hands should be raised to grasp the slate', then 'at the word "slates", the slates should be smartly lifted and placed in the groove in front of the desk without noise. The hands should then be lowered.' Eventually the class was standing in Indian file beside their desks in the gangways awaiting the command, ' " Quick march", the word "quick" being used simply as a caution. At the word "March", all the files move off with the *left* foot, taking care that regular paces be maintained. When the last scholar in each file has reached the front of the desks, the word "Halt" or "Right turn" may be given.' To avoid an unruly irruption into the classroom the drill could be carried out in the reverse order.[26]

The assembling of up to a thousand children in an urban board school raised a number of problems concerning the prevention of the spread of infectious diseases. A recent survey of the architecture of English schools has pointed to the hygienic deficiencies of the board schools built on the centre-hall system, that is those schools that had the classrooms leading off from a central assembly hall. This arrangement, an architectural legacy of earlier days when the master had supervised his pupil-teachers in a single schoolroom, allowed the head teacher to exercise a similar measure of control from the assembly hall

169

through a judas window. The gain in discipline was made at the expense of classroom ventilation as only one set of windows opened on to the outside of the school. The atmosphere of an inadequately aired classroom could be further vitiated not only by the smell of unwashed children but by the fact that 'It is a very common experience in the poorer elementary schools, especially when the frost comes, that quite a number of children during the . . . first session in the morning become sick and vomit. Of course some of them may be sickening for measles or scarlet fever.' More usually they were retching from sheer hunger. Early in the twentieth century the Board of Education, under pressure from doctors and architects, sanctioned a design with classrooms leading off from corridors, an arrangement that allowed fresh air into the rooms from opposite sides. The Board's chief architect visited the first school built on this pattern on a cold February morning. In almost all other schools he would have found a fug in such weather. Instead he wrote, 'It was remarkable that when I walked into the classroom there was no smell.'[27]

Bad workmanship compounded the hygienic shortcomings of the central-hall type school in the London area. During the late 1880s and early 1890s the Board received a number of alarming reports about the sanitary condition of some of its schools. For instance at the Princess Road Board School in Marylebone, one of the more prosperous districts of the Metropolitan Board, a high incidence of sore throats amongst the staff was traced to a leakage of sewerage gas from faulty joints in the main sewer. At another school part of the playground subsided to expose a cesspool. A smoke test at yet another school revealed seepage of sewerage gas into the caretaker's room, the infants' classrooms and their lavatories. The Board spent £100,000 between 1888 and 1891 on repairs, including £1,800 on the Princess Road School to stop it from falling down, only to discover that there were a further twenty-one schools needing 'a great deal to be done'. With its debates reported in *The Times* the London School Board worked in a glare of publicity that other boards were able to avoid. To some extent the revelation of these shortcomings is a measure of the high standards the Board set itself. It would be naïve to suppose that similar deficiencies did not exist elsewhere.[28]

Apart from the defects of the buildings, a number of other factors facilitated the spread of infectious disease. The practice of making diseases notifiable developed slowly. From 1875 to 1889 only cholera had to be reported to the health authorities. The first major act, the

Notification of Infectious Diseases Act of 1889, compulsory in London and adoptive elsewhere, extended the range of notifiable diseases. By 1899, when most of the country had adopted the act, a further amending act closed the remaining loopholes by making notification compulsory throughout England and Wales. The effectiveness of such legislation depended on the capability of all concerned to make a correct diagnosis of any symptoms from which a child was suffering. It also implicitly imposed an obligation on parents not to make any attempt at concealment through a sense of shame. Poor parents had the additional difficulties of obtaining medical assistance and producing medical certificates to excuse their children from attendance at school. Although the Education Department ruled that when a school board required a medical certificate the board should pay, boards did not always obey the injunction. Hence parents sent their children back to school before they should have done through fear of the attendance officer. On the other hand doctors indicating that they were not the servants of the school boards were reluctant to issue a certificate without payment. The medical profession further argued that the issue of a certificate specifying the disease breached the confidentiality that was supposed to exist between a doctor and his patient but had to admit that the 1889 Act breached this principle. Last, the system by which a child earned exemption from school by making 250 attendances a year for five years – raised to 350 for five years in 1900 – put further pressure on parents. If an irregular attender became ill towards the end of a school year his absence might ruin his chances of reaching his target of 250 for that year.[29]

Thus much depended on the ability of the teacher to recognize the symptoms of infectious diseases. Unfortunately only a minority of teachers received the necessary instruction at their training colleges in the nineteenth century. However, the Board of Education acted on the recommendations of the *Report of the Inter-Departmental Committee on Physical Deterioration* published in July 1904 by making a course in hygiene compulsory for all training college students. It attempted to remedy the deficiencies of existing teachers by offering grants to local authorities to provide them with evening classes in the subject. Less than half a century earlier an inspector had written,[30]

I once saw a boy in a Welsh school with his head tied up. I asked what was the matter. 'Mumps' said the clergyman, 'but mumps is not infectious.' I appealed to the parish doctor; the parish doctor took the clergyman's view.

By 1914 teachers were being equipped to take an informed interest in the health of the children so that they could hold a watching brief for the school nurse and doctor by referring pupils to them between visits or to the out-patients' department of a hospital.

There was one working-class grievance that most of the poorest did not share. They were not worried about possible infractions of the safeguards to religious liberty built into the 1870 Act. They were more concerned about their children having to go to school at all, and thought that arguing about the type of religious instruction provided was irrelevant to solving the basic family problem of how to survive without running foul of authority. Indeed two witnesses to the Cross Commission thought that many parents in the poorest parts of Manchester and London had never even heard of the conscience clause, that great confused battlefield of Victorian England. The outcome of the parliamentary struggle, fought at times across party lines, was that voluntary schools could give denominational teaching subject to the safeguard that parents could withdraw their children if they so desired. At first Forster's bill had required any such request to be made in writing thereby putting a considerable obstacle in the path of many working-class parents. The government withdrew this condition but, to avoid disrupting lessons as much as possible, stipulated that religious instruction was to take place at the beginning or end of the day. In board schools the Cowper-Temple clause forbade the teaching of any 'religious catechism or formulary which is distinctive of any particular denomination', a phrase that did not exclude the teaching of doctrinal beliefs. As Forster explained, 'You may have sectarian teaching without sectarian formularies and catechisms.' The defeat of Jacob Bright's amendment, with Conservative assistance which more than outweighed Liberal defection, that 'In any [board] school . . . the teaching shall not be used or directed in favour of or against the distinctive tenets of any religious denomination', aroused nonconformist fears for the future. In 1870 the chances were that this sectarian education was going to be Anglican, for 1,700 training college students out of 2,171 were in colleges affiliated to the Church of England.[31]

The struggle at Westminster was taken to the provinces when the school boards drew up their syllabuses of religious instruction. A few cut the Gordian knot altogether, seven in England and 50 in Wales by 1888, by banning any form of religious teaching in their schools. Many followed the lead of the London School Board by vetoing any attempt to attach children to a particular denomination. Others such as the

Anglican dominated board at Manchester allowed denominational teaching. It remains one matter to know what instruction a teacher was expected to give, it is another to know what he actually taught and how he taught it. The effectiveness of a particular board's supervision, or local authority after 1902, must have varied between one place and another and been conditional on such factors as the strength and bitterness of local sectarian rivalries, and the vigilance of all concerned.

There were two parties to the conscience clause. Normally one thinks of the plight of the nonconformist parent who found the safeguards inadequate. However, Anglicans had a conscience as well. To omit any part of the Church's doctrine or liturgy was seen as a breach of trust for 'The religion of the Church is one and indivisible, it embodies "the faith once delivered to the saints", the teacher of that religion must teach it in its integrity or not at all . . . .'[32] The doctrinal struggle took place at two levels, the well-documented one of politicians and ministers of religion, the less illuminated one of school manager and parent. Undoubtedly both sides were guilty of some cant and humbug. In addition to those parents who had never heard of a conscience clause there were those who stood silently at the touchline in this struggle of faiths. They chose a school not on account of its religious affiliation but for 'the efficiency with which such things as tend to the advancement in life of their children are taught in it, and by its general tone and discipline'. James Fraser, later Bishop of Manchester, informed the Newcastle Commission that parents who judged schools solely by these secular criteria were 'too ignorant of the distinctions of religious creeds to make it ever probable that . . . they will . . . raise a special objection to the character of religious instruction.' Working men and women did not always see church and chapel as mutually exclusive institutions. They attended both and gave an accomplished preacher a support that at times transcended denominationalism. Furthermore, Professor Laqueur's study of the Sunday-School movement shows that they supported the Sunday Schools for the wide variety of social and cultural functions they offered in the absence of the mass organized entertainment of a later age. Last, even an articulate artisan could show an astonishing indifference, if not ignorance, of the sectarian variety that existed. The Cross Commissioners asked H. Williams, a jobbing printer who was one of the three working-class representatives they examined, whether the school his children attended was in connection with the Church of England. He replied, 'I think it is. I would not be sure.' Yet this man was a

Sunday School teacher of impeccable Anglican background for he had attended the National Society school in Baldwin's Gardens, Holborn. His children had gone to the almost equally famous Home and Colonial School, Gray's Inn Road, attached to the training college of that name controlled by the Church of England Independent Society.[33]

There was then some justification for the argument put by one inspector that 'the religious difficulty, as it exists, does not appear to exist in this district, at least, as far as the schools with which I am acquainted are concerned.'[34] When examined by the Cross Commissioners, a number of school inspectors in Holy Orders, together with representatives of the Anglican, Wesleyan, and Roman Catholic churches, attested to the effectiveness of the conscience clause. They knew of no cases of its violation, a tribute more to working-class quiescence and indifference than to the effectiveness of the law in protecting a parent who wished to exercise his right of withdrawal.

Returns made to the National Society by the diocesan inspectorate showed that out of 2,000,000 children on the registers of Anglican schools, parents withdrew 2,200 from all religious instruction and a further 5,960 from part of it, usually the Church's teaching on infant baptism. Apart from the ignorant and indifferent there were an unknown number of sincere dissenting working-class parents who preferred not to exercise their legal rights. The 'fear of incurring the displeasure of their superiors in the neighbourhood and imperilling their employment' was enough to deter them. Similarly small shopkeepers and artisans working on their own account were dependent on the goodwill of their social superiors, the locally influential, for their livelihood. They feared the loss of trade that might ensue if their rejection of the Church's teaching branded them as troublemakers. Others hesitated for it seemed churlish and ungrateful to reject the Church's teaching when it had been for so long the provider of education. Parents also hesitated to withdraw their children from religious instruction for the same reason that makes many think twice today, they thought that their action would make their children stand out and be seen as different to others. In addition they had good reason to fear petty acts of tyranny and unkindness from the teachers.[35] In this respect even the London School Board was not blameless.

Amongst the most vulnerable to these pressures were the Primitive Methodists whose faith contained within it a social and political protest. The economically close connection that their ministers maintained with

174

their congregations enhanced this sense of working-class solidarity. In a century that had witnessed a rise in the incomes of many incumbents in the Established Church, their ministers started at £50 a year and reached £100 after ten years. The highest salary in the Connexion was £150. Parental readiness to withdraw their children from the teaching of the Anglican Church must have varied not only between one sect and another but also between one village and another. Those circumstances that made the Church of England weak allowed dissent to flourish and its adherents to be self-assertive. Freest of all were those who lived in an open village with some absentee landowners. Hardest hit were the inhabitants of a close village where, in extreme cases, the landowner could curb dissent by refusing to lease or sell land for a chapel. In 1876 the Rev. Gervaise Smith, the president of the Wesleyan Conference, maintained that there were 2,000 villages that did not enjoy perfect religious freedom. He also drew attention to the practice of landowners refusing to let farms or houses to tenants who were not Anglicans, a practice that must have become difficult to sustain later in the century when tenants became harder to find.[36]

The Education Department's policy of letting sleeping dogs lie was another handicap that told against nonconformist parents. Unless a parent complained of an infringement of the conscience clause, the Department did nothing. Similarly, although an inspector had to take action if he received a specific complaint, it was not his duty to search for evidence of violation. Thus in 1897 when an MP drew the House's attention to a case in Honiton the Department took no action at the time as no parent had yet complained. Not until one did so later, did the Department act. Last, the Department's view that the Lord's Prayer, the ten commandments and the Creed were not distinctive of any one denomination added further restrictions to the sphere of possible complaint.[37]

Infringements of the spirit of the 1870 Act provided further grounds for nonconformist discontent. In rural areas the managers of voluntary schools avoided the operation of the Cowper-Temple clause even when they had handed their schools over to a board. An inspector of schools in the Taunton area blandly wrote,

The religious objection to boards I believe to be rapidly disappearing. It has become an almost universally accepted arrangement that 9 to 10 is the religious hour . . . . Church schools are in many places let to boards at a nominal rent, after 10 o'clock in the morning, the incumbent of the parish maintaining his right to the first hour of the day.

There was little to choose between a rural board and a voluntary school in many instances. 'The difference . . . is very slight, as far as the management is concerned, the boards are mostly so only in name, and the school is practically under the charge and supervision of the clergyman.' Even the teacher might be the same despite the change of management. An incumbent, concerned for the immortal souls of dissenters' children in his school, could quite legitimately try to persuade them to abjure the faith of their parents. Passages from a catechism, *Some Questions of the Church Catechism and Doctrines Involved Briefly Explained* were quoted in the House of Commons in 1876 and again in 1891. The catechism, said to have been used in National Society schools, contained such passages as:

Q. Is it very dangerous to leave the Church?
A. Yes; and it is also a grievous sin.
Q. Is it very wrong to join in the worship of dissenters?
A. Yes, we should only attend places of worship in connection with the Church of England.

The catechism was evidently a popular one. First published in 1870, it had reached its thirteenth edition by 1896 despite Archbishop Benson's condemnation of it in 1889 as not being in keeping with the mind of the National Church. What mattered to children more, was not learning a formula that they may not have understood in the first place, but the way in which the incumbent could bring other sanctions to bear. It was a common practice to exclude the children of known nonconformist parents from treats provided by the Church. The largesse of the charitable, coal, blankets, shoes, and other gifts was withheld from their parents as well. With limited resources at their disposal it was understandable, but not necessarily condoneable, that incumbents should look after the faithful in their flock first. In this struggle of faiths both parties were equally justified in invoking their consciences. Unfortunately for the nonconformist or atheist parent the struggle often took place between men who were politically, economically, and socially unequal.[38]

The Elementary Education Act, which the churches had so long resisted, ushered in a golden age of religious instruction. Between 1870 and the end of the century the average attendance in Church schools more than doubled from 844,344 to 1,855,802. The corresponding figure for board schools, where religious instruction covered the spectrum from doctrinal teaching without the formularies to a mere exposition of the Bible, was 2,201,049. With another half million children in Wesleyan, British, and Roman Catholic schools, quantitatively religious education flourished as never before. In both Wesleyan and Anglican schools an average daily ration of forty-five minutes ensured that it received as much attention as ever. The Church of England built up a network of diocesan inspectors to cover the whole country. Church schools were allowed to close for two days, as far as secular instruction was concerned, to allow the inspection of religious education to take place. As a result clerical control was far more extensive than before 1870 when the government inspector had made it just one of his concerns. Much has been written about the school inspector as being the teacher's bogeyman yet A. J. Mundella, when Vice-President of the Committee of the Privy Council on Education, maintained that the schoolmaster feared the diocesan inspector more. Many school boards with their detailed syllabuses, examinations and prize schemes showed an equal enthusiasm. Yet the children had the last word. If church attendance and membership are taken as a measure of religious commitment, its slight rise between 1871 and 1911 suggests that the effort made was out of all proportion to the result and that the teaching fell largely on deaf ears.[39]

Although not all incumbents took the attitude that they were going to teach nonconformist children the whole of the Anglican Catechism – some left out the Church's teaching on infant baptism – the incumbent remained in sole charge of religious instruction in his school until 1902. The Act of that year deprived him of his previously unfettered control of the religious education of his parish. It put the control of religious education in the school into the hands of the managers, a predominately lay body, and gave them the power to supervise the content of religious teaching in Church schools. Colonel Kenyon-Slaney, MP for the Newport division of Shropshire, moved the relevant amendment to the bill, not primarily to curb the independence of the incumbent, but to curb the teaching of 'extreme and eccentric' doctrine that was alien to the English Puritan tradition. An alliance of anti-Ritualists within the Established Church and nonconformists without – the latter seizing any opportunity to bring rate-aided Church schools under some measure of public control – passed the amendment by an overwhelming majority, 211 to 41, in a House of Commons that possessed a large Conservative majority thanks to the 'Khaki' election of 1900.[40] Kenyon-Slaney's success is indicative of the weakening effect that half a century's internal doctrinal dissension had had on the prestige of the

Church, a factor that had in turn contributed to its loss of influence over the educated laity. Not only was the stature of the village incumbent being diminished in an increasingly secular age but the breakdown of rural isolation helped to erode his authority in the community as well. Before the invention of the bicycle and the motor car the village saw few strangers; the school only the government and diocesan inspectors. By 1914 a village school might be visited by the school doctor, the school nurse, the dentist as well as officials and educational advisers from the county council; any one of whom might have something to say on the running of the school.

Despite the preoccupation of contemporaries with the religious issue, secular instruction took up roughly five-sixths of school-time. As we have seen, in many respects there was little to choose between a rural board and voluntary school. Often the much more important distinction was between town and country schools. Throughout the period under survey the rural boy was under pressure from the farmer, wanting cheap labour, and his parents, needing his wages, to leave school as soon as possible. The forces of a rural society and economy limited the education he received by shortening his stay at school. Even if a village boy could have stayed on at school there was little point in his doing so for there were no higher grade schools in the countryside. The majority left after reaching Standard IV, a level of attainment within the reach of a ten-year-old. If he remained at school longer the teacher, attempting to deal with a number of younger groups at the one and same time, had little hope of giving him special attention. Many rural teachers were ill-equipped to cope for the countryside had little to offer the capable or ambitious. The school building was but one of a number of drawbacks to a job in a rural school. By 1900 a male head teacher could be earning as much as £500 a year in a large board school in London or another major city, the head of the girls' department could be on £400. Male assistants could find boards offering a graduated scale rising from £120 at 20 to £250 after fourteen years' service, women the slightly lower one of £100 to £200. On the other hand 10 per cent of all women headmistresses in rural schools received less than £1 a week in the early 1890s. Women teachers in the countryside were frequently forbidden to live alone for fear of causing scandal and gossip. Consequently they had few friends, little privacy, and limited access to any social life for their private life required 'a delicate and discriminating hand'. The infants' mistress of Long Sutton, Lincolnshire, who lodged in a public house where 'she made herself useful and interesting out of school hours', had a freedom that many others must have envied.[41]

Although nearly a third of all masters and a fifth of the mistresses had rent-free accommodation, this perquisite could prove a mixed blessing for the country teacher. The *Schoolmaster* complained that once the schoolmaster's house had been erected to the Education Department's specifications, one parlour 12 foot by 12 foot, a kitchen 10 foot by 10 foot, and two other rooms 9 foot by 8 foot, officialdom took no further interest. In this cramped accommodation a married couple might have had to rear a family. Many teachers did not have access to pure drinking water in the country. When the storage tank fed from the gutters on the roof ran low, the water was brackish and no longer potable. The *Lancet* reported the case of a master of a rural board school who, after the local medical officer of health had condemned the water, was dismissed for complaining. That such teachers enjoyed a status little above that of a servant is further illustrated by an advertisement of 1897 offering £50 a year with a furnished house and fuel to a 'widow with son, or sister and brother, who could be employed as outdoor servant'. Similarly a Buckinghamshire Nursing Association showed it knew the economic worth and the social esteem attached to the rural schoolmaster when it stipulated that 'gardeners, keepers, coachmen, grooms, butlers, estate carpenters, brick-layers, smiths, railway employees, schoolmasters, and quite small tradespeople should pay as artisans'. The transfer of the rural school to the county councils after 1902 improved the lot of the lowest paid. By 1914 county councils were paying certificated women heads an average salary of £103 4s a year. This was still less than half, however, of the London County Council's £209 6s.[42]

A series of revisions to the Revised Code brought changes in the subjects taught in elementary schools in the last three decades of the century. Broadly speaking the Education Department recognized three groups of subjects, obligatory, class, and specific. The distinction between them was not so much pedagogic as administrative. The same subject could attract a grant as either an obligatory or a class subject. Similarly the Department occasionally transferred a subject from one category to another. The obligatory subjects were the three Rs together with needlework for all the girls. This remained the irreducible minimum until 1891 when the Department added drawing for older boys. Two years later it added one class subject to be taught throughout the school. In 1895 it required object lessons and suitable occupations to be taught to Standards I to III.

179

The three R's together with the later compulsory additions represented the maximum that many children received. Chronologically the first addition to the obligatory minimum had come in 1867 when schools could earn a higher grant by teaching additional subjects. When these subjects became known as specific subjects in 1875 they provided a wider education for no more than a small minority of the children. Confined to children in Standards IV to VI they broadened the education of just over 3 per cent of those on the registers, 89,186 out of 2,943,774. From time to time the Department changed the regulations but the highest proportion of children tested in these subjects never rose above the 4·4 per cent of 1883; although there were 30 subjects to choose from in 1895 the proportion tested in them went down to 2·4 per cent.

For the fortunate few the Code offered the prospect of reaching a modest competence. For example, Standard VI Latin required a mastery of Caesar's *De Bello Gallico* Book I, mathematics included algebra as far as quadratic equations. Literary subjects, the cheapest to teach since they required no special equipment, unlike elementary science, were the most popular. Geography, grammar, and literature were the subjects of nearly nine-tenths of the tests administered. Latin attracted more entries than mechanics, mensuration, physics, chemistry, and zoology put together. Finally, whereas 55,590 were examined in two subjects, only 374 attempted three.

The third category, class subjects, came into existence when the 1875 Code created the third element of the trinity by transferring the popular history, elementary geography, and grammar to this new group. To earn a grant under this head a school had to offer two of these subjects above Standard I. Since the obligatory needlework could be counted under this head girls, in effect, could be restricted to one extra subject. By 1880 most schools were taking advantage of the offer with nine-tenths of those eligible, 1,708,374 out of 1,876,105, having an education consisting of more than just the three Rs. The schools that contented themselves with the basic minimum, roughly 5 per cent with an average attendance of under 50, were mainly small rural ones. More serious was the low level of attainment in the three Rs, the result of irregular attendance. Less than half the scholars who ought to have been presented in Standards IV to VI, because they were more than ten years old, were so presented: 52·39 per cent (508,116 out of 969,839) were examined in standards suitable to children of the age of seven (67,741, 6·98 per cent), eight (171,035, 17·64 per cent) or nine (269,340, 27·77 per cent).[43]

To search the successive editions of the Revised Code to discover what schools were expected to teach is a comparatively simple but tedious task. To determine how a teacher actually behaved and taught is another matter. However, it is possible to suggest how training colleges expected their students to teach when they left. A collection of reports from the master of method at St Peter's College, Birmingham, covering the years 1876 to 1896, provides some examples of what were considered good and bad teaching. The following is based on comments made by the master after seeing the student's criticism lesson, the equivalent of the apprentice's masterpiece. The tutor's remarks show that the teacher of 1875 was expected to do more than present a class with a mass of half-digested information. He was required to illustrate his lesson with clear blackboard work and use models and specimens to interest his class. For instance a lesson on 'Tea' in 1875 met with the comment that the content was 'too much in the catalogue style – more [material] than possible to teach and consequently dealt with in an imperfect manner'. A lesson on the river Nile was 'too dry and heavy' while another on sugar was described as a 'dry uniform lecture'. On the other hand a lesson on the spinal column was 'clear and forcibly presented'. The student had questioned the class briskly and forcibly so as to lead them from one point to another as the lesson proceeded. In addition, he had used the blackboard and his diagram effectively. However, his attitude to the children was criticized for he was authoritarian and inclined to be unsympathetic. Comments on two of the best students of the year are equally illuminating. One who was 'on the whole an excellent teacher' had a lively and impressive manner and was cheerful and patient. Neither over severe nor unduly lax, he had controlled the boys easily and readily, managing to keep a class of 'really troublesome boys in good order without much effort'. Another earned his tutor's commendation for having kept all the class busy, seeing that the brighter boys were not idle if they finished their work early and assisting the weaker ones.

The reports for 1895–6 inevitably show that the weaker students were making the same mistakes as their predecessors of twenty years earlier. However the teaching was now more advanced and ambitious. While science lessons in 1875 had been confined to natural history – leaves, the camel, the elephant – and such topics as the barometer, and 'solid, liquid, and gas', all taken in one lesson (sic!); the later student was leading his class to investigate the composition of the atmosphere, the principles of the mariners' compass, the electric bell and capillary action. Again the class was not expected just to learn by rote but by observation and experiment. The student who gave a lesson on the electric bell had

plenty of suitable apparatus and a properly fitted model. He taught the use of each part inductively and experimentally; but made the mistake of announcing the results of his experiments instead of leading the boys to make their own discoveries.

Despite the final adverse comment this had been one of the better lessons of the year. At the other end of the scale a lesson on the Spanish Armada contained 'very little to raise it above the level of mediocrity'. It had been a recapitulation of the bare outline of the facts in which the student had made little attempt to supplement the material in the textbook used by the class.[44]

By the time these students were examined in the mid-1890s the Education Department had produced an expanded Revised Code that gave teachers more opportunity to engage in lively teaching than they had had twenty-five years earlier. The newly introduced object lessons, compulsory for Standards I to III, illustrate the point. Now that children could be taken on visits to museums and other places in school time, the Department urged schoolmasters to use their new found freedom. To cater for a new need educational suppliers began to put chests containing specimens on the market for these lessons. Some of the recommendations of the Department such as that children should count the rings of a felled tree to estimate its age, grow mustard on flannel, collect, press and label leaves are still acted on today. However, the suggestion 'Note effect of heavy rain in tearing up roads. Note the channels so made, and the arrangement of the sand and pebbles washed to a distance' is a reminder of an age that had yet to experience the motorcar and macadamized roads. Alongside object lessons were 'suitable occupations'. These included

modelling, simple geometrical drawing, weaving, plaiting, building with cubes, drill, singing, recitation, and other exercises such as will relieve the younger children, especially during the afternoon, from the strain of ordinary lessons, and train them to imitate and observe.

Instructions to inspectors show the Department's concern to wean teachers from a soul-destroying mechanical approach. The geography syllabus was to start with the children making a plan of the school and playground, an introduction to the subject still used. The school had to have a globe and good maps of the county and immediate neighbourhood of the school. The teacher had to know the exact distance of a few near and familiar places. Teachers were encouraged to mark the meridian line of true north on the floor of the classroom so that children could learn the points of the compass in relation to the school. History consisted of stories and biographies working chronologically forward from the ancient Britons to great inventions, and for those who stayed at school long enough, the Crimean War, the Indian Mutiny, and the growth of the colonies. In an attempt to eliminate the recital of tedious detail during the lessons, teachers had to agree their syllabus for the year with the inspectorate. As well as encouraging visits to places of interest that related to the lessons, inspectors were also asked to promote the use of public libraries by urging school teachers to take their children round them.[45]

To sum up: by the mid-1890s schools had to provide education in the three basic subjects of reading, writing, and arithmetic. Girls had to take needlework, older boys drawing and Standards I to III object lessons. Schools could earn additional grants by teaching singing and recitation throughout. The requirement for the latter subject varied between 20 lines of poetry and 150 lines of Shakespeare, Milton or some comparable author in Standard VI. To make it more than a mechanical rote-learning exercise, candidates were expected to understand the meanings and allusions properly. Schools had also to present their pupils in one or two class subjects. As needlework and object lessons could come into this category, many children actually only took one, at the most, of English, Geography, Elementary Science, History, Suitable Occupations in Standards I to III, or Domestic Economy if they were girls. Last, schools could offer not more than two specific subjects. As we have seen, only one child in every forty did so.

Girls could make cookery, laundry work, or dairy work their second specific subject; boys could choose gardening. As girls had to sacrifice the chance of taking one of the more academic subjects if they wished to follow the course in cookery, it is worth asking if their act of immolation prepared them adequately for their future role in a working-class family. As early as 1832 the young Dr Kay, later Sir James Kay-Shuttleworth, had written of Manchester, 'Domestic economy is neglected, domestic comforts are too frequently unknown'. Despite his recognition of the possible political and social consequences of this state of affairs,[46] the Department he set up was slow to take remedial action. In 1875 it allowed girls to attend cookery lessons in school time. Seven years later it gave direct encouragement by offering a grant for the teaching of cookery. A girl had to be over the age of twelve at the end of the school year and to attend lessons for 40 hours, of which 20 had to be practical work, a year. This compared unfavourably with the four hours a week, 160 a year, that girls normally spent on needlework. In a two-hour practical lesson an individual girl, one of a batch of 24, a number later reduced to 18, might do no more than peel an apple as her contribution to making an apple dumpling. An additional drawback was that the practical lesson did not necessarily bear any relationship to the teacher's demonstration lesson she had witnessed a week or so earlier.

Other factors eroded the value of these lessons as a means of preparing a working-class girl for motherhood. Children seldom learned the kind of basic cooking with inexpensive foods that they would need to practise in their own homes once they were married. They found out how to make a beefsteak pie but not how to use the cheaper cuts of meat. Country children did not learn how to make attractive dishes from potatoes and other vegetables or from what could be gleaned in the fields. Town children did not find out how to deal with cheap and popular sea foods such as bloaters, kippers, whelks, or mussels complained Mary Davies after she retired from her post of inspector of cookery. As school managers valued most the cookery teacher who ran her courses at the least cost to the school, children spent too much time making small items that could easily be sold afterwards such as rock cakes or sausage rolls. The Education Department must bear some of the blame for it reassured thrifty minded school managers. 'A very useful lesson may be given and practised with only two ounces of meat used for making a stew or pie or a gill of milk used for making a rice pudding'. However, the Department partly redeemed itself by showing sufficient sense of reality to suggest that children should learn to measure quantities by the cup or spoonful as many of them came from homes that did not possess kitchen scales. Because of this same concern to see that food was not wasted many teachers did not allow children to put the dishes they had prepared into the oven. Their fear was that it might spoil if the oven were too hot or too cold. At a time when cooks had to learn largely by experience whether an oven was at the correct temperature, children missed an important part of their training.[47]

Unfortunately the Education Department had encouraged the development of cookery lessons without first ensuring that there were sufficient and adequately trained teachers. In the early years schools relied on teachers trained privately in cookery schools, the most important of which was the National Training School of Cookery, founded at South Kensington in 1874. This school and others established by local enthusiasts gave a training in high-class cookery, household cookery for prosperous middle-class homes, and artisan cookery. Only the last was likely to prove useful in elementary schools. The Education Department accepted certificates from these schools that initially devised courses as they wished, trained and examined their pupils as they desired. The London School Board's regard for these certificates was so slight that they retrained their possessors before appointing them as cookery teachers. However, the institution of government inspection of the cookery training schools and the drafting of the Cookery Teacher's Examination Scheme in the late 1890s helped to raise standards. In 1907 the Board of Education carried the process of ensuring uniformity still further by issuing regulations for the teacher's diploma in domestic subjects, an omnibus qualification that included cookery, housewifery and laundry-work. Thus it was not until shortly before the First World War that schools were able to recruit adequately trained teachers with a two-years' course behind them.[48]

With the passage of time the number of girls receiving some form of domestic training in elementary schools gradually increased. In the late 1870s the school boards of Leeds, Liverpool, and London had been among the early pioneers. The work had proceeded slowly. In 1887 there were 8,000 to 9,000 girls in London learning basic cookery, 'making beef tea and mutton broth, and drinks for sick people; and also porridge, and coffee, and cocoa, and bread, and cooking vegetables of various kinds. Also in season . . . jam'. In 1895 the Education Department paid grants for 134,930 girls learning cookery and 11,720 girls taking laundry-work. By 1913–14 the numbers had risen to 379,095 for cookery, 182,342 for laundry work, 55,490 for housewifery, and a further 21,598 on mixed courses.[49] With more than one and three-quarters of a million children aged eleven or over on the registers, many of the girls eligible to take one of these courses never did so. Even if they were amongst the chosen, they still only had forty hours, divided equally between demonstration lessons and practical ones, a year. Headmistresses usually picked their older pupils to go to the classes, despite the Board's new ruling that girls as young as eleven could attend. Yet the older girls who stayed at school the longest needed the classes least for they came from the more prosperous working-class families. Poorer parents still withdrew their children from school as soon as they could.

Given the unsuitability of much of the teaching one should not feel unduly sorry for the poorer girls who missed their cookery lessons. Even the London County Council, despite the down-to-earth approach of the preceding school board, did not minister to their needs for its course of domestic-science instruction was based on family budgets of £3, £1 15s, and £1 8s a week for a family of six. Yet contemporary estimates put the earnings of between a third and a half of all adult men at less than £1 5s 9d with a substantial proportion of these under £1 a week. A survey of the homes of the respectable poor, earning between 18s and £1 10s shortly before 1914, revealed a dearth of basic kitchen equipment. Often one kettle, one frying pan, and a couple of burnt saucepans completed the tally. Not all the homes investigated had gas laid on. Where there was no gas stove, cooking was done on a kitchen range with an oven as small as ten inches by twelve. Where there was no oven, food was sent on Sundays to the neighbouring bakehouse.[50]

To explain the improvement in working-class diet one must look not to the work of the elementary school but to the rise in real wages between 1875 and 1896 that enabled families not only to buy a more varied and wholesome diet but also to purchase the equipment with which to cook. Before 1880 the sale of gas for domestic purposes was mainly confined to middle- and upper-class homes. Gas stoves costing between £4 4s and £5 5s were beyond the reach of working class families. However, the invention of the penny slot-meter opened up a new market for gas companies to exploit, the working-class consumer. They could now begin to sell gas in penny instalments, knowing that they were safe from bad debts, to families that could neither have coped with the cost of installing gas pipes nor with a quarterly bill. Not only did they fit the new meters but they also hired out gas rings and stoves.

Gas companies supplying industrial towns near the coalfields were particularly aggressive in their sales drive. Companies in some Lancashire towns made no charge at all for their stoves. At Rochdale, an exception to this rule, the company levied a rent of 10 per cent of the cost of the stove per annum; as compensation it metered the gas for cooking at a lower price than gas for lighting. St Helens required its customers to pay only an initial charge of 2s or 3s, the cost of the pipes used for installing the cooker. This town with a population of 84,410 in 1901 had over 6,000 gas stoves and 4,500 boiling rings in use by 1905. The growth of these large markets encouraged the production of cheaper cookers. The Gas Light and Coke Company, serving North London, developed a mass produced, cast-iron, easy to maintain cooker, the 'Horseferry', which remained in use in some homes until the 1930s. At the same time the design of cooking utensils improved with the introduction of enamelled cast-iron ware. Stamped out by a hydraulic press, a process that obviated the need for soldering, pots and pans became cheaper and easier to clean. Thus by 1914 the working-class housewife, outside the ranks of the poorest, had a gas stove, a cleaner, more convenient and more easily adjusted device than the coal-fired kitchen range. She had a greater number of cooking utensils with which to prepare food that was cheaper, more varied and better in quality than that available to her mother in 1870.[51] These factors, rather than vague memories in adulthood of a few cookery lessons attended at the age of twelve or thirteen, contributed to the improvement in the quality of working-class life during the decades immediately before 1914. However, cookery lessons do no more than provide an extreme example of the shortcomings of the education offered in the elementary schools. It was too little and ended too soon for the majority of children.

VIII

◆◆

Unwillingly to School

◆◆

To some extent the government's tardiness in introducing universal compulsory education helped to mitigate the sufferings of the poorest families. Indeed it was not until 1918 that full-time education to the age of 14 became the general rule in England and Wales. The Education Act of that year finally closed a series of loopholes that had allowed roughly half the children in elementary schools to leave between the ages of 12 and 14 in the years just before the First World War. The oldest concession to be withdrawn was the half-time system, a practice that dated back to the Health and Morals Act of 1802. The same act also withdrew the two-mile 'distance' excuse, whereby children living more than two miles from school were excused attendance. Finally, the act stopped the practice of granting part-time exemption because the child had reached a certain level of proficiency or had made a stipulated number of attendances.[1]

At the other end of the school, full-time attendance between the ages of 5 and 10 did not become universally compulsory in law until 1880 and in practice even later. The 1870 Act had done no more than give school boards the power to introduce bye-laws. For the next six years the boards were under no necessity to enforce them. Until the Education Department drafted model bye-laws in the same year, 1876, the boards produced a bewildering mosaic of rules that gave employers, parents, and children every reason to feel contempt for the law and every excuse to evade it. However, the first step after 1870 towards effective compulsion came in 1873 when attendance became mandatory for children whose parents received the payment of school fees as part of their outdoor relief. Thus the pauper family, one of the least politically articulate but one of the most suspect elements in society, was amongst the first to feel the full rigour of the new legislation.

In 1876 less than half of the population of England and Wales, 46 per cent, lived in areas in which school attendance was at least nominally compulsory. The overwhelming majority of them, 8,609,740 out of 10,531,011, lived in London and other large cities and towns. Less than 20 per cent were country folk. The Elementary Education Act, 1876, attempted to remedy the situation while paying due deference to the prejudices of the landed classes. The Act gave the managers of voluntary schools the best of both worlds, the means of improving attendance yet keeping the school board at bay. The creation of yet another unit of local government, the school attendance committee, safeguarded local dignitaries from that intrusion of democracy, dissent, and tenant control over landowner that a directly elected school board seemed to make possible. The act had the further advantage of giving a conservatively minded countryside a ready-made excuse for doing nothing. The bye-laws of a school attendance committee could only become effective when a particular parish requested it. Moreover, the proviso whereby objectors could demand a poll of the ratepayers at the expense of the parish put a further brake on change. Thus in 1879 there were still 6,000,000 people, nearly all of whom were living in rural areas, outside the bye-law system. The 1880 Act imposed compulsory attendance on the inhabitants of 450 recalcitrant school boards, of which only two had a population of over 5,000, and on the overwhelming bulk of the rural parishes in the school attendance committees. Out of 584 poor law unions possessing such bodies, there were only fifteen in which all the parishes were covered by bye-laws.[2] Thus ended a curious four-year interlude during which there had been two Englands, one in which local authorities were obliged to enforce such bye-laws, regarding school attendance as they might have made, and another in which children were free to come and go from school as they pleased.

Apart from the Elementary Education Acts there were at least fifteen acts in force in 1876 regulating the working conditions of children in factories and workshops, some of which required children to attend school outside working hours. Of all the clauses of this complex legislation the hardest to enforce were the educational ones. The Royal Commission on the Factory and Workshops Acts reported[3]

So far as children are concerned the shortcomings of the Factory Acts . . . appear to be chiefly on the educational side of the question. The protection afforded by the existing law, both from unsuitable labour and from too long hours of work, is in most cases satisfactory.

189

Two of the main obstacles to the law's successful implementation had their roots in the parent act, the Factory Act of 1833, which had preceded both the establishment of the school inspectorate and the beginnings of the compulsory registration of births, deaths, and marriages. In the absence of birth certificates the 1833 Act had introduced a surgeon's certificate as evidence of a child's age. With professional standards not yet fully established amongst medical men the surgeon, the social inferior of the physician at that time, proved an inadequate surrogate for the registrar. Surgeons were under considerable temptation to issue certificates because they thereby earned their fee; in contrast the medical examination carried no fee. Thus the surgeons who rejected a child as being under age found that their conscientiousness went unrewarded. Moreover, they were under considerable pressure both from employers and parents to pass the children as being of the requisite age. Since even an experienced surgeon could make a genuine mistake as 'the dental development is not absolutely reliable' as an indicator of age, the certificate was at best one of opinion, not one of fact. Given these hazards, it is not surprising that one factory inspector reported in 1869 that he had annulled certificates 'by the score'.[4]

Since the children employed in textile mills form an easily identifiable group whose parents strongly opposed attempts to lengthen their school careers and thereby stop them from working, they merit special attention. Of all the children employed on a part-time basis in the mid-1870s, the Royal Commission thought that the educational clauses of the factory acts worked best with them. As the school inspector who covered the Stockport area found that the children were seldom required to make good any time they might have lost at school, this judgment is more of a testimony to the ineffectiveness of the legislation in other industries than to the law-abiding nature of mill owners or parents. In the textile industries as a whole the tradition of the cottage industry, in which children assisted their parents as soon as they were able, died hard although technological changes made earlier in the century now required operatives to look outside their families for all the juvenile labour they required. Thus in Lancashire and Yorkshire children worked in the mills because 'it was the proper thing to be done', not because of poverty – the dominant motive elsewhere. On the contrary textile workers were regarded as a comparatively affluent working-class group in the mid-1870s. 'There are hundreds of overlookers, spinners, and others earning themselves 28s to 40s per week, their wives and daughters also earning good wages, whose little children are nevertheless attending school but part-time.' Moreover, other parents in the textile towns followed the lead of those working in the mills. They saw that the custom of the district offered them an opportunity of increasing the family income. Similarly employers welcomed the cheap child labour that was so readily available. Half-time certificates were readily obtained for children who were never going to work in the mills. Elsewhere this practice was rare. In the whole of the London School Board area, for instance in 1892, only 693 part-time certificates were issued.[5]

From the late 1880s onwards factory inspectors began to report a decline in the number of part-timers employed in some industries and a standstill in others, changes that preceded the raising of the minimum school-leaving age from ten to eleven in 1891. In the textile industries factory owners were beginning to find young children more trouble than they were worth. For instance, one Manchester mill that had employed 500 in 1879 had less than 40 on its books ten years later. Although millowners were convinced that the dismissal of the young part-timer could increase output, such a policy conflicted with the interests of their workers, the actual employers of the part-timer. Two half-timers were cheaper than an older full-timer. Whereas in the late 1880s a Bolton spinner paid two half-timers 3s 6d or 4s a week each, he had to find as much as 9s 6d or 10s for the older full-timer. Even twenty years later, by which time many of the new mills had either ceased to employ part-timers or had never ever had them, managers of older mills hesitated to dispense with the part-timer whom they now regarded as superfluous. They feared to 'run counter to the custom of the district, and incur unpopularity with some of the parents and operatives.'[6]

Workers opposed the abolition of the part-time system for a number of reasons. Most important was their fear that they would suffer financially twice over. As parents they would lose the earnings of their children; as workers they would not receive a compensatory increase in wages to enable them to employ the more expensive full-timer. Furthermore, they believed that the abolition of the part-time system would make the full-timer even more expensive than he was already. In the eyes of the adult worker the part-timer's merit was that he took some of the drudgery out of the daily round. He was expected, quite illegally, to arrive in the mill before the start of the shift to set up the machinery for the operative. At the bottom of the industrial hierarchy he could not pass on the kicks he received from above. In Bolton where the little piecer is under a piecer and the piecer is under a minder, it is a tradition among minders to do as little work as they can themselves, and to put as much as they can on the piecer. The piecer in turn puts the work on the little piecer, who is sometimes terribly overworked. In some cases it really amounts to white slavery.

Thus self-interest gave parents every reason to adopt the attitude. 'What has been good enough for me is good enough for you'.[7]

As with other educational reforms, trade union leaders were readier to condemn the part-time system than were the rank and file. The Inter-Departmental Committee on Partial Exemption from School Attendance pointed out in its report in 1909 that at a recent conference of Trades' Councils and Trades Unions members had voted by 186 to 27 in favour of the abolition of the part-time system, but cotton operatives in Lancashire had voted 151,032 to 34,120 against. There had been a similar split in opinion in Yorkshire. On balance the poorer worker favoured the retention of the system, a sentiment that was particularly strong in Macclesfield where work in the silk trade was intermittent. Here the weavers, often averaging less than 15s a week and 'tainted with poverty', realized that any extra source of income was of some service to them. In Bradford where male labour had few outlets and the wages of wool-combers were low, the child's earning potential was again an important factor in working-class budgets. A difference of attitude could exist even within a town. In Oldham the native Oldhamer, descended from those originally employed in the home industries, was said to have formed 'the better class of population' by the early twentieth century and favour abolition. Those descended from children imported into the city from London and elsewhere and later supplemented by the Irish immigrants were held to have produced a 'very low class' who supported retention. Lastly, Huddersfield provides an example of a town in the West Riding of Yorkshire whose school board had been able to abolish the part-time system. Despite this one success and the recommendation of the 1909 Inter-Departmental Committee that the rest of the country should follow Huddersfield's lead from 1911 onwards, the part-timer lingered on until 1918. The Act of that year gave the quietus to a method of combining school and employment that had once won the accolade of Karl Marx's endorsement of Nassau Senior's approval. In 1895, the year of a Factory Act that required factory owners to make a return of their employees, there had been 55,625 part-timers in textile factories in England and Wales. By 1897 the total had fallen to 45,993 and ten years was just over

30,000. By 1914 the number working in *all* factories was 31,140. Despite this gradual decline proposals made before 1914 to end the system were regularly opposed by representatives of the cotton workers both inside and outside parliament. In February 1914 six Labour members, five of whom represented Lancashire constituencies, had voted against a private member's bill.[8]

The combination of work and school made the part-timer's day a long one and effectively denied him access to secondary education. It is not surprising that the accident rate for children in the mills was nearly double that for adults and young persons. Long hours not only made them more accident prone; their education and that of their school fellows suffered as well. Part-timers often fell asleep over their lessons. Children at school full-time found their education held back as the teacher had to cope with them as well as two sets of part-timers, one coming in the morning, the other in the afternoon.[9] From the late 1870s onwards children's official hours were from 6.00 a.m. to 12.30 p.m. in the mill. Unofficially they often arrived earlier. After leaving the mill, where they could have been working in a humid atmosphere varying between 80°F and 110°F, they had to hurry home for a meal before starting afternoon school. Although the hours worked in a textile mill fell by half-an-hour to a weekly average of $27\frac{3}{4}$, after the beginning of 1902 the commitment of 13 to 14 hours schooling remained. Yet the Yorkshire boy who stuck this regime out for a weekly wage of 3s or 4s frequently did no more than qualify to become an unskilled labourer. His chances of permanent employment in a worsted mill, for example, were slight. Only in lowly paid combing did men outnumber women by about three to two. In spinning and weaving women were in a majority of four or five to one. The vast majority of boys, except for a few who became overlookers, left the mill in their teens to seek employment elsewhere.

In contrast to the children in the textile factories, many of those in workshops and non-textile factories were hardly touched by the remedial legislation before the late 1870s. The biggest problems facing the factory inspectorate were the sheer size of their workload and their need to rely on unofficial sources of information. For instance an inspector, covering Cornwall, Devon, and half Somerset, had to turn to the local trade directories to discover that he had 10,000 to 12,000 workplaces in his area. In the course of three years he visited 4,000 of them. Another inspector based on Nottingham found a further difficulty. The lace and stocking manufacture were carried on in places so

193

obscure and multitudinous as to escape the most vigilant attention. At times employers and employees deliberately obfuscated this obscurity. The inspector for the Rugby area complained,

As soon as an inspector pays one of his rare visits to a 'stocking' village, his coming is at once made known, and children are quickly hidden away, under skeps or baskets and in cupboards and holes, and when his back is turned, employers and parents congratulate themselves on their good luck and adroitness in escaping detection.

The members of the Royal Commission who accompanied R. A. Cross, their chairman, to the Luton and Dunstable area to look for straw-plaiting schools had similar experiences. On making enquiries about such schools they were directed to one in a small hamlet but on their entrance they found the children doing nothing. 'In other villages we were unable to find the strawplait schools though informed of their existence, our enquiries appearing to excite suspicion.' The small countryside workshops, in which hats and bonnets were made up from the plaited straw proved equally elusive. They reported

The workshops in the country places are so seldom visited and . . . the coming of the inspector is so well known, that the law is almost a dead letter . . . . There appears to be a general disposition among the work-people at this trade to evade the law. The children at the schools will not tell how they work; the existence of the plait schools is concealed; the arrival of a stranger is telegraphed about.

Even in a larger centre such as Luton 'Many small workshops . . . eluded detection by having notice of the rare visits of the inspector to the town.'[10]

Generally speaking, some of the strongest opposition to the new Education Acts and the labour laws came from those districts in which cottage industries supplemented the earnings of the agricultural labourer. Although the 1876 Royal Commission on Factory and Workshop Acts found widespread support for their proposal to raise the age for beginning full-time employment from eight to ten they met resistance from 'the straw-plait trade of Bedfordshire and the neigh-bourhood, pillow-lace making, stocking seaming, hat and bonnet sewing, winding for handloom weavers and framework knitters, the needle and fish hook manufacturers, and glove sewing trades'. Many parents sent their children, engaged in such trades, to so-called schools not to learn their three Rs but to ensure that they maximized their output. As one observer delicately explained, 'The mother would not make the child work so hard as the plaiting-school mistress' as 'she did not choose to exercise the amount of compulsion that was necessary to get the amount of plait out of the children.' The scholastic standards of these schools were far inferior to those recognized as efficient by the Education Department. Gross overcrowding, earthen floors, inadequate lighting, heating, and ventilation and in the gloving schools in parts of Somerset, skin diseases caught from the pelts, added to the misery of the children. Yet one inspector gilded the lily when he wrote of the lace-making schools in South Devon.

Here hard by ruddy cliffs and a blue sea in a land of luxuriant foliage, and under a roof which, even if delapidated, is probably picturesque, a party of little maids, demure and cleanly employ their tiny fingers after a fashion, which however irksome in reality, looks more like a pastime than serious work . . . ill-treatment there is none, while cleanliness is usual and order invariable.

He ended on a less eulogistic note, 'It cannot be denied that to economise space, the little stools - are usually placed very close together, so that the position of the bodies is necessarily rather cramped . . . and that the ventilation is far from perfect.'[11]

It was far harder to gloss over the conditions under which children worked in bakehouses and brickworks in the late 1860s and 1870s. Children put in a sixteen-hour stint at the biscuit firms of Carr's of Carlisle and Powell's of Preston, an arrangement that the Royal Commissioners stated was 'facetiously described as "putting them into the hot house to mature".' The inspector under whose jurisdiction Huntley and Palmer's factory at Reading fell found that complaints of overwork were frequent. He did not know of any workplace that required inspection more than did this particular factory.[12]

The brickfield provided many a child with a refuge, albeit surely one of last report, from the ministrations of factory inspector and schoolmaster. Brickmaking, when carried on in the open, was a difficult trade to control because of its intermittent nature. Not only was it seasonal but brickfields were seldom worked for the whole week. Since the earlier acts required children to have worked the whole week before they came under the labour laws, the brickfield provided a legal sanctum for all who wished to evade the law. The structure of the industry and the scattered nature of the work added to the inspector's difficulties. If an inspector appeared at one end of a field, girls banned from working in brickfields from 1872 onwards, and boys had plenty of time in which to disappear. One inspector recalled that in the early 1870s little girls were concealed on his approach. 'Report has it that once I stepped on a girl hid under some matting without discovering her.' To deceive him the brickmakers resorted to 'every possible device'. He found that 'Both masters and parents frighten the children by telling them that the Inspector will take them to prison, or eat them.' As soon as he got out of his train, news was sent to every brickfield, a watch kept, and the girls concealed on his approach. He resorted to driving in a closed gig by a circuitous route only to find that he could get to only one brickfield without being discovered first. He had a similar problem with unfenced iron mills. The boys dropped their tongs and ran like rabbits. Another inspector recalled that, in the early 1870s, it was often not without some danger of personal injury, or, at least, insult, that a Factory Inspector performed his duties, and on more than one occasion he had been threatened with violence. Even if an inspector discovered a child working illegally, the collusion of those present made it difficult for him to discover the actual employer. The custom of the trade was to sub-let the work to a foreman, who again sub-let the actual making of the bricks to moulders, each of whom had a trench and employed his labour with scant regard for the law. Yet the child put to treading clay in a brickfield needed effective legal protection. Where pug mills were not in use a boy trod a mixture of clay and water, a process that was said to make a horse totally unfit for work after two seasons.[13]

As a general rule, law enforcement in the industries based on workshops or the putting-out system was extremely difficult. Apart from restrictions in the Workshops Regulation Act of 1867 on their powers the inspectorate had the difficult task of proving a negative. They had to show that a boy had not attended school. Furthermore, to convict a parent who might possibly have been illiterate, they had also to show that the parent knew of the act's requirements and of his child's absence from school. Similarly the legal confusion over the person of the errand boy gave parents and employers the best of both worlds. Errand boys were outside the jurisdiction of the various factory acts. If the parents were prosecuted under these acts, they could plead that he did not actually work on the premises. Contrariwise, a prosecution under the education acts brought the plea that the boy made up parcels and therefore came under the aegis of the factory acts. The infrequency of the visits of the inspectorate, together with the difficulties of bringing a successful prosecution, encouraged all concerned to break the law with virtual impunity. If a parent was so unfortunate as to be fined, it was a small loss to set against a child's total earnings.

Moreover, a reading of the reports of the factory inspectors suggests that they were loath to prosecute unless they were faced with flagrant breaches of the law or open defiance. Not only was the number of summonses issued small but some of the inspectorate saw virtue in a policy of Fabian gradualism. When Alexander Redgrave, an inspector of factories, pointed out that the Elementary Education Act, 1876, 'restricted the manufacturer in his supply of labour, and deprived the parent of the earnings of his children', he drew the conclusion that 'the act must be enforced with tenderness, and both parties led up, rather than be driven, to compliance.' One sub-inspector saw virtue in his heavy caseload because 'The present size of the sub-divisions acts as a wholesome check upon premature and undue pressure . . . improvement is a plant of slow growth, and great national improvements are not perfected in one generation', an attitude that was liable to become a self-fulfilling prophecy if allowed to flourish unchecked. Moreover the appointment of gentlemen, rather than low-born careerists was seen as a way of protecting employers from the tyranny of the executive. If the local sub-inspectors were of 'inferior grade and receiving small salaries', the same official argued, they would be too zealous in seeking promotion and 'too anxious to ride to fame upon the backs of the employers of labour. Work under the Workshop Regulation Act . . . however irksome the work may be at times . . . can be better done by a gentleman'.[14]

The eventual salvation of many children from long hours of illegal toil in the country workshops came not through a change of heart of either parent or employer, nor did it come from more effective administrative action. It came through technological innovations and other factors that made these rural crafts no longer economically viable. For instance, around 1870 machinery used for the weaving of cocoa fibre and horse hair in the Long Melford area made redundant the child who had earlier put the horsehair on the reed. In the 1880s the boot and shoe industry around Kettering began to move into the factories. This eliminated the need for the services of a part-time errand boy who took the boot from the riveter, who put the sole on, to the factory for inspection before it was taken by another boy to the finisher. Under the earlier fragmented and under-capitalized system errand boys had quickly set themselves up in business and become the employers of other boys younger than themselves, hiring a stand for a few pence a week in a central workshop and employing their own runners.

Other children became the unintended beneficiaries of the free-trade era. Imports of French machine-made lace ruined the pillow-lace industry of Bedfordshire and Buckinghamshire by the late 1880s. The glove trade of Yeovil fell on hard times when German and Italian imports left only the quality trade to the home producer. Similarly a combination of mechanization and cheap imports destroyed the cottage-based industries of hat making and straw-plaiting in Bedfordshire and Hertfordshire. By the late 1870s the sewing machine had driven the hat industry from the cottage into the small factory whose owner could afford the initial outlay of £50 or so for a good quality machine. At the same time the importation of Chinese plait at a lower price than the villagers could buy unplaited English straw put the cottage plaiter out of business as well.[15]

During the closing decades of the century the urban industrial areas shared the experience of the rural regions in which the cottage type industries had been carried on. With the increasing cost and complexity of machinery the demand for unskilled juvenile labour fell. The total prohibition of the practice whereby children cleaned machinery in motion, contained in the Factory and Workshops Act of 1878, lessened the usefulness of children to law-abiding employers. In addition a slow improvement in the effectiveness of law enforcement made the illicit employment of children more bothersome and financially less rewarding to all concerned. Thus the employment of half-time children in Birmingham, for example, had practically ceased in all businesses except the button trade by 1890 where girls could still earn about 1s 6d a week. Similarly during the 1880s the number of children at work on a half-time basis had shown a decline throughout the iron manufacturing districts of Staffordshire. Thus by 1897 a return put the number of half-timers in non-textile factory and workshops at 8,498. In addition there were those working half-time outside the Factory and Workshop Acts. According to a return of the Education Department for the following year these brought the total to 103,678. Such figures err on the side of caution as it is improbable that they are complete.[16]

Before attendance at school became generally compulsory in 1880 the earlier factory and workshop acts, as well as being ineffectively administered, had a further disadvantage. There was no guarantee that children would go to school before they came into the orbit of the part-time system. If anything, contemporaries thought the opposite was true. Parents either tried to put their children into jobs that were not regulated by legislation or, failing that, into those that required the minimum amount of schooling. Thus in the countryside agriculture provided an alternative to the cottage industries covered by the Workshop Regulation Act. The boy over the age of twelve in a coalmining district went down the pits where he could work full-time instead of going part-time to a factory or workshop. Other parents were credited with having adopted the attitude that since their children would have to go to school on entering certain occupations, there was no point in anticipating that evil while their children could still earn a few pence running errands, holding horses' heads, or hawking. One enactment, the Agricultural Children's Act of 1873, attempted to remedy this situation.

As well as making provision for the education of rural children the act regulated their conditions of work. The age at which they could start work in agricultural gangs was raised from 8 to 10. Elsewhere they could not normally work in agriculture under the age of 8. Between the ages of 8 and 10 children could only work if they produced a certificate showing that they had made 250 attendances at a school recognized as efficient by the Education Department. Between the ages of 10 and 12 the smaller quota of 150 attendances or 15 weeks sufficed. Once a child passed Standard IV he became exempt from further attendance. In addition the local justices of the peace could suspend the operation of the act for a period not exceeding eight weeks a year. Last, the act exempted children over the age of eight 'employed in the operations of the hay harvest, corn harvest, or gathering of hops'.

The act came into force on 1 January 1875. Despite its many concessions to the farming interest, it became a dead letter within twelve months. In 1876 Viscount Sandon, then Vice-President of the Privy Council on Education, admitted that 'As no one was bound to enforce the Act, it was put in force in only some eleven or twelve counties, and there was generally worked by the police.' Even this seems an exaggeration. A return made to the House of Commons of 'correspondence between the Home Office and Justices of Quarter Sessions relative to the Agricultural Children's Act' does not give a single example of a clerk of the peace stating that the justices had instructed the police to enforce the Act. So little account was taken of the Act that only twenty of the clerks of the peace in England and Wales even bothered to reply to the Home Office circular. The countryside had followed the lead of the new Conservative administration of 1874. Disraeli had been one of the Buckinghamshire justices to vote against instructing the police to enforce the act. R. A. Cross, the Home Secretary, had acted likewise by instructing the Metropolitan Police not to enforce the act.[17]

The government's ministers had mirrored the opinion of the countryside. The *Field*, the journal of county society, saw defying the law as no crime. 'What we fear is that the police may look upon the offenders as though they belonged to the criminal classes . . . . No greater mistake could be made by them . . . .' Country teachers found it impolitic to attempt to operate the act. A schoolmistress who attempted to bribe a village policeman to round up local truants was told 'Now miss if you want to keep your situation, take my advice, it is no use going against the farmers. Teach those who come to school, and if they employ the boys, don't pretend to know it.' A schoolmaster complained that he and his family 'had been subject to the grossest indignities and abuse'. He had approached the magistrate's clerk for police protection without success. As a result he found that 'People may kick at your door and turn over your soft-water vats' with impunity, such was the strength of popular protest when given the tacit support of local social leaders.[18]

A confluence of social and economic factors ensured the unpopularity of the education acts in the countryside at all levels of society. At certain times of the year farmers wanted the maximum amount of help available. Traditionally they had seen the labourers as their dependents on whose services and those of whose families they could call at will. The Education Acts, with their regulation of children's labour, cut across this informal traditional relationship between master and man; in the same way it cut across the parent's traditional practice of sending his children to work in the fields as soon as they were able to earn a penny or so a day. Moreover the statutory limitations on the supply of juvenile labour came at a time when the farmer was already experiencing a labour shortage. Between 1850 and 1870 the number of full-time agricultural labourers fell by 15 to 20 per cent. More important was the decline in the number of casual and temporary harvest labourers, the result of growing employment opportunities in the urban areas, the decline of cottage industries, the increasing reluctance of women to work in the fields, and the fall in the amount of available migrant labour. To cap it all had come the Education Acts. In the short term they further restricted the amount of immediately available juvenile labour. In the long term farmers feared that education would widen the minds of the young thereby encouraging them to forsake the fields altogether for the cities or the colonies. The farm labourer, in common

200

with every other working-class parent, suffered the double burden of losing his children's earnings and having to find the weekly school pence when he was in a trough of the poverty cycle with a young family on his hands. To make matters worse many small rural Church schools, progressively feeling financial strains, are said to have taken advantage of the introduction of compulsory education by raising their fees. Thus the lot of the labourer earning 2s 3d a day and subject to stoppages for wet weather, paying perhaps 2s a week for his cottage, was a parlous one if he had a large family and the board of guardians refused to pay the school fees for him.[19]

In the countryside the general picture is one of an apathy that bordered on passive resistance. Occasionally resistance became active when the proposed school board met the hostility of the very incumbent whose shortcomings the Education Department was attempting to remedy. In one or two cases in Northumberland angry incumbents tore down from the church door the notices the Department had issued. One inspector commented:

To the farmer of the old-fashioned type it seems little short of adding insult to injury, first to make him pay a man for doing a boy's work, and then to make him pay a rate for the said boy being taught nothing that will make him a better ploughman or carter in the future, and this at a time of high wages, bad harvests, trade unions, and general discontent.

Farmers and others frequently rationalized their opposition to the Education Acts by blaming them for the poor state of the roads. Now that they could no longer employ the children in the fields on stone picking, the roads could not be kept in a proper state of repair because the necessary stones were not readily available. However, the comments of an inspector responsible for another farming area reminded one how dangerous generalizations about the attitude of social classes and occupational groups in the nineteenth century can be. Around Taunton farmers made the best of a bad job, arguing that since they had to pay the school board rate they might as well have their money's worth and see that the children attended and reached the requisite standards of the bye-laws. Similarly in the Dunmow Union, near Colchester, the inspector in charge found 'every appearance of zealous work on the part of the school attendance committee, a hearty co-operation with them on the part of the magistrates.' Yet the nearby Lexden Union had the 'only school attendance committee in the district . . . to have systematically and wilfully endeavoured to avoid the proper performance

of their duties . . . up to the present they have been signally successful.'
Clearly much depended on the attitude of the locally influential. There
is the suggestion that the least amount of illegal employment occurred
in close villages. On the other hand such villages probably contained
proportionately fewer children than did open ones. The landowners in a
close village could prevent the building of cottages thereby restricting
the number of labourers' families who might at some time become a
charge on the poor rate. Labourers accordingly had to live in the
nearest conveniently sited open village to rear their families. Yet such
villages making a heavier demand for educational services were often
the ones that had lacked schools before 1870. In a close village the
predominant landowner usually continued to support any Church
school he had already built or provided one *de novo* after 1870 if only
to keep the school board at bay.[20]

In rural England the school attendance officer was frequently the
relieving officer, a combination of duties that gave working-class
parents added reason for resenting the new legislation. In addition he
might act as an assistant overseer, tax collector, and registrar of births,
deaths, and marriages. His district, if thinly populated, could be an
extensive one in which difficulties of travelling added to his burden.
The Bootle school attendance committee's boundaries enclosed $12\frac{1}{2}$
square miles and a population of 4,523 in 1881. Their two officials,
paid a salary of £6 a year for a day's work a week, had not issued their
first summons by 1883. They seem to have taken to heart the advice
that one school inspector averred was offered another attendance
officer, 'It is privately reported to me that in one instance a man was
given 2s a week and told to do as little as he could.' Similarly despite
the introduction of general compulsion in 1880, another school
inspector wrote two years later, 'The clerk of the Thrapston [near
Peterborough] school attendance committee states "they regret that
they are unable to inform me how many schools are under their super-
intendence".' The following year HMI S. G. Tremenheere found that
only 68 per cent of the children in Whitehaven attended school
regularly. For the town's population of 20,000 there was one part-time
attendance officer; for the country districts another who had not
entered some of his schools for at least the last twelve months. Neither
official was required to make any kind of return to his committee.[21]

As late as 1890 there were still 40 parishes that had never introduced
any bye-laws to extend education beyond the age of 10. Even the later
acts of 1893 and 1899 which raised the school-leaving age to 12 left

them unaffected, thanks to a loophole in the legislation. However, the Education Department persuaded all except two, Little Stukely in Huntingdonshire and Therfield in Hertfordshire, to follow the Government's lead. These two parishes continued to release their children from school at the age of ten until the 1902 Act swept their school boards away.[22] In addition, the Education Act of 1899 made special concessions to the farming interest. Whereas other children could not start part-time work until they were twelve, farming children could start a year earlier. At thirteen they could leave school for ever to work on the land. Between the ages of eleven and thirteen they had to make 250 attendances a year if working part-time, other children having to make 300 attendances between the ages of twelve and fourteen. However, few authorities made use of these special concessions granted in 1899. By 1909 they were claimed mainly for the fruit picking in parts of Kent. In agricultural districts, as in the textile regions, official sentiment was turning against the part-time system. The Inter-Departmental Committee of 1909 which investigated the problem condemned it in the countryside on the grounds that the children had a disruptive influence on the schools as they picked up adult tastes, habits, and language while working. In rural areas,[23]

One of our witnesses said he had been told by teachers that they had to give their biggest half-timers a thrashing regularly each October. Where, as is frequently the case in rural schools, the head teachers are women, a state of affairs which calls for such drastic remedies is even more serious.

Growing dissatisfaction with a part-time system of education that pleased neither the schoolmaster nor the employer is indicative of the way in which the great drive to bring the nation's children into the schools was nearing its successful conclusion by the end of the nineteenth century. As long as it was a struggle to get the children into the schools at all, concern over the deficiencies of the part-time system or over working out of school hours was something of a luxury. The criminal statistics of the period, albeit they may be better evidence of the incidence of authority's readiness to prosecute than of juvenile breaches of the law, suggest a readier acceptance of the new laws by the early twentieth century. The number of prosecutions fell from a peak of nearly 100,000 in 1883 (97,274) to under half that figure (36,823) by 1910. However, truancy was the second most common offence from 1888 to 1916. During the last two years of the First World War, thanks to the halving of beer consumption, it finally overtook its judicial rival, offences against the intoxicating liquor laws.[24]

With a more efficient administration of the law parents realized that the only way in which they could safely use their children's services to supplement the family budget was to send them to work outside school hours. During school-time the child not in school was an easy prey to the police or the school-attendance officers. No longer could parents emulate the example of those of Raunds, a village between Thrapston and Higham Ferrers, where they found that if they never sent their children to school in the first place, their names never became known to the authorities. Although it had been possible as late as 1890 to find families here who had never sent a child to school, such parents became increasingly rarer. By the mid-1890s the Education Department estimated that 99 per cent of the seven to eleven year-old group eligible to attend elementary schools were on the school registers.[25]

Unfortunately for the child working outside school hours, legal safeguards were meagre. Under the Elementary Education Act, 1876, it was possible to prosecute an employer if the child's work interfered with his efficient education. The act, invoked solely against those who employed children during school hours, proved something of a broken reed. It was not used against those who required children to work such excessive hours, before or after school, that they fell asleep in the classroom.[26] Similarly the Shop Hours Act, 1892, which imposed a limit of 74 hours a week on youngsters under the age of 18, was of little help. It left children working in the family shop, the commonest form of retail unit at the time, unprotected. The Prevention of Cruelty to Children Act, 1894, did little to stop excessive juvenile labour. The act forbade street selling and performing by children under the age of eleven. It restricted these activities to the hours of 6.00 a.m. to 9.00 p.m. for boys under the age of 14 and girls under 16. In practice these clauses were generally ignored in London, if not elsewhere, by the turn of the century. A further weakness of the Act was that it only covered children who were employed to sell, thereby excluding those trading on their own account, and children performing such tasks as delivering goods and knocking up workmen.[27] Last, a number of provincial cities, including Birmingham, Bradford, Hull, Manchester and Sheffield, had obtained special powers under private acts to restrict street trading in the 1880s. In 1898 the city of Liverpool secured powers to introduce a licencing scheme for young street traders. The Corporation laid down age restrictions, limited the hours of work, and banned children from trading in public houses and music halls. Within a few years other cities followed the Liverpudlian example. Effective enforcement was another matter. In Liverpool there were no more than three inspectors, yet the city possessed over 3,000 grocer's shops alone. Prosecutions were usually instituted for failing to display a notice of the Act, not for breaches of regulations restricting conditions of work.[28]

In 1897, a year before Liverpool received its corporation act, Mrs E. F. Hogg had published an article on the school child wage earner in the *Nineteenth Century*. Its evidence came from a committee she had set up on the subject. For a number of reasons she found a ready audience. The closing years of the century were those of the beginning of the growing concern over the question of national efficiency, a debate that encompassed both the moral and the physical well-being of the young.[29] Hence part of the crusade against the street trader was a moral one. At a time when youth workers became increasingly worried about the prevalence of street gambling, the boy newspaper seller was a ready target for their attention. In particular those who sold racing papers were thought to be at special risk, possessing as they did both the knowledge, the contacts, and the cash with which to place small bets. For the same reason lather boys working in barber's shops, a common venue for the passing of betting slips, also became subjects of special concern. Alarm grew apace. By 1910 an official report described the moral effects of street trading as tending 'to create a restless disposition, and a dislike of restraint which makes children unwilling to settle down to any regular employment', a comment that re-echoes the anxiety expressed about the part-timer in the mills qualifying himself for the unskilled labour market. For the young street trader the pathway to vagrancy and crime was seen to be an easy one; the newspaper seller took to gambling, the match seller became a beggar. In any case many saw matchbox selling as no more than a disguised form of begging. For a girl the consequences of street trading were dire, 'she almost inevitably was taking a first step towards a life of immorality'. Such was the same report's worry about the older trader, the boy of 14 to 16 who became a loafer and one of the *'gamins* of our large towns', that it recommended the banning of all boys under 16 and girls under 17 from street trading.[30]

Moreover demographic change and the enforcement of compulsory school attendance made street children conspicuous out of school hours. Unlike the 1860s and early 1870s when street gangs and children roaming the street to make a casual living had been a part of everyday life, the streets were now relatively free of children during school hours. The streets filled when the schools disgorged their contents. In addition there were more children to fill the streets than ever before; the 5 to 15 year-old cohort had increased by 75 per cent between 1851 and 1911, from 4,005,716 to 7,196,484.[31]

Following the publication of Mrs Hogg's article an Inter-Department Committee had reported in November 1901. The outcome was the Employment of Children Act, 1903, which allowed local authorities to frame bye-laws regulating street trading and other juvenile forms of employment. Since the Act was adoptive it proved of limited value. Out of a total of 329 authorities there were still 98 without bye-laws regulating general employment and 198 without restrictions on street trading in 1914. Employers, newspaper proprietors, farmers, shopkeepers, and others took advantage of a procedure that required objections to be heard at a quasi-judicial enquiry. Since this was held at the expense of the originating authority the threat of employers' opposition was sufficient to blackmail the more frugally minded boroughs into quiescence. Even if an authority passed the necessary bye-laws there was no guarantee that it would take steps to enforce its regulations. Cities such as London, Bolton, Bradford, Bristol, Leeds, and Liverpool, that attempted to make a good job of it were exceptional. Consequently an optimistic estimate puts the decline in the number of children earning wages between 1903 and 1914 around 10 to 15 per cent. Where there was some discernible improvement, it was seen in the fall of the numbers of very young children trading or those selling very late at night on the streets.[32] To add to its drawbacks the 1903 Act touched only the fringe of the problem, for the 1902 Committee had reported 'The severest work, the longest hours, and the hardest conditions, are often to be found in the case of children who are employed without wages in doing housework in the homes of their parents.' Girls in particular did an enormous amount of unpaid work that never appeared in any parliamentary return for they were 'more tractable than boys, and . . . more easily made into drudges.' Their main work was that of doing other people's housework and looking after their babies. The belief that this was a natural extension of their role in their own homes accounted for the great disparity between boys' and girls' rates of pay shown in Table 7. Usually the girls were helping neighbours in or a little above their own circumstances.[33]

Outside the home the biggest employers of school children were the shops. In an unorganized and highly competitive labour market retailers

TABLE 7   *Children not employed by parents*

		Children not employed by parents	
	Number	*Weekly hours*	*Weekly wages without meals*
Boys	984	23·2	1s 11½d
Girls	78	17·18	7¾d
	Number	*Weekly hours*	*Weekly wages with meals*
Boys	368	24·85	1s 10½d
Girls	194	20·88	10¼d

		Children employed by parents	
	Number	*Weekly hours*	*Weekly wages*
Boys	120	21·25	7¾d
Girls	48	13·3	2d

Source: Report of the Interdepartmental Committee on the Employment of School Children, Parliamentary Papers, 1902, XXV, pp.422—7.

used children's services lavishly. They could give their more prosperous working-class customers a service that today's middle-class housewife would envy. Grocers, butchers, and other retailers, all sent their boys early in the evening to call for orders which they subsequently delivered the same day. With this service the mother whose credit was good needed to do no more than sally forth weekly to be greeted deferentially by the local traders while she paid her bills. Apart from taking, making up, and delivering orders, children acted as barkers outside the shop, served, or just watched goods on display on the pavement. For this they received about a penny an hour. The luckier ones who worked in a food shop might get a meal or some odds and ends to take home. A survey of London schools in 1897 found the following rough approximations, 'delivering newspapers and milk, 1d to 1¼d; street selling, ¾d; shop boys, 1d to 1¼d; carrying and delivering coal, 1d.' An analysis made in London schools four years later showed that boys working 25 hours or less a week averaged 1·45d an hour, while those working 40 or more hours a week made only 0·81d an hour. It was alleged that shopkeepers readily exploited familial misfortunes and paid the children of widows or invalid fathers less than the going rate. 'Mentally feeble' children suffered similarly.[34]

TABLE 8   *Family income of school children in employment*

Weekly income	Number of children at work	
	London	*Leeds*
Less than 10*s*	25	6
10*s* to 15*s*	58	16
15*s* to 20*s*	60	28
20*s* to 25*s*	189	77
25*s* to 30*s*	154	67
30*s* to 35*s*	175	102
35*s* and more	141	187*
Totals	802	483

* 60 families earned between 35*s* and £2; 127 earned £2 a week or more.

Source: Report of the Interdepartmental Committee on the Employment of School Children, Parliamentary Papers, 1902, XXV, pp.374-5.

With these exceptions the children who usually secured jobs after school were not from the poorest families. Employers wanted 'sharp lads' who were physically fit and respectably enough dressed to win the confidence of their customers. The poorest children shared the fate of their parents. At the bottom of the occupational and social pyramid, they stayed there picking up such casual labour as might come their way. Jobs went to children from homes already enjoying sufficient prosperity to feed and clothe the family adequately enough to impress potential employers. Thus in Kentish Town, London, an area of heavy employment of children outside school hours, the parents of these children were said to be 'well-to-do' by working-class standards. Most of the fathers of working children were in regular employment in the local railway company depots or with the pianoforte makers that congregated there. Table 8 shows that the median family income for child workers in London was 20*s* to 25*s* a week. The same table substantiates a point made earlier, the readiness with which comparatively affluent working-class parents sent their children out to work in the textile towns.

Among the more onerous tasks was that of delivering milk, an activity that was often combined with knocking up workmen and which could start as early as 5.00 a.m. Working as a lather boy in a barber's shop could require five hours each evening, together with fifteen on Saturdays and a further six to eight on Sundays. Newspaper rounds might need only an hour each morning and evening. However, the launching of the *Daily Mail* in 1896 made life harder for the boy selling papers. This paper, aimed at a working-class market that had not previously bought a daily paper, made no attempt to supply its reader-ship with the latest news. It was published before the more expensive papers to catch the workman on his way to his place of employment. Boys could be taking the *Daily Mail* out on delivery as early as 5.30 a.m. while the penny papers and *The Times* did not go out from the shop before 7.00 a.m. or later. Many of the paper boys combined delivery with selling. Such lads were out in the streets before school, sold mid-day editions during their school dinner hour, and then the evening papers after school. The more sensational the news, the greater were the sales and the longer the hours worked. As one boy said, 'a big race, football match, or a good divorce, or a fairish murder, it pays to stop out pretty late, and I does.' If he had been speaking after August 1914, he would have added war news as well. Profits were low for the boy in the street who came at the end of a distribution chain that stretched from him to the newspaper office via an agent and a middle-man. Making $3\frac{1}{2}d$ profit on a shilling's sales when newspapers retailed at a halfpenny each was a slow job. The newspaper boy had one con-solation. In the variegated bustling street life of late Victorian and Edwardian England he stood a cut above the matchbox seller, an occupation put by many on a par with begging. While newspaper selling enjoyed a certain respectability, matchbox sellers bore a social stigma. This stigma was shared by organ grinders, icecream sellers, and their assistants, men following pursuits deemed more suitable for Italians than English working men. Older school children joined the groups of unemployed hanging around railway stations looking for casual employment. Even this group had its own hierarchy. The boys who offered to carry bags and parcels for a small tip were the inferiors of those who possessed handcarts in which they could wheel heavier loads.[35]

In the country agricultural work continued to make heavy demands on a child's time. School children were out in the Kentish fields early picking perishable fruit to catch the trains to the London markets. Lincolnshire children could start pea picking as early as 2.00 a.m. before going to school. Because of the greater distances that had to be travelled errand boys had to be out earlier than their urban brothers delivering or collecting milk and taking bread and newspapers to customers. In Devonshire labourers boarded their children out at farms where in return for their keep the children, as young as ten or eleven, worked on the land before and after school without any payment in cash. Children from the East End of London had their taste of country life when they missed the first three or four weeks of the autumn term hop picking and lived in primitive conditions that no school inspector would have tolerated in their schools.[36]

Even with the improvement in the enforcement of the laws regulating school attendance and juvenile working conditions that took place during the period under discussion, there were still at least half a million children dividing their energies between school and work in 1914. The disquiet expressed about this state of affairs and the concern shown over the physical condition of the people that made the Education (Provision of Meals) Act a political possibility were part of a greater whole, an anxiety about the debilitating effects on urbanization, the scale of which was still a comparative novelty at the end of the nineteenth century. There was also a xenophobic streak running through the debate which blamed the worst conditions of employment on 'The continuous pumping of alien filth from the kennels and ghettos of Europe, Asia and America into the East End of London through the sewage-pipes of the steamship companies.'[37]

Although the main emphasis of this study has been on families with little or no tradition of school going, it is well to remember that the tripartite division with which we started in the 1860s remains meaningful for 1914 and to some extent today. The skilled artisan who made use of the schools regularly before 1870 because he saw they offered his children the means of upward occupational mobility had his peer in 1914. 'A quite remarkable proportion of the children of elementary schoolmasters is now knocking at the doors of the older Universities', wrote C. F. G. Masterman, 'and those who effect entrance are taking off the highest honours.' A few of the sons of small shopkeepers, artisans, and others of comparable income now had access to the provincial universities and, thanks to the building of non-collegiate halls of residence, Oxford and Cambridge as well. Similarly a study of 88 working-class children of Huddersfield who completed their sixth-form courses shortly after the Second World War shows that they came mainly 'from the upper strata of the working class, from small families who lived in favourable, socially-mixed districts. Further, over a third of the parents had connexions with the middle class themselves and shared many of its aspirations', a group whom the investigators described as 'sunken middle class'. From this sample 54 had gone to university.[38]

The pre-1870 middle stratum of the working classes consisted of those who were sending their children to school as and when they could. There was no clear division between these parents and those above and below, one group faced imperceptibly into another. After 1870 we can equate these parents with those 'respectable' ones who sent their children to school regularly and obeyed the new laws. The more prosperous and committed of them were able to provide that extra ingredient of parental encouragement that enabled their children to stay at school a little longer than legally required and enter the burgeoning clerical and minor supervisory occupations.

There still remained in 1914 the equivalent of our third group, those who had never sent their children to school before 1870. Although no longer able to avoid it altogether, their concern was to see that their children performed the minimum possible. To them compulsory education far from being the gift of a beneficent state was an infliction that reduced living standards, disrupted the normal pattern of life, and exacerbated the social problems that *ad hoc* voluntary agencies and the state eventually alleviated. As we remarked earlier the Plowden Report of 1967 was able to identify a group that could see little or no occupational or economic advantage in schooling. For many working class parents the proviso whereby a child could leave school on reaching the necessary Standards led to an inversion of the values of today's middle-class educationalist. In the working-class home the bright child was the one who demonstrated his academic prowess by leaving as early as legally possible.[39]

For the majority of children the new laws had lengthened their period of dependence and deferred their entry into the adult world. However, the extra control parents gained over their children in chronological terms was offset largely by the restrictions put on their children's wage-earning capacity. Children found the delay of their entry into the adult world of wage earners irksome for until they achieved that status their opinion counted for little in many a working-class home. One wonders how many shared the acute sense of shame felt by one nine-year-old fenland boy whom Sybil Marshall tells us hid in the ditches on his way to school to avoid the ridicule of the farm labourers in the mid 1870s.[40] Thus opponents of any extension of the period of elementary education could always justifiably point to the eagerness with which children looked forward to the day when they could leave; contrariwise proponents deplored the early age at which parents lost the means of restraint over their children and the readiness with which boys could spend their money on cigarettes and music halls, in disfavour by the 1900s as causes of ill-health and venues of vice respectively.

In this rough and ready tripartite division of the working classes the ever-present factor has been the attitude of the parents whether it be supportive, neutral, or negative, a factor that recent research has reaffirmed as playing an important role in determining the extent of a child's success at school. For the bulk of working-class children attending school firm support was lacking. Parental attitudes were determined largely on practical, knife and fork criteria. A rejection thesis based on political ideology is hard to sustain. On the contrary the group to whom we might plausibly attribute the greatest degree of political sophistication, the skilled artisan and his economic equals, was one that made the greatest use of the schools and campaigned for the state to provide a pathway from the elementary school to the university. Those who see nineteenth century elementary education as designed to keep a working-class child in his allotted place overlook the very real difficulties the poorest parents faced in sending their children to school at all let alone for the extended time that would have been required for a wider curriculum. Similarly the obstacles facing the working-class voter at school-board elections explain only part of the poor showing of candidates devoted to his cause. With a succession of local government elections only the more politically committed were going to turn out for school board elections for ' "The difficulty in England", the Fabians complained in 1896, "is not to get more political power for the people, but to persuade them to make use of the political power they have".'[41] When one couples the general lack of parental support with the irregularity of many children's attendance one may legitimately wonder whether the excellence of the grounding in the three Rs popularly attributed to the schools of this period was more myth than fact. Despite the teacher's heavy concentration on these subjects, nearly a third of the children were not reaching the level expected of them at the age of ten in 1890. Complaints by potential employers at the beginning of the twentieth century that school leavers could not write decently, spell correctly, or work simple calculations accurately have a familiar ring.[42]

Last, one may ask just when did the practice of sending a child to school with daily regularity finally become established. Whereas one is not surprised to find a rise in the incidence of illegal juvenile employment in the First World War, by 1939 another generation had gone

212

through the schools. Yet with the disruption of the normal pattern of life there was a resurgence of older attitudes especially in some of those agricultural areas where observance of the law had been lax before 1914. Similarly in the large cities an extra 2 to 8 per cent stayed off school where, if both parents were absent during the day, the oldest girl reverted to her pre-1870 role. She stayed at home to look after her sick brothers or sisters, deal with tradesmen, and perform other similar tasks. Children who returned to London after the raids of the winter of 1940–1 did not always seek out the schools; an expanded force of school enquiry officers had to seek them out.[43] Thus almost three-quarters of a century after Forster's Bill had become law, some parents still acquiesced in rather than accepted the legal requirements that had changed the pattern of a family life that dated back to a pre-industrial society. What to one social group had appeared to be remedial legislation had added a burden to another.

Notes

Part One   The Working Classes and the 1870 Act

Chapter I   Our Future Masters

[1] *Report of the Schools' Inquiry Commission (Taunton Report)*, Parliamentary Papers (hereafter P.P.) 1867–8, XXVIII, A, 'Memorandum by Dr W. Farr', Appendix II, pp.6–10.

[2] *Ibid.*, D. C. Richmond, 'Estimate of the Number of Boys . . .', pp.15–27; *ibid.*, vol. H, J. G. Fitch, 'General Report on the West Riding of Yorkshire', Appendix I, pp.333–8.

[3] R. D. Baxter, *National Income* (1868), *passim* especially pp.14, 21 and 52.

[4] *Reports of the Committee of the Privy Council on Education (Reports on Education)*, P.P. 1857 (session II), XXXIII, pp.443–4.

[5] *Taunton Report*, P.P. 1867–8, XXVIII, A, pp.2–3.

[6] *Ibid.*, pp.20, 90.

[7] *Reports on Education*, P.P. 1896, XXVI, p.65.

[8] *Taunton Report*, P.P. 1867–8, XXVIII, A, pp.339, 345, 431, 434.

[9] *Ibid.*, P.P. 1867–8, H. pp.714, 737, 749–51, 759 footnote.

[10] *Ibid.*, P.P. 1867 8, G. pp.231, 271–2.

[11] *Ibid.*, P.P. 1867–8, H, p.246.

[12] *Ibid.*, p.248–9.

[13] P.P. 1862, XLI, p.5.

[14] *Report of the R.C. on the State of Education in England (Newcastle Report)*, P.P. 1861, F, Q 623

[15] *Ibid.*, P.P. 1861, A, pp.73–4; *Minute of 31 December 1857*, P.P. 1857–8, XLV, p.6.

[16] *Newcastle Report*, P.P. 1861, XXI, F, Q1546.

[17] *Supplementary Rules to the Revised Code*, P.P. 1864, XLV, p.lxvi.

[18] *Reports on Education*, P.P. 1867–8, XXV, p.197.

[19] *Ibid.*, pp.10–11.

[20] *Reports on Education*, P.P. 1865, XLII, p.135.

[21] *Reports on Education*, P.P. 1867–8, XXV, p.347.

²² *Reports on Education*, P.P. 1866, XXVII, p.29; P.P. 1867–8, XXV, pp.306–7; P.P. 1865, XLII, p.71.

²³ *Hansard*, CLXXXII, 38, 12 March 1866.

²⁴ *Hansard*, CLXXXVI, 7, 18 March 1867.

²⁵ *Hansard*, CLXXXII, 59–60, 12 March 1866.

²⁶ *Hansard*, CLXXXVI, 7, 18 March 1867.

²⁷ *Hansard*, CLXXXVIII, 1546, 15 July 1867.

²⁸ M. Cowling, 1867: *Disraeli, Gladstone and Revolution* (Cambridge, 1967), *passim*; F. B. Smith, *The Making of the Second Reform Bill* (Cambridge, 1966), pp.236–7.

²⁹ *Hansard*, CXC, 75, 19 November 1867: *Ibid.*, 49, 19 November 1867.

³⁰ *Hansard*, CXC, 750, 14 February 1868.

³¹ *Hansard*, CXCI, 105–29, 24 March 1868. The Bill is printed in *House of Lords Sessional Papers*, 1867–8, IV, 233–76. See also A. Bishop and W. Jones, 'The Act that never was: the Conservative Bill of 1868', *History of Education*, I (1972), 160–73.

³² *The Times*, 10–29 October 1868 *passim.*

³³ *Hansard*, CXCIV, 81, 16 February 1869.

³⁴ *Hansard*, CLXXXVI, 62, 18 March 1867.

³⁵ *Hansard*, CLXXXVIII, 1539–50, 15 July 1867.

³⁶ H. Perkin, 'The Origins of the Popular Press', *History Today*, VII (July 1957), pp.425–55; R. K. Webb, *British Working-Class Reader, 1790–1848* (1955) and the same author's 'Working-Class Readers in early Victorian England', *English Historical Review* XXXIII (1954), pp.333–51.

³⁷ J. Alexander and D. G. Paz, 'The Treasury Grant, 1833–9', *British Journal of Educational Studies* XXII, pp.78–89.

³⁸ N. Roper, 'Towards an Elementary Education Act for England and Wales, 1865–8', *British Journal of Educational Studies* (XXIII, 1975), pp.181–208.

³⁹ *Hansard*, CLXXXVI, 1351, 10 July 1867.

Chapter II   The Parental Consumer

¹ *Census of Great Britain: Reports and Tables on Education in England and Wales (Education Census, 1851)*, P.P. 1852–3, XC, pp.xxiv, xxvii.

² *Ibid.*, p.xl.

³ *Newcastle Report*, P.P. 1861, XXI, B, p.223; *ibid.*, vol. A, p.666. The reference is to O. Goldsmith, *An Abridgement of the History of England* (1774), based on his four-volume work of 1771. The *Abridgement* underwent numerous revisions and extensions. Its forty-sixth edition appeared as *Whittaker's improved edition of Pinnock's Goldsmith's History of England* in 1858. It was translated into French, German, Spanish, and Bengali. A cram book, *History for Woolwich and Arsenal Candidates of December 1874. From Goldsmith's Text*, appeared as late as 1874.

⁴ *Education Census, 1851*, P.P. 1852–3, XC, p.xli.

⁵ *Children and their Primary Schools* (The Plowden Report), (HMSO 1967), vol. I, p.50.

⁶ *Education Census*, 1851, P.P. 1852–3, XC, p.xli.

[7] *Newcastle Report*, P.P. 1861, XXI, C, p.87; *ibid.*, vol. A, p.177; *ibid.*, vol. C, p.242; *ibid.*, vol. B, p.147; *ibid.*, vol. B, p.58; *ibid.*, vol. B. pp.350–1.

[8] *Reports on Education*, P.P. 1870, XXII, p.347.

[9] *Newcastle Report*, P.P. 1861, XXI, C, pp.249, 253–4, 268.

[10] *Newcastle Report*, P.P. 1861, XXI, C, p.399.

[11] *Ibid.*, P.P. 1861, XXI, A, p.662, 664.

[12] *Ibid.*, P.P. 1861, XXI, C, pp.87–8.

[13] *Ibid.*, P.P. 1861, XXI, A, p.245.

[14] *Ibid.*, P.P. 1861, XXI, B, p.58.

[15] R. Thabault, *Education and Change in a Village Community* (1971), pp.3 4.

[16] *Newcastle Report*, P.P. 1861, XXI, A, p.243.

[17] B. S. Rowntree, *Poverty: A Study of Town Life* (1902), pp.133, 298.

[18] *Newcastle Report*, P.P. 1861, XXI, A, pp.179, 188, 189.

[19] *Newcastle Report*, P.P. 1861, XXI, A, pp.383–4.

[20] *Newcastle Report*, P.P. 1861, XXI, B, p.10.

[21] W. B. Stephens, 'An Anatomy of Illiteracy in Mid-Victorian Devon', in J. Porter (ed.), *Education and Labour in the South-West* (University of Exeter, 1975), pp.7–20.

[22] *Second Report of the Children's Employment Commission*, P.P. 1865, XXII, p.lxv; *Report of the Royal Commission on the Housing of the Working Classes*, P.P. 1884, XXX, Qs 14856–15054 *passim*.

[23] *The Times*, 12 August 1899.

[24] *First Report from the Commissioners on the Employment of Children and Young Persons in Trades and Manufactures* (Children's Employment Commission) P.P. 1863, XVIII, pp.24–8.

[25] *Second Report, Children's Employment Commission*, P.P. 1843 XIV, C38, C39, C43; *First Report, Children's Employment Commission*, P.P. 1863, XVIII, p.30.

[26] *First Report, Children's Employment Commission*, P.P. 1863, XVII, p.xxvi, *Second Report, Children's Employment Commission*, P.P. 1864, XXII, p.33.

[27] *Second Report, Children's Employment Commission*, P.P. 1864, XXII, p.97. *Newcastle Report*, P.P. 1861, XXI, A, p.34.

[28] *Sixth Report, Children's Employment Commission*, P.P. 1864, pp.x and xi.

[29] *Third Report, Children's Employment Commission*, P.P. 1864, XXII, p.x; *Second Report, ibid.*, P.P. 1864, XXII, p.x; *Second Report, ibid.*, P.P. 1864, XXII, p.xlvi; *Third Report, ibid.*, P.P. 1864, XXII, p.xxvii.

[30] *First Report, ibid.*, P.P. 1863, XVIII, p.xxxiv.

[31] H. S. Tremenheere, 'The Extension of the Factory Acts', *Transactions of the National Association for the Promotion of Social Science* (1866), pp.291–2.

[32] *Reports of the Inspectors of Factories*, P.P. 1871, XIV, pp.13, 57, 58.

[33] *First Report, Children's Employment Commission*, P.P. 1842, XIV, pp.195, 804, 859–60.

[34] *Reports on Education*, P.P. 1868–9, XX, pp.280–1; *Factory Times*, 7 December 1894.

[35] L. W. Evans, *Education in Industrial Wales* (Cardiff, 1971), pp.297–8.

[36] *British Miner and General Newsman*, successively *British Miner* and *Miner*, 18 October 1862, 17 January, 1863.

[37] *Report from the Select Committee on Accidents in Coal Mines*, P.P. 1854, IX Qs 1251–81 *passim*.

[38] *Report of Inspectors of Coal Mines*, P.P. 1857 (Session II) XVI, p.115; *Report from the Select Committee on Mines*, P.P. 1866, XIV, Q. 3073.

[39] *Workman's Advocate*, 23 September 1865.

[40] *Newcastle Report*, P.P. 1861, XXI, B, pp.348–53. *Annual Reports on Education*, P.P. 1871, XXII, pp.110–11.

[41] *Report from the Select Committee on Mines*, P.P 1866, XIV, Qs 38, 117, 1609–15, 2235, 4071–4, 4083, 9681.

Chapter III   The Coercion of the Parental Non-consumer

[1] *Newcastle Report*, P.P. 1861, XXI, A, pp.84, 178, 382.

[2] *Report from the Select Committee on the Education of Destitute Children*, P.P. 1861, VII, Q.365.

[3] *Hansard*, CLXX, 1198–9, 5 May 1863.

[4] T. P. Allen, *An Enquiry into the existing state of education in Battersea*; Allen, *Inquiry into the Existing state of education in Richmond, Twickenham, Mortlake, and neighbourhood*; Allen, *Report to the Council of the Society of Arts on the existing state of education in Ealing and Brentford*; G. C. T. Bartley, *One Square Mile in the East End of London*. All four reports are bound at the end of *Journal of the Royal Society of Arts*, XVIII (1869–70).

[5] *Reports on Schools for [the] Poorer Classes in Birmingham, Leeds, Liverpool, and Manchester*, P.P. 1870, LIV, p.174.

[6] C. J. Montagu, *Sixty Years in Waifdom* (1904), pp.196–9, 213, 293. J. R. Howarth, *Then and Now: a sketch of 50 years' work* (1894), pp.243–4. *The Ragged School Magazine*, XXIII (June 1870), p.124. For a recent account of the Ragged School Movement, see E. A. G. Clark, 'The Early Ragged Schools and the Foundation of the Ragged School Union', *Journal of Educational Administration and History I*, no. 2, (June 1969), pp.9–21.

[7] *Report from the Select Committee on Destitute Children*, P.P. 1861, VII, pp.iii, iv, v, Q.3933.

[8] *Return showing the number of children . . . chargeable to the poor rates . . .* , P.P. 1856, XLIX, p.405; *Newcastle Report*, P.P. 1861, XXI, F, p.404: *Return relating to Pauper Children*, P.P. 1870, LVIII, pp.5 and 120.

[9] F. Adams, *Lecture on Education delivered at Huntingdon 17 February, 1870* (Cambridge, 1870).

[10] *Report of the First Meeting of the Members of the NEL* (Birmingham, 1869), p.66.

[11] *Authorised Report of the Education Congress held . . . on 3 and 4 November 1869* (London and Manchester, 1869), pp.5, 268 (original italics).

[12] W. L. Sargant, 'On the Progress of Elementary Education', *Journal of the Statistical Society*, XXX (1867), p.122.

[13] *The Times*, 28 August 1868.

[14] *Bee-Hive*, 16 January, 1867, 12 February 1870.

[15] *NEL Circulars*, 1869–70, 'Circulars from Robert Applegarth', Birmingham University Library, sq. L18. N3 C5; A. W. Humphrey, *Robert Applegarth* (1913),

pp.212, 228, R. Applegarth, *Compulsory Education at School: The Working Man's View* (Birmingham, 1870); *NEL Verbatim Report of the Proceedings of a Delegation to W. E. Gladstone* (Birmingham, 1870), p.19.

[16] E. A. and G. H. Radice, *Will Thorne: Conservative Militant* (1974), p.35.

[17] *Co-operator*, March 1861, 1 June, 15 June, 15 July 1865, 16 April 1866.

[18] A. F. Taylor, 'Birmingham and the Movement for National Education 1866-77', (University of Leicester Ph.D. thesis, 1961), pp.337, 352; *Birmingham Daily Post*, 14 October 1869.

[19] *NEL Monthly Paper*, January, September 1870.

[20] *The Times*, 16 and 27 June 1870.

[21] H. W. Holland, *Proposed National Arrangements for Primary Education* (1870), p.2.

[22] *Reynold's Newspaper*, 25 August 1867, 13 February 1870; T. P. Allen, *An Enquiry into the Existing State of Education in Battersea (Supplement to the Journal of the Society of Arts)*, 12 August 1870.

[23] *Reports on Education*, P.P. 1873, XXIV, pp.111-12, *ibid.*, P.P. 1875, XXIV, p.39.

[24] R. Gregory, 'Hints to Managers', *National Society Monthly Paper*, *December 1870*, pp.202-10.

[25] *Schoolmaster*, 17 December 1872.

[26] M. G. Grey, 'Meeting of Working Men and Women at the Cadogan Rooms 28 November 1870', in *The School Board of London, Three Addresses of Mrs William Grey* (1871).

[27] *Reports on Education*, P.P. 1876, XXIII, p.404; W.E. Marsden, 'Social Environment, school attendance, and educational achievement in a Merseyside town, 1870-1900', in P. McCann (ed.,) *Popular Education and Socialization in the Nineteenth Century* (1977), pp.193-230. See also the same author's 'Historical Georgraphy and the History of Education', *History of Education,* VI (February 1977), pp.21-42.

Chapter IV   School Boards for All

[1] *The Times*, 15 July 1870.

[2] There were many other points at issue as the need to print three versions of the Bill in each House attests.

[3] *Bee-Hive*, 30 May 1868, 15 January and 12 February 1870: *Reynold's Newspaper*, 26 June 1870.

[4] H. Silver, *English Education and the Radicals, 1780-1850* (1975), p.82: *Newcastle Report*, P.P. 1861, XXI, p.211.

[5] E. P. Hennock, *Fit and Proper Persons: Ideal and Reality in Nineteenth-Century Urban Government* (1973), pp.17 and 75; C. Gill, *History of Birmingham: vol. I, Manor and Borough to 1865* (1952), p.35.

[6] C. Gill, *op. cit.*, pp.33-4, 68, 217; T. R. Tholfsen (ed.), *Sir James Kay-Shuttleworth on Popular Education* (New York and London, 1974), pp.147-8.

[7] NEU, *Authorised Report of the Education Conference held on 3 and 4 November 1869* (London and Manchester, 1869), pp.76, 105-6, 121-2, 204.

[8] University of Birmingham Library, Chamberlain Papers, JC/27/13, 2 March

1870. I acknowledge the permission of the University of Birmingham to make this quotation.

⁹ *Hansard*, CCIII, 313, 14 July 1870. S. and B. Webb, *English Local Government: English Poor Law History*, Part II, vol. I (London, 1929), p.234, Fn. I; *op. cit.*, *Statutory Authorities for Special Purposes* (London, 1922), p.452.

¹⁰ *The Times*, 28 October 1870.

¹¹ W. P. McCann, 'Trade-Unionist, Co-operative and Socialist Organizations in relation to Popular Education, 1887–1902' (University of Manchester, Ph.D. thesis, 1960), p.263 quoted by B. Simon, *Education and the Labour Movement*, 1870–1920 (1965), p.152.

¹² *Reports of Inspectors of Factories*, P.P. 1876, XVI, pp.82–3.

¹³ *Luton Advertiser and Dunstable Herald*, 3 December 1870, 18 February 1871, *Luton Times*, 11 February 1871; J. G. Dony, *A History of Education in Luton* (Luton, 1970), p.21.

¹⁴ *Hertfordshire Advertiser*, 25 February 1871.

¹⁵ *Report from the Select Committee on Parliamentary and Municipal Elections (Hours of Polling)*, P.P. 1877, XV, p.68.

¹⁶ *Ibid.*, Qs. 190–3, 978; Appendix III, 'Letter from J. H. Lockwood, secretary of the Old Society of Operative House Painters, Leeds', dated 16 June 1878; 'Letter from Thomas Moore, secretary of the National Association of Operative Plasterers, Leeds', dated 18 June 1878.

¹⁷ *Ibid.*, Qs. 1288–93, 2270–1.

¹⁸ *Ibid.*, Qs. 3, 391–413, 441, 447–8, 1050; *The Times*, 28 November 1873.

¹⁹ *The Times*, 30 November, 5 December 1870; *Bee-Hive*, 3, 10, 24 December 1870.

²⁰ *The Times*, 2 December 1870; see reference 15, Q. 120; *The Times*, 28 November 1873, 5 October 1894.

²¹ *The Times*, 15, 20 October, 2 November 1870.

²² *Birmingham Daily Post*, 12, 14, 16, 18 November 1870.

²³ *Ibid.*, 19, 24 November 1875.

²⁴ *Ibid.*, 7 November 1876, 4 November 1885, 7 November 1888, 11 and 24 November 1891.

²⁵ *Leeds Mercury*, 8 October, 30 November 1870; *Yorkshire Post and Intelligencer*, 22 November 1870.

²⁶ For instance, George Smart, a painter 'who claims specially to represent the working classes', was seen as the odd man out at Salford in 1885. When he was elected the mayor, the returning officer publicly commented, 'it remained to be seen whether the election of Mr. Smart would prove of sufficient benefit to the ratepayers to justify the expenditure of £700 which the election would cost', *Manchester Guardian*, 6 November 1885.

²⁷ *Bradford Daily Telegraph*, 18 November 1870; Bradford Educational Services Committee, *Education in Bradford since 1870* (Bradford 1970), pp.1–2, 32.

²⁸ *Nottingham and Midland Counties Daily Express*, 24 November 1870.

²⁹ *Nottingham Daily Express*, 25 November 1892.

³⁰ *Leeds Mercury*, 3, 7, 12, 13, 16, 18, 21 November 1891.

³¹ *Factory Times*, 20 November 1891: *Report from the Select Committee on School Board Elections (Voting)*, P.P. 1884–5, XI, Q1049; *The Times*, 1 December 1876.

[32] A. Gill, 'The Leicester School Board, 1870–1903', in B. Simon (ed.), *Education in Leicestershire, 1540–1940* (Leicester, 1968), p.162; *Nottingham Daily Express*, 12 November 1889.

[33] For an account of the Manchester School Board, see C. B. Dolton, 'The Manchester School Board', (University of Durham, M.Ed. thesis, 1959).

[34] *Liverpool Mercury*, 7, 18 November 1891, 20 November 1897, 9, 17 November 1900; J. A. Picton, *Memorials of Liverpool* (Liverpool, 1903), pp.353–4.

[35] *Manchester Guardian*, 6, 20 November 1894.

[36] F. Rogers, *Labour, Life and Literature: Some Memories of Sixty Years* (1973), with an introduction by D. Rubinstein, p.52. For other evidence of his opinion that the working classes had little interest in education, see pp.53, 67–8, 99–102, 139.

[37] *Brighton Herald*, 23, 30 September, 7 October, 11 November, 16 December 1893; 10 October, 14 November 1896; 7 October 1899.

[38] *Birmingham Daily Post*, 20 November 1894.

[39] *Schoolmaster*, 4 November 1893.

[40] *Women's Suffrage Journal*, 1 October 1879; S. and B. Webb, *English Local Government: English Poor Law History*, Part I, vol. I (1929), p.234, fn. II.

[41] In practice there was not always a clear-cut division. For instance, some Anglicans of a Liberal persuasion supported the school-board party and opposed their fellow Anglicans.

Part Two   The Schools and the Social Services

Chapter V   After Bread, Education

[1] *After Bread, Education: A Plan for the State Feeding of School Children*, Fabian Tract 120 (1905).

[2] *Fifth Report, Children's Employment Commissioners*, P.P. 1866, XXIV, p.xxvi.

[3] J.N. Clarke, *Education in a Market Town: Horncastle* (1976), p.19: G.A.N. Lowndes, *Margaret McMillan* (1960), p.56: *Report of the Inter-Department Committee on Medical Inspection and Feeding of Children Attending Public Elementary Schools*, (*Report on Medical Inspection of Children*), P.P. 1906, XLVII, Q. 3963.

[4] M. E. Bulkley, *The Feeding of School Children* (1914), pp.3–5.

[5] *School Board Chronicle*, 11 March 1871; G. A. N. Lowndes, *op. cit.*, pp.56–7; *Social Trends*, (HMSO, 1976), p.152.

[6] *Reports on Education*, P.P. 1870, XXII, pp.151, 318.

[7] *The Times*, 14 September 1904 quoted by J. L. Brand. *Doctors and the State* (Baltimore, 1966), pp. 184–5.

[8] *Schoolmaster*, 18 November 1899.

[9] B. B. Gilbert, *The Evolution of National Insurance in Great Britain*: pp.106–12: H. Iselin, 'The Story of a Children's Care Committee'. *Economic Review*, XXII (1912), pp.42–64: *Medical Inspection of Children Report*, P.P. 1906, XLVII, Q. 5172.

[10] On the difficulty of obtaining milk in some rural areas, see *Report of the Royal Commission on the Housing of the Working Classes*. P.P. 1884–5, XXX, Qs 1469–701. *Report of the Inter-Department Committee on Physical Deterioration* (*Report on Physical Deterioration*), P.P. 1904, XXXII, Qs 307–9, 369–70, 1256, 5371, 5374, 5452, etc.

[11] *Report on Medical Inspection of Children*, P.P. 1906, XLVII, p.57.

[12] *Ibid.*, Qs 238–332, *passim.*

[13] One example of the exaggerated importance attached to overpressure is that of a boy, suffering not from overpressure in school, but from the effects of an accident when a horse trod on his head.

[14] *Lancet*, 15 November, 20 December 1884.

[15] *The Times*, 22 February, 1 November 1884.

[16] *Report of Dr. Crichton-Browne to the Education Department upon the alleged Overpressure of Work in Public Elementary Schools*, P.P. 1884, LXI, pp.8–11 (266–9), 76–7 (334–5): *The Times*, 16 September 1884; for a fuller discussion of the controversy, see A. B. Robertson, 'Children, Teachers, and Society: The Over-Pressure Controversy, 1880–6', *British Journal of Educational Studies*, (XX 1970), pp.315–23.

[17] *The Times*, 13 March 1884.

[18] Greater London Council Record Office (GLCRO), S.B.L. 1469, *Underfed Children Attending School, 1898, Report of the General Purposes Committee*, p.18: *The Times*, 5 March 1887: *Report on Medical Inspection of Children*, P.P. 1906, XLVII, Q. 5768.

[19] H. Bosanquet, *Social Work in London, 1869–1912: A History of the Charity Organisation Society* (1914), pp.230–55.

[20] COS, *The Better Way of Assisting School Children* (1893), pp.8, 17, 18, 27, 28: H. Bosanquet, *The Standard of Life* (1906), pp.168, 225.

[21] S. D. Fuller, 'Penny Dinners', *Contemporary Review* (XLVII, 1885), pp. 424–32.

[22] *Report on Medical Inspection of Children*, P.P. 1906, XLVII, Qs 5176–7, 6227, 6277.

[23] GLCRO, S.B.L. 1469, *op. cit.*, p.20.

[24] *Report on Medical Inspection of Children*, P.P. 1906, XLVII, Qs 965, 5107, 5128.

[25] *Report on Physical Deterioration*, P.P. 1904, XXXII, p.40, Qs 942–5.

[26] *Special Report from the Select Committee on Education (Provision of Meals) Bill*, P.P. 1906, VII, p.iv (74).

[27] *Report on Medical Inspection of Children*, P.P. 1906, XLVII, Q 5646.

[28] *Ibid.*, Qs 1933, 3181–7, 4947–50, 4968; *Report on Physical Deterioration*, P.P. 1904, XXXII, Qs 7834, 7845. The headmaster of the school in Walworth had no difficulty in obtaining crusts from a baker's shop, as bakers were legally obliged to give full weight. On selling a quartern loaf they weighed the bread and added pieces from other loaves as makeweights. M.S. Pember Reeves, *Round About a Pound a Week* (1914), pp.94–5.

[29] *Report on the Medical Inspection of Children*, P.P. 1906, XLVII, Qs 5207, 5209.

[30] *Ibid.*, pp.35–7, Q.4354. B. S. Rowntree, *Poverty: A Study of Town Life* (1902), pp.99–110.

[31] *The Times*, 8, 11, 13 December 1884.

[32] G. H. Sargant, *Farthing Dinners* (Birmingham, 1886, second edn., 1887). *Special Report from the Select Committee on the Education (Provision of Meals) Bill 1906*, P.P. 1906, VIII, Q.2838. *Report of the Medical Superintendent of Elementary Schools for the Year ending 31 December 1910* (Birmingham, 1911), p.45. *Report on Physical Deterioration*, P.P. 1904, XXXII, Q.13239.

[33] P.P. 1906, VIII, Qs 2847–8.

[34] *Report of the Medical Superintendent for Birmingham* (Birmingham, 1911), p.45. P. S. Winder, *The Public Feeding of Elementary School Children* (London, 1913), p.43.

[35] GLCRO, S.B.L. 1468. *Report of a Special Committee on Underfed Children Attending School, 7 November, 1895*, pp.iv, 8, 9, 22, 39; SBL 1469, *Underfed Children Attending School, 1898–9*, pp.12–14.

[36] *Report on the Medical Inspection of Children*, P.P. 1906, XLVII, pp.78, 81, Qs. 1189–95.
The Report gives the following details of income for the voluntary feeding agencies:

Counties	£1,004
London	£10,299
County boroughs	£17,912
Boroughs	£3,089
Urban districts	£1,264
Total	£33,568

Not only is this return incomplete but some of the figures refer to 1903–4 and others to 1904–5. Furthermore, during the winter of 1904–5, one of 'abnormal distress from want of employment', civic authorities in a number of industrial towns made a special effort to raise money.

[37] GLCRO, S.B.L. 1468, p.iii; *Report on Medical Inspection*, P.P. 1906, XLVII Q.1420. Some observers justified this uncertain state of affairs whereby children did not know beforehand if they would get a meal on a particular day as it kept parents up to the mark. If 'irresponsible' parents knew for certain that a meal would be provided on a particular day they would not give their children any breakfast before sending them to school. GLCRO S.B.L. 1467, *Meals for Schoolchildren Report . . . 25 July 1889*.

[38] *Report on Physical Deterioration*, P.P. 1904, XXXII, pp.66–7.

[39] *The Times*, 16, 24 March, 6, 29, April 1905.

[40] M. E. Bulkley, *op. cit.*, p.41 footnote 2, B. B. Gilbert, *op. cit.*, p.109, *Report of the Royal Commission on the Poor Laws*, P.P. 1909, XXXVII, p.195, *Birmingham Schools Cheap Dinner Society, Report for 1900–1*.

[41] *Special Report from the Select Committee in Education (Provision of Meals) Bill*, P.P. 1906, VIII, pp.ix–xi (74–9).

Chapter VI   Cleansing the Augean Classrooms

[1] M. Stocks, *A Hundred Years of District Nursing* (1960), p.83; B. Abel-Smith, *A History of the Nursing Profession*, (1960), p.125.

[2] The above summary is based on *Report on Medical Inspection*, P.P. 1906, XLVII, pp.2–29.

[3] *Report on Physical Deterioration*, P.P. 1904, XXXII, Qs 440–545 *passim*.

[4] GLC Record Office, File PH/SHS/3/8.

[5] *Annual Report of the Chief Medical Officer of the Board of Education for 1911* (hereafter cited as *CMO's Report for 1911*, etc.), P.P. 1912–13, XXI, pp.54, 129.

[6] GLC Record Office, File PH/SHS/3/8; *CMO's Report for 1913*, P.P. 1914, XXV, pp.36, 367.

[7] GLC Record Office, Files PH/SHS/3/6, PH/SHS/3/10, PH/SHS/3/60.

[8] For the medical condition of ATS recruits, see R. M. Titmuss, *Problems of Social Policy* (1950), p.128; other statistics are derived from *The Health of the School Child, 1939–45* (HMSO, 1947), pp.35–9, 87; *The Health of the School Child, 1972* (HMSO, 1974), p.44; *The Times*, 1 September 1977.

[9] *CMO's Report for 1918*, P.P. 1919, XXI, p.2.

[10] *CMO's Report for 1914*, XVIII, pp.267–8.

[11] *CMO's Report for 1909*, P.P. 1910, XXIII, pp.36, 51; *CMO's Report for 1914*, P.P. 1914–6, XVIII, pp.166–9.

[12] *CMO's Report for 1913*, P.P. 1914, XXV, pp.135, 137.

[13] A. H. Hogarth, *Medical Inspection of Schools* (1909), p.41.

[14] C. E. Hecht (ed.), *Rearing an Imperial Race* (1913), p.92; M. Loane, *From their Point of View* (1908), pp.141–2.

[15] A. H. Hogarth, *op. cit.*, pp.226–30; *Lancet*, 7 April 1900.

[16] *Report of the Medical Superintendent of Elementary Schools and Superintendent of Special Schools for the Year ending 31 December 1909* (Birmingham, 1910), pp.25–6. Birmingham's other main hospital, the Queen's, required a shilling registration fee and saw a restricted quota of patients a day. The General Hospital had no separate opthalmic department. Glasses could only be obtained when cases were referred to the ophthalmic surgeon by the medical staff. Although the City introduced a scheme whereby parents could obtain glasses at a reduced cost varying between 1*s* 9*d* and 4*s*, half the children needing them did not get them because of poverty.

[17] *CMO's Report for 1913*, P.P. 1914, XXV, p.207; *CMO's Report for 1918*, P.P. 1919, XXI, p.97.

[18] GLC Record Office, File PH/SHS/2/5.

[19] *CMO's Report for 1911*, P.P. 1912–13, XXI, p.141; *CMO's Report for 1914*, P.P. 1914–6, XVIII, p.163. In May 1913 the Leicestershire Education Authority prosecuted a parent for refusing permission for the removal of his daughter's adenoids. The case reached the High Court where Mr Justice Darling found in favour of the education authority on the grounds that the fact that the parents did not believe in operations showed that they were persons whose opinions were of little weight. *CMO's Report for 1912*, P.P. 1914, XXV, p.366.

[20] *British Dental Journal* (XXII 1901), p.582; *ibid.*, (XXIV 1903), p.261; (1904 XXV), pp.687, 768, (XXVII 1906), p.294, (XXVIII 1907), pp.75, 1326. *British Journal of Dental Service* (XLVII 1904), p.357, *ibid.* (LI 1908), p.308. *CMO's Report for 1910*, P.P. 1910, XXIII, pp.128–9; *CMO's Report for 1911*, P.P. 1912. 1912–3, XXI, p.154; *CMO's Report for 1914*, P.P. 1914–6, XVIII, pp.176–7. The contemporary spelling 'tooth-brush' is a further indication of the

limited extent to which the article was in general use before 1914. The *British Dental Journal* began to carry advertisements for children's tooth-brushes from 1910 onwards.

[21] *CMO's Report for 1913*, P.P. 1914, XXV, pp.3, 108, 135, 158, 183; *CMO's Report for 1918*, P.P. 1919, XXI, p.50.

[22] GLC Record Office, S.B.L. 289, *School Board for London, First Annual Report of the Joint Committee on Underfed Children* (June 1901); GLC Record Office, S.B.L. 290, *Second Annual Report . . .* (June 1902), p.35.

[23] Quoted from the *LCC Report of Joint Committee on Underfed Children for the Season, 1906–7* (1907), p.3, by the *Report of the Royal Commission on Poor Laws*, P.P. 1909, XXXVII, p.197; *The Times*, 17 December 1908.

[24] P.P. 1909, XXXVII, pp.198, 830–45 *passim*. The Minority Report's concern for administrative efficiency and the elimination of overlapping provided a splendid example of how to lie with statistics.

In the Metropolis it was found in 1907–8 that 3·29 per cent of the 49,000 children fed were at the time in receipt of outdoor relief, whilst no fewer than 13·46 per cent had recently been in receipt of such relief, though it had been brought to an end before the date of the investigation. Thus, it would appear that of the 10,000 children of school age on any one day maintained by the Metropolitan Boards of Guardians on Outdoor Relief, *something like 1,600, or one in every six were actually being fed, in the winter of 1907–8, by the Local Education Authority* (original italics).

The context of this passage suggests that the children were receiving relief simultaneously from both the Poor Law Guardians and the Local Education Authorities. Given the intermittent nature of both forms of relief, the assumption is quite unwarrantable.

[25] H. Iselin, *op. cit.*, pp.42–64.

[26] *CMO's Report for 1913*, P.P. 1914, XXV, p.21.

[27] The Board of Education's circular, dated 1 January 1907, is reprinted in L. S. Bryant, *School Feeding: Its History and Practice at Home and Abroad* (Philadelphia and London, 1913), pp.302–11: P. Winter, *The Public Feeding of Elementary School Children* (1913), pp.29–30, 56–62.

[28] *CMO's Report for 1914*, P.P. 1914–6, XVIII, p.244: M. McMillan and A. Cobden Sanderson, *London's Children: How to Feed Them and How not to Feed Them* (1909), p.10; J. H. Palin, *Bradford and Its Children: How They are Fed* (Bradford, 1908): A. J. Marder, *From Dreadnought to Scapa Flow*, vol. I (1961), p.9.

[29] *CMO's Report from 1913*, P.P. 1914–6, XVIII, p.21: *CMO's Report for 1918*, P.P. 1919, XXI, pp.175–7: *The Times*, 18 and 20 July 1912.

[30] *Report on the Working of the Education (Provision of Meals Act), 1906, for the year ending 31 March 1910*, P.P. 1911, XVIII, p.4. Official statistics give an unduly flattering picture of the school meals service. For instance, some of the 38,943 children fed in these cities may have received meals for no more than a fortnight or so. Similarly many of the 358,306 fed in 1912 were strikers' children given meals for a few weeks at the most. Furthermore, a breakfast of cocoa, bread and margarine constituted a meal for statistical purposes.

[31] M. E. Bulkley, *The Feeding of School Children* (1914), pp.104–5. In many instances the food remained monotonous throughout the period under discussion.

An authority such as Bradford which provided a four-week schedule of meals was the exception. Few authorities attempted more than a weekly programme so that every West Ham child, for example, knew that Thursday was the day for mince and suet pudding. A further cause of tedium was that there was little difference in practice between stew, mince, and soup. For specimens of diets, see *ibid.*, pp.231–6.

[32] *CMO's Report for 1918*, P.P. 1919, XXI, pp.175–7.

[33] *The Health of the School Child* (HMSO 1936), pp.27–30; *ibid.* (1939), p.22; *The Health of the School Child, 1939–45* (HMSO 1947), pp.23–6; R. Titmuss, *op. cit.* p.509.

Part Three   In and Out of the School

Chapter VII   Schools, Parents and Children

[1] *The Times*, 27 November 1875.

[2] *Reports of Inspectors of Factories*, P.P. 1876, XVI, pp.10–11; Birmingham School Board, *Report on Compulsion as applied to school attendance in Birmingham* (Birmingham, 1878); *The Times*, 26 March 1876.

[3] *The Times*, 13 October 1874; 36 and 37 Vic. c. 86 s 24 (iv), 24 (viii).

[4] *Reports on Education for 1875–6*, P.P. 1876, XXIII, p.260; P.P. 1879, XXIII, p.432; P.P. 1890–1, XXVII, p.311. *Report of the Royal Commission on the Elementary Education Acts (Cross Report)*, P.P. 1888, XXXV, p.196–7; *ibid.*, P.P. 1887, XXIX, Q. 26540.

[5] *Report for 1875–6*, P.P. 1876, XXIII, p.246; *Cross Report*, P.P. 1888, XXXV, p.196.

[6] *Report for 1890–1*, P.P. 1890–1, XXVII, pp.300, 318.

[7] *Report for 1891–2*, P.P. 1892, pp.ix, 314.

[8] *The Times*, 1 August 1872; 13 February 1873.

[9] G. R. Sims, *How the Poor Live* (1883), p.23.

[10] *Cross Report*, P.P. 1887, XXIX, Q. 29821.

[11] *The Times*, 16 September, 4 October 1886; *School Board Chronicle*, 23 March 1878.

[12] *The Times*, 5, 9, 13, 15, 19 October 1886.

[13] *Ibid.*, 8 August 1891; D. Rubinstein, *School Attendance in London: A Social History* (University of Hull publications, 1969), pp.83–9.

[14] *Monthly Paper of the National Society* (1868), pp.158, 199, 201.

[15] R. Roberts, *The Classic Slum* (Harmondsworth, 1973), p.46.

[16] *Schoolmaster*, 25 September 1880; 30 October 1880 quotes instances where this happened.

[17] *Ibid.*, 14 November 1878; 18 September 1886 gives examples of schoolmasters whom the parents probably correctly suspected of having been unnecessarily brutal being escorted from school under police protection.

[18] All these cases were reported in *Schoolmaster*, a journal professionally sympathetic to the teacher charged with assault. See the issues of 21 July 1877; 10 July 1880; 10 December 1880; 1 July 1882; 19 November 1898; 18 November 1899 for the cases discussed above. They have been selected from a wide sample of similar reports.

¹⁹ A. R. Skelley, *The Victorian Army at Home* (London 1977), pp.147–50; *Supplemental Conversazione to the Englishwoman's Domestic Magazine* (April to December 1870), *passim*; M. Seaborne and R. Lowe, *The English School; Its Architecture and Organization, volume II, 1870–1970* (London, 1977), p.46.

²⁰ *Hansard*, fourth series, LXXXVII, c. 1375, 11 May 1900; *ibid.*, XCIV, c. 593, 20 May 1901. Gorst's announcement came after a protest that 378 cases of the use of corporal punishment had been recorded at an infants' school in three months.

²¹ *Schoolmaster*, 23 January 1892; *Lancet*, 16 July 1892. Little is known of the victims' point of view except for what they wrote in later life. Usually such authors were public-school men. However, there was a series of schoolboy strikes in October 1889, doubtless inspired by the gasworkers' and dockers' successes in London that summer. In a number of short-lived strikes boys in Barnet, parts of London – where the Street Masons, Paviors, and Stone Dressers' Amalgamated Union gave moral support – Leeds, Liverpool, Northampton, and elsewhere struck for shorter hours, one meal a day, and the abolition of the cane, school fees and home lessons. *The Times*, 10–19 October 1889.

²² *Schoolmaster*, 24 September and 8 October 1894.

²³ *Report of the Royal Commission on the Housing of the Working Classes*, P.P. 1884, XXX, Qs 1907–14; 2100–5; 5940–3; 5960–2; 10709; 10755–7. *Hansard*, fourth series, vol. LXXIII, c. 1397–1402, 4 July 1899; *ibid.*, vol. LXXV, c. 848, 31 July 1899. D. Rubinstein, 'Socialization and the London School Board 1870–1914: aims, methods, and public opinion' in P. McCann (ed.), *Popular Education and Socialization in the Nineteenth Century* (1977), pp.231–64.

²⁴ For a protest deputation to the London School Board, see *The Times*, 19 January 1883. House of Lords Library, Evidence on Opposed Bills, vol. XIII (1888); vol. VII (1895); vol. VIII (1898); House of Commons Select Committee on Private Bills, 1884, vol. LXXVII give examples of local opposition to the London School Board's intention to build a school nearby.

²⁵ *Schoolmaster*, 30 January 1897.

²⁶ For an example of Hammer's advertisement, see *School Board Chronicle*, 8 May 1875.

²⁷ M. Seaborne and R. Lowe, *op. cit.*, pp.75–8, 83; *Report of the Interdepartmental Committee on Physical Deterioration*, P.P. 1904, XXXII, Qs 12422–3.

²⁸ *The Times*, 6, 13 December 1889; 3 July 1891; 28 January 1893; 24 February 1893; 25 January 1895. E. R. Robson, architect to the London School Board, narrowly escaped legal action from his employers. His talent for survival was such that he obtained employment with the Education Department. M. Seaborne and R. Lowe, *op. cit.*, p.8.

²⁹ C. F. Brockington, *A Short History of Public Health* (1966), p.47; *Lancet*, 16 July 1881; 16 February 1895.

³⁰ *Report for 1873–4*, P.P. 1874, XVIII, p.221.

³¹ *Cross Report*, P.P. 1887, XXX, Qs 51,608, 53,002; J. Murphy, *Church, State and Schools in Britain*, 1800–1970 (London, 1971), pp.58–60.

³² J. G. Hubbard, *The Conscience Clause of the Education Department illustrated by the evidence taken by the Select Committee* (1865), p.14. I am indebted to my colleague, Dr J. M. Hull, for this reference.

[33] *Newcastle Report*, P.P. 1861, XXI, A, pp.33–4. T. W. Laqueur, *Religion and Respectability: Sunday Schools and Working-Class Culture, 1780–1850* (New Haven and London, 1976), pp.175–9. *Cross Report*, P.P. 1887, XXX, Qs 48, 457–48, 606 *passim*.

[34] *Report for 1876–7*, P.P. 1877, XXIX, p.429.

[35] *Cross Report*, P.P. 1888, XXXVII, p.381; *ibid.*, P.P. 1887, XXX, Qs 52645–6.

[36] *Ibid.*, P.P. 1887, XXX, Qs 44608–11; *Hansard*, third series, vol. CCXXX c. 1200, 27 July 1876.

[37] *Hansard*, fourth series, vol. XLIX, c. 498, 916.

[38] *Report for 1880–1*, P.P. 1881, XXXIII, p.259; *Report for 1884–5*, P.P. 1884–5, XXIII, p.310; W. H. Mackintosh, *Disestablishment and Liberation* (London, 1972), pp.259–61; *Hansard*, 3rd series, vol. CCXXX c. 1980, 27 July 1876; *ibid.*, vol. CCLIII, c. 490–1, 676–7, 11 and 14 May 1891.

[39] Cross Report, P.P. 1888, XXXV, pp.292–3; *Hansard*, third series, vol. CCXCIX c. 707, 14 June 1885. The number of Easter Communicants rose from 8·2 per cent of the adult population over the age of 15 in 1871 to 9·8 per cent in 1911. For these figures and details of the membership of other denominations, see A. D. Gilbert, *Religion and Society in Industrial England* (1976), pp.28–32.

[40] *Hansard*, fourth series, vol. CXIII, c. 1303–62, 31 October 1902.

[41] *Schoolmaster*, 4 February 1893; 16 June 1893, 14 February 1908.

[42] *Schoolmaster*, 10 June 1893; 16 June 1894; 9 January 1897; *Lancet*, 29 April 1893.

[43] *Special Reports on Educational Subjects*, P.P. 1898, XXIV, 'Public Elementary Education in England and Wales, 1870–95', pp.1–78, especially 33–44, is the main source of much of the above. For the results in testing the three Rs in 1879–80, see *Report for 1880–1*, P.P. 1881, XXXII, p.xv. By 1889–90, the last year of the examination of individual children in these subjects 440,131 (31·22 per cent) of those over the age of ten were still being examined in the first three standards. *Report for 1890–1*, P.P. XXVII, p.xvi.

[44] Collection of reports from the master of method on students' work at St Peter's College, Saltley, Birmingham for 1876, 1878, 1878–9, 1880–1, 1882–3, 1895–6, *passim*.

[45] *Report for 1896–7*, P.P. 1897, XXVI, 'Revised Instructions, 1879', pp.481–570, *passim*.

[46] T. G. Tholfsen (ed.), *Sir James Kay-Shuttleworth on Popular Education* (New York and London, 1974), p.45. The term 'domestic economy' in Dr Kay's pamphlet, *The Moral and Physical Condition of the Working Classes of Manchester in 1832* (1832) had a moralistic connotation. Training in domestic economy was a means of gentling the poor. His pamphlet described the eventual fate of the cotton operative denied home 'comforts: 'he generally becomes debilitated and hypochondriacal, and unless supported by principle, falls the victim of dissipation.' Cookery was good for girls too. When Miss F. Calder, honorary secretary of the Liverpool Training School of Cookery, was asked by the Cross Commissioners 'Do you think that when girls acquire the art of cooking it develops the taste for manual labour?', she replied, 'Very much indeed. In various schools girls who would not think of going to work or to service, and who would think any manual labour rather beneath them, . . . have been found . . . very much anxious to go out to work.' *Cross Report*, P.P. 1887, XXIX, Q. 19,023.

[47] M. Davies (formerly Miss M. Harrison, inspectress of cookery), 'The Teaching of Cookery', *Contemporary Review* (LXXIII, 1898), pp.106−14; M. Davies, 'Physical Deterioration and the Teaching of Cookery', *Contemporary Review* (LXXXVII, 1905), pp.88−94; see also the brief 'Annual Reports of the Inspectress of Cookery' in the *Reports ofthe Department*, 1894−6 by Miss M. Harrison, 1896−7 *et seq.* by Miss Hyacinthe M. Deane. Mrs Davies's description of working-class diet is similar to that given by E. Roberts in 'Working-Class Standards of Living in Barrow and Lancaster, 1890−1914', in *Economic History Review*, XXX (May 1937), pp.306−21. Thermostatically controlled gas stoves were not in general domestic use until the inter-war years. Before their development the cook had to regulate the temperature of her oven by a rule-of-thumb setting of the gas tap.

[48] H. Sillitoe, *A History of the Teaching of Domestic Subjects* (1933), now inevitably dated, provides a useful background study of the subject matter of its title.

[49] *Cross Report*, P.P. 1887, XXIX, Qs 29, 149, 34,551. *Statistics of Public Education in England and Wales*, 1913−14, Cd 8097, pp.56 7, 201. With one exception cookery was a girls' subject. Boys over the age of twelve, living in seaport towns, were allowed to take cookery as a preliminary to serving in that male reserve, the mercantile marine. In 1913−14 there were 387 boys following this subject, *ibid.*, p.45.

[50] M. Loane, *The Queen's Poor: Life as they find it in town and country* (1906), p.136; M. S. Pember Reeves, *Round About a Pound a Week* (1914), pp.57−9, 222, 312.

[51] T. C. Barker, J. C. McKenzie, J. Yudkin (eds), *Our Changing Fare* (1966), pp.88−9, S. Everard, *The History of the Gas Light and Coke Company*, 1812−1949 (1949), pp.178, 197, 277, 307, 346. For the improvement in milk, especially to London, as an example of the improvement in food supplies see M. W. Beaver, 'Population, Infant Mortality and Milk', *Population Studies*, XXVII, pp.243−54; E. H. Whetham, 'The London Milk Trade, 1860−1900' in *Economic History Review* (XVII 1964), pp.369−80 and the same author's 'The London Milk Trade, 1900−30' in D. Oddy and D. Miller (eds), *The Making of the Modern British Diet* (1976), pp.65−76. *Report . . . by the Board of Trade into working-class rents . . . in the United Kingdom*, P.P. 1908, CVII, pp.394 and 400 for the number of gas cookers etc., in Rochdale and St Helens. Further information about the extent to which gas cookers and slot meters were in common use can be gleaned from the same source for the following towns. In each case the 1901 population is given as a means of estimating the proportion of households that might be considered to be so equipped. Barrow-in-Furness, pop. 57,586, had 5,774 slot or automatic meters and 3,836 ordinary meters in 1906; Blackburn, pop. 127,626, 14,500 slot meters; Bristol, pop. 328,945, slot meters were first introduced in 1892. By 1906 there were 16,157 slot and 31,459 ordinary meters. Burnley, pop. 97,043, nearly 8,000 gas stoves and 9,500 'gas breakfast-stoves' (i.e. boilers and grillers) in use by 1906. *Ibid.*, pp.91, 95, 113, 120, 122, 349, 353. In South London the South Metropolitan Gas Company had 93,164 consumers by the end of 1898 using 80,115 slot meters to pay for gas supplying 62,845 stoves of which 40,601 were on hire. *Report from the Select Committee on Metropolitan Gas Companies*, P.P. 1899, X, pp.297−8.

Chapter VIII   Unwillingly to School

[1] On 31 January 1913 there were 641,365 children aged 11 to 12 and 615,640 aged 12 to 13 on the registers. A year later the number aged 12 to 13 was 616,101 and 437,199 were between 13 and 14, a loss of 203,675. These figures probably underestimate the total loss because of the time lag between a child leaving and his name being struck off the registers. In addition an unknown number left before the end of the summer of 1914. Board of Education: *Statistics of Public Education, Part I, 1912–13, 1913–14* (Cd 7674, Cd 8097), pp.20–1.

[2] Report for the Education Department for 1875–6 (*Report for 1875–6*) P.P. 1876, XXIX, p.xxi; *Report for 1880–1*, P.P. XXXII, p.xxvi.

[3] *Report of the Royal Commission appointed to inquire into the working of the Factory and Workshops Acts*, P.P. 1876, XXIX, p.lii.

[4] *Ibid.*, Appendix C, p.30; *Reports of the Inspectors of Factories*, P.P. 1870, XV, p.17.

[5] *HMI J. Lomax's Report*, P.P. 1875, XXIV, p.39 (351); *Reports of Inspectors of Factories*, P.P. 1876, XVI, p.10; *Report of the Departmental Committee Appointed to Inquire into the Conditions of School Attendance and Labour*, P.P. 1893–4, LXVIII, pp. 21, 24.

[6] *Report of the Chief Inspector of Factories*, P.P. 1888, XXVI, p.16; *Report of the Royal Commission on Labour*, P.P. 1892, XXXV, Qs 3749, 3778–81; *Report of the Inter-Department Committee on Partial Exemption from School Attendance (Committee on Partial Exemption)*, P.P. 1909, XVII, p.10.

[7] *Ibid.*, Qs 5366, 5375–6.

[8] *Ibid.*, p.12, Qs 5384, 5909–12; *Committee on Partial Exemption*, P.P. 1909, XVII, p.3; K. Marx, *Capital* (1891 edn), pp.488–9; R. Barker, *Education and Politics* (Oxford, 1972), pp.23–4.

[9] *Committee on Partial Exemption*, P.P. 1909, XVII, p.10. A practice described by Horace Mann fifty years earlier (p.27) still prevailed in the cotton industry. Children in the Burnley mills and possibly elsewhere had to wait to be noticed by a tacker or weaver before being taken into regular employment. The median period of waiting for twenty-five children in one sample was three-and-a-half months. Reachers-in and warehouse boys did not have to wait more than three or four days without pay before being offered employment. *Ibid.*, Qs 44–450. In 1914 children employed part time in textile factories on the alternate week system worked 33 hours one week and $32\frac{1}{2}$ the second, on the alternate day system they worked 30 hours one day and $26\frac{1}{2}$ the next. Children in non-textile factories worked 34 and $32\frac{1}{2}$ hours in alternate weeks or 30 and $27\frac{1}{2}$ hours alternate days. These hours excluded statutory minima meal times. F. Keeling, *Child Labour in the United Kingdom* (1914), p.xxv.

[10] *Report of the Royal Commission on Factory and Workshops Acts*, P.P. 1876, XXIX, pp.14, 188, 196–7, 203.

[11] *Ibid.*, pp.lix, 173.

[12] *Ibid.*, pp.xviii, 88 (218).

[13] *Reports of the Inspectors of Factories*, P.P. 1876, XVI, pp.71–4; P.P. 1888, XXVI, p.70; *Report on the Royal Commission on Factory and Workshops Acts*, P.P. 1876, XXIX, pp.31, 113.

[14] *Ibid.*, p.44; *Reports of the Inspectors of Factories*, P.P. 1877, XXIII, p.7.

[15] *Reports of the Inspectors of Factories*, P.P. 1873, XIX, p.27; P.P. 1878, XX, pp.7–8; P.P. 1888, XXVI, 58–9.

[16] *Reports of the Inspectors of Factories*, P.P. 1887, XVII, p.11: P.P. 1888, XXVI, p.50; P.P. 1898, XIV, p.153.

[17] *Correspondence relative to the operation of the Agricultural Children's Act*, P.P. 1875, LXI, pp.1–15, especially p.13.

[18] *Field*, 8 January 1876; *Schoolmaster*, 12 June 1875, 19 February 1876.

[19] E. L. Jones, 'The Agricultural Labour Market in England, 1793–1873', *Economic History Review* 2nd series, XVII (1964), pp.327–63; for the difficulties facing the agricultural labourer, see *Report of the Royal Commission on the Housing of the Working Classes*, P.P. 1884–5, XXX, Qs 14694–707; *Report from the Royal Commission on Agriculture*, P.P. 1882, XIV, Q. 59398.

[20] *Report for 1874–5*, P.P. 1875, XXIV, p.388; *Report for 1880–1*, P.P. 1881, XXXIII, pp.396–8; for a discussion of demographic patterns in open and close villages, see Obelkevich, J., *Religion and Rural Society, South Lindsay, 1825–75* (Oxford, 1976), pp.11 *et seq*.

[21] *Report for 1877–8*, P.P. 1878–9, XXIII, p.681; *Report for 1881–2*, P.P. 1882, XXIII, p.237; *Report for 1883–4*, P.P. 1884, XXIV, pp.415–16.

[22] For Therfield's struggle with officialdom, see J. S. Hurt, 'The Development of elementary Education in the Nineteenth Century: the roles of the Committee of the Privy Council on Education and the Hertfordshire Gentry' (London University, Ph.D. thesis, 1968), pp.483–8.

[23] *Committee on Partial Exemption*, P.P. 1909, XVII, p.6. The same report summarizes the conditions determining exemption from school attendance by this date. At the age of 12 a child could claim partial exemption if (1) he was employed under the Factory Act, (2) if he had reached the standard of proficiency prescribed by the local authority, usually Standards III, IV, or V, or had made 300 attendances in any 5 years since the age of 5 in not more than 2 schools. A child of 12 could claim total exemption if he had reached the standard prescribed by the local authority, usually Standards V, VI, or VII. If, however, he was employed under the Factory Act he still had to attend school part-time until the age of 13. A large number of authorities granted total exemption at the age of 13 to children who had made 350 attendances in any 5 years at not more than 2 schools since the age of 5. For the majority of children the attendance test, 350 attendances a year was little more than 75 per cent of those possible, was the operative one. The Report showed that 1,352 Burnley children had recently qualified to leave school on the basis of their attendance record and only 106 by passing their Standards.

[24] For prosecutions under the Elementary Education Acts, see *Judicial Statistics*, P.P. 1895, CVIII, p.122, P.P. 1920, L, p.8. For the decline in beer consumption, see A. J. P. Taylor, *English History, 1914–45* (1965), p.37.

[25] *Report of the Inspector of Factories*, P.P. 1881, XXIII, pp.25–6; Report for 1896–7, P.P. 1897, LXVIII, pp.xxiii–xxiv.

[26] ILP (City of London Branch), *Commercialism and Child Labour* (1900), pp.11, 15.

[27] Workmen on early morning shifts who could not afford alarm clocks paid children to rouse them. Some firms employed their own knockers-up until 1939.

[28] *Report of the Interdepartmental Committee on the Employment of School*

Children, (Committee on School Children), P.P. 1902, XXV, Appendix 36, pp.411–13.

²⁹ As early as 1891 the *Contemporary Review* had expressed disquiet, 'The children belong to their parents, but they also belong to the nation. In a few years they will enter into the material of which adult society is made, and we have to be on our guard against a damaged article.' H. Dunckley, 'The Half-Timers', *Contemporary Review*, LIX (1891), pp.798–802. For the change in moral attitudes, see J. R. Gillis, 'The Evolution of Juvenile Delinquency in England, 1890–1914', *Past and Present*, No. 67 (May 1975), pp.96–126.

³⁰ *Report of the Departmental Committee on the Employment of Children Act, 1903*, P.P. 1910, XXVIII, pp.11–16.

³¹ *Census of England and Wales, 1911*, P.P. 1912–13, CXIII, p.425.

³² F. Keeling, *op. cit.*, pp.31–2, 57–9.

³³ *Report of the Interdepartmental Committee on the Employment of School Children*, P.P. 1902, XXV, pp.13, 14, 17.

³⁴ E. F. Hogg, 'School Children as Wage Earners', *Nineteenth Century*, XLII (1897), pp.235–44.

³⁵ For the impact of the publication of the *Daily Mail* on the hours worked by newspaper boys, see *Committee on School Children*, P.P. 1902, XXV, Qs 3915–91; for social distinctions amongst street children, see C. E. B. Russell, 'The Education, Earnings, and Social Condition of Boys engaged in street-trading in Manchester', *ibid.*, pp.456–61.

³⁶ *Ibid.*, Qs 2746–946, *passim*, 5296–400, *passim*.

³⁷ R. H. Sherard, *The Child-Slaves of Britain* (1905), p.65.

³⁸ C. F. G. Masterman, *The Condition of England* (seventh edition, 1912), p.76; B. Jackson and D. Marsden, *Education and the Working Class* (Harmondsworth, 1976), pp.162, 171, and 211.

³⁹ For the inversion of values see B. Jackson and D. Marsden, *op. cit.*, p.75.

⁴⁰ Quoted by M. Spufford, 'The Schooling of the Peasantry in Cambridgeshire, 1575–1700' in J. Thirsk (ed.), *Land, Church, and People: Essays presented to Professor H. P. R. Finberg* (1970), pp.112–47, from S. Marshall, *Fenland Chronicle* (1967), pp.17, 21.

⁴¹ Quoted by M. Bruce, *The Coming of the Welfare State* (1961), p.139.

⁴² *Special Reports on Educational Subjects: Report on the School Training and Early Employment of Lancashire Children*, P.P. 1904, XIX, p.20.

⁴³ P. H. J. H. Gosden, *Education in the Second World War: A Study in Policy and Administration* (London, 1976), pp.68, 81–2.

Index

Acland, A.H.D., 47

Acts of Parliament: Agricultural
Children's Act, 1873, 199–200;
Bleach and Dye Works' Act,
1860, 57; Children's Act, 1908,
131, 132, 133, 146; Children
in Receipt of Outdoor Relief
Act, 1855, 58, 61; Education
Act, 1902, 177; Education
Act, 1918, 188; Education
(Administrative Provisions)
Act, 1907, 128, 131; Education
Department Provisional Order
Confirmation Act (London),
1895, 166; Education (Provision of Meals) Act, 1906,
108, 114, 123–4, 130–1, 144,
146, 148–51, 210; Education
(Provision of Meals) Act, 1914,
151; Elementary Education
Act, 1870, 3, 14, 21, 24, 51,
59, 69–74, 75, 103, 128, 157,
163, 169, 172, 176, 180;
Elementary Education Act,
1870 and Representation of
the People Act, 1867, 16–24,
61, 67–9, 76–7; Elementary
Education Act, 1873, 101,
157, 188; Elementary Edu-
cation Act, 1876, 159, 189,
197, 204; Elementary Edu-
cation Act, 1880, 189;

Elementary Education Act,
1891, 161; Elementary
Education Act, 1899, 203;
Elementary Education
(Defective and Epileptic
Children) Act, 1899, 128;
Employment of Children Act,
1903, 206; Endowed Schools
Act, 1869, 21; Factory Act,
1802, 23, 101, 188; Factory
Act, 1819, 23; Factory Act,
1833, 57; Factory Act, 1834,
57; Factory Act, 1844, 44;
Factory Act, 1864, 45, 57;
Factory Act, 1867, 45, 57;
Factory Act, 1895, 192;
Industrial Schools Act, 1857,
23, 58, 61; Industrial Schools
Act, 1861, 23, 59, 61;
Industrial Schools Act, 1866,
23; Lace Factories' Act, 1861,
57; Liverpool Corporation Act,
1898, 204–5;
Local Education Authorities
(Medical Treatment) Act,
1909, 131; Local Government
Act, 1888, 158; Local Government Act, 1894, 81; Metropolitan Management Act,
1855, 81; Metropolitan Poor
Act, 1867, 81; Mines Act,
1842, 49; Mines Act, 1860, 50;

233

Acts (*cont.*)
  Notification of Infectious
  Diseases Act, 1889, 171;
  Notification of Infectious
  Diseases Act, 1899, 171; Poor
  Law Amendment Act, 1844,
  61; Poor Law Amendment
  Act, 1848, 61; Prevention of
  Cruelty to Children Act, 1892,
  204; Printworks Act, 1845, 48,
  57; Public Schools Act, 1868,
  21; Reformatory Schools Act,
  1854, 23, 58; Reformatory
  Schools Act, 1857, 23, 58;
  Reformatory Schools Act,
  1866, 23; Representation of
  the People Act, 1832, 23, 24;
  Representation of the People
  Act, 1867, 17, 18, 24, 67–8,
  76; Shop Hours Act, 1892,
  204; Unemployed Workmen
  Act, 1905, 145; Workshops
  Regulation Act, 1867, 57,
  196, 197, 199; *See also*
  Bills
Airy, HMI, Dr O., 117, 118–19
Anglesey, 58
Applegarth, Robert: on education,
  62–3, 65
Arnold, E.P.: and school fees, 15,
  69
Arnold, M.: and school fees,
  15
Ashton-under-Lyne, 137

Baker, Robert, 82
Band of Hope, 56
Barnsley, 46
Battle of Britain, 152
Baxter, R.D.:
  National Income (1868),
  6–7
Becker, Lydia, 97–8
Bedfordshire, 147, 198
Bee-Hive, 62, 76, 85
Bills: Education Bill, 1807, 23;
  Education Bill, 1820, 23;
  Education Bill, 1868, 19–20,

80; Education of the Poor
Bill, 1867, 24; Manchester
and Salford Bill, 1852, 61;
Reform Bill, 1866, 16, 65;
Schools of Industry Bill,
1796, 23
Birmingham, 32, 40, 53, 77, 78,
  80, 148–9, 150, 156, 158,
  198, 204; demand for juvenile
  labour, 43–4; Education Aid
  Society, 54, 58, 60; education
  census of, 54–6; medical
  treatment in, 138–9, 141, 223
  n 16; National Education League,
  65–6; New Meeting Sunday
  Schools, 42–3; Schools Cheap
  Dinner Society, 117–19, 120,
  123; dinner menus, 118–19,
  125, 126–7; third-grade schools,
  9
Birmingham School Board, 61,
  83, 95; and working men,
  87–9
Black Country, 32–3, 42
Bolton, 191, 206
Booth, Charles, 105, 112, 113,
  161; and London School
  Board, 71–4
Bootle, 74, 103, 202
Boys' Shoeblack Brigade, 56–7
Bradford, 29, 53, 77, 135, 136,
  143, 148, 150, 192, 204,
  206; citizens petition House of
  Commons, 79; Medical
  Inspection of children, 103;
  school dinners in, 116, 123
Bradford School Board: and
  working men, 89, 90
Bread and Food Reform Society,
  119
Breconshire, 137
Bright, Jacob, MP for Manchester,
  88, 172
Brighton: School Board and
  working men, 96, school
  meals in, 127
Bristol, 33, 53, 143, 150, 206;
  ragged schools, 4, 54

Liverpool School Board: and workmen, 94

London: general, 6, 27, 54, 75, 143, 144, 147, 156, 158, 162, 172, 192, 213; Charing Cross Hospital, 140-1; errand boys, 207-9; Great Exhibition of 1851, 56-7; National Education League, 66-7; ragged schools, 4, 52, 54; Statistical Society, 61; third-grade schools, 9; districts: Ann Street, Gray's Inn Road, 166; Bermondsey, 105, 112, 113; Charing Cross, 130; Chelsea, 33, 53, 85, 106, 115; Covent Garden, 166; East End, 210; Finsbury, 107; Greenwich, 86; Hampstead, 142; Holborn, 140; Kentish Town, 208; Lambeth, 85, 122, 130; Limehouse, 112; Lisson Grove, 112; Marylebone, 85; Norwood, 141; St George in the East, 33, 53, 146-7; St Pancras, 33, 53; Seven Dials, 115; Southwark, 53, 86; Stepney, 103, 134; Stockwell, 85; Strand, 169; Tower Hamlets, 85, 92; Trafalgar Square, 160; Walworth, 115; Wandsworth, 133; Waterloo, 85, 115; West End, 160; West Ham, 150, 151; Westminster, 85, 86, 102, 158; Whitechapel, 133; Woolwich, 85; schools: Baldwin Gardens School, Holborn, 174; Chaucer School, Bermondsey, 112, 113; Home and Colonial School, Gray's Inn Road, 174; Johanna Street School, Lambeth, 122, 130; Lant Street School, Southwark, 165; Monnow School, Southwark, 74; National Training School of Cookery, South Kensington, 185; Northey Street School, Limehouse, 112, 130; Orange Street School, Southwark, 74, 106, 161; Princess Road School, Marylebone, ix, 170

London Board School Free Dinner Fund, 117

London, City of, 75, 80

London County Council, 114, 121, 129, 139, 140, 150, 179, 186; toothbrushes, 142; verminous children, 132-4, 145-6

London School Board, 63, 70, 104, 112, 121, 128, 155, 172, 174, 191; cookery classes, 185; election of 1870, 71, 81-2, 85-7; fees in schools, 71-4; hours of polling, 84-6; Joint Committee on Underfed Children, 144; remission of fees, 158, 159-61; secret ballot, 75, 80; tested children's eyesight, 138; women members, 97

London Vegetarian Society, 119

Long Melford, 197

Longton, 40

Lowe, R.A., 17, 20; 'our future masters', 21-3, 67-8; Revised Code, 8; school attendance, 53

Lucraft, Benjamin, 66, 67, 88, 92, 160

Luton, 83, 194

Macclesfield, 192

MacDonald, Alexander, 64

Mackworth, Herbert, Inspector of Collieries, 49

Mair, R.M.: *The School Boards* (1873), 93

Manchester, 10, 53, 60, 61, 121, 136, 150, 156, 172, 183, 204; Educational census of, 54-6; and Salford Education Aid Society, 54

Manchester School Board, 128, 173; school dinners, 116; working men, 94

Mann, Horace: education census
  of 1851, 25–30
Marlborough, 6th Duke of:
  Education Bill of 1868, 19–20
Marshall, Sybil, 211
Marx, Karl, 63, 192
Masterman, C.F.G., 210;
  The Heart of Empire (1901),
  104
Merthyr Tydfil, 53
Metropolitan Radical Federation,
  86, 160
Miner, 47–8
Moncreiff, Rev. G.R.: children
  in Standard VI, 14
Morell, J.D.: school fees, 12–13
Morocco, French: education in,
  35–6
Morten, Honnor, 120
Mundella, A.J., 177

National Education League, 77,
  158; and 1870 Act, 60, 62;
  petitions to the House of
  Commons, 80; working men,
  65–7
National Education Union, 60,
  78–9
National Society, 4, 59;
  Monthly Paper of, 162; poor
  children, 69–70; school
  attendance, 52–3; withdrawal
  of children, 174
National Union of (Elementary)
  Teachers, 96–7, 120, 168
Newcastle, 53
Newcastle Commission, 4, 19, 29,
  30, 31, 34, 58, 173; free
  education, 12, 36–8; school
  attendance, 52–4
New Imperialism, 104
Newman, Dr George, Chief
  Medical Officer to the Board
  of Education, 148
Nineteenth Century, 205
Normansell, John, 49
Norris, HMI, Rev. J.P., 53
Northamptonshire, 58

Northumberland, 39, 201, 202;
  colliers in, 31, 46
Nottingham, 193
Nottingham School Board: and
  working men, 90, 93

O'Connor, Feargus, 40, 90
Oldham, 192
Overpressure controversy, 106–8,
  221 n16

Pankhurst, Emmeline, 95, 98
Parez, C.H., 69
Peabody buildings, 107
Peek, Sir Francis, 105, 110
Peel, Sir Robert, 67
Penny Banks, 56
Penny Magazine, 22
Pickard, W., 50
Plowden Report, 30, 211
Plymouth, 33
Potter, George, 85;
  Birmingham election of 1873,
  88; London election of 1870,
  86–7
Preston, 136; Powell's biscuits,
  195
Public Assistance Committees,
  145

Queen Victoria Jubilee Institute
  for Nurses, 129–30

Ragged School Union, 4, 52, 56–7
Rathbone, William, 20
Reading, Berkshire, 130; Huntley
  and Palmers, 195
Redgrave, Alexander, 45, 197
Referee: Children's Free Breakfast
  and Dinner Fund, 106
Relief (School Children) Order,
  1905, 122–3
Residuum, 4, 59, 69, 103, 111
Revised Code, 11, 14, 32, 106;
  1875 Code, 96, 180; 1879 and
  1880 Codes, 107; in the 1890s,
  182–3; Standard VI, 8
Reynold's Newspaper, 68–9, 76

For Product Safety Concerns and Information please contact our EU
representative GPSR@taylorandfrancis.com
Taylor & Francis Verlag GmbH, Kaufingerstraße 24, 80331 München, Germany